The Impossible

The Impossible

An Essay on Hyperintensionality

Mark Jago

OXFORD
UNIVERSITY PRESS

OXFORD
UNIVERSITY PRESS

Great Clarendon Street, Oxford, OX2 6DP,
United Kingdom

Oxford University Press is a department of the University of Oxford.
It furthers the University's objective of excellence in research, scholarship,
and education by publishing worldwide. Oxford is a registered trade mark of
Oxford University Press in the UK and in certain other countries

© Mark Jago 2014

The moral rights of the author have been asserted

First Edition published in 2014
Impression: 1

Published in the United States of America by Oxford University Press
198 Madison Avenue, New York, NY 10016, United States of America

British Library Cataloguing in Publication Data
Data available

Library of Congress Control Number: 2013956084

ISBN 978-0-19-870900-8

As printed and bound by
CPI Group (UK) Ltd, Croydon, CR0 4YY

For Dad, with love

Contents

Acknowledgements

This book grew out of work on my Australian Research Council *Discovery Projects* postdoctoral grant DP0880437, 'Rationality and Resource Bounds in Logics for Intentional Attitudes', which ran at Macquarie University, Sydney from July 2008 to January 2011. Although the book was written in 2011 and 2012 whilst lecturing at Nottingham, many of the ideas in it developed during my stay at Macquarie. Huge thanks to the department at Macquarie for hosting my stay and, in particular, to Peter Menzies for his time and advice as my postdoctoral mentor.

During my stay at Macquarie, I benefitted greatly from being a part of the magnificently supportive Australian philosophical community. Thanks to the philosophers at Sydney University for making me feel very at home and, in particular, to David Braddon-Mitchell, Mark Colyvan, Kristie Miller, Nick Smith and Huw Price for their friendship and invaluable advice, both philosophical and gastronomic. I met many wonderful early career researchers in Australia, with whom I discussed many of the ideas in this book and from whom I learnt so much: Jamin Asay, Jens Bjerring, Rachael Briggs, Kenny Easwaran, Alison Fernandes, Aidon Lyon, Dave Ripley, Wolfgang Schwarz, Lionel Shapiro, Mike Titelbaum and Alistair Wilson. I'm sure there are others who should be in this list: if so, apologies and thank you very much!

Many of the ideas discussed here were presented, in various stages of development, in talks at conferences and workshops: the *Hyperintensionality and Impossible Worlds* workshop, ANU, Canberra, 22–23 November, 2008; University of Sydney Philosophy Research Seminar, 20 May 2009; Macquarie Philosophy Research Seminar, 28 April 2009; ANU research seminar, Canberra, 28 October 2010; *Prague Colloquium on Epistemic Aspects of Many-Valued Logics*, 13–16 September, 2010; *Philosophy of Information Workshop*,

University of Hertfordshire, 10 May 2012; *10th Formal Epistemology Workshop*, LMU Munich, 29 May–2 June 2012; *Logica 2012*, Hejnice, Czech Republic, 18–22 June 2012; *Foundations of Logical Consequence* conference, St Andrews, 8–10 June 2012. I'd like to thank all of the audiences at these talks, who contributed valuable feedback on my ideas. Particular debts of gratitude are owed in this regard to Rachael Briggs, Jens Bjerring, David Chalmers, David Etlin, Hannes Leitgeb, Ole Hjortland, Peter Menzies, Greg Restall, Graham Priest, Jonathan Schaffer, Sebastian Sequoiah-Grayson, Robbie Williams and Timothy Williamson.

Some of the arguments in the book have appeared in previously published articles. My discussion of the problem of information in §2.2 draws on 'Imagine the possibilities: Information without overload', *Logique et Analyse* 49 (2006), 345–71. The discussion of Yagisawa's theory of worlds in §4.3 follows 'Against Yagisawa's modal realism', *Analysis* 73 (2013), 10–17. Chapter 5, on impossible worlds (in particular, §5.2, §5.3, §5.5 and §5.6), draws on 'Impossible worlds', forthcoming in *Noûs*. An earlier version of an argument in §5.3 appeared in 'Constructing worlds', *Synthese* 189 (2012), 59–74. The material on negative facts in §5.4 was worked out jointly with Stephen Barker, and appeared in our joint 'Being positive about negative facts', *Philosophy and Phenomenological Research* 85 (2012), 117–38.

The negative parts of chapter 6, in which I argue against various responses to the logical omniscience problem (§6.2 and §6.3), draw on 'Hintikka and Cresswell on logical omniscience', *Logic and Logical Philosophy* 15 (2007), 325–54. The discussion of vagueness that follows, §6.4, draws on 'The problem of rational knowledge', forthcoming in *Erkenntnis*. The ideas behind my construction of epistemic space in §7.1 and §7.2 first appeared in developed form in 'Logical information and epistemic space', *Synthese* 167 (2009), 327–41; a much earlier form of the idea was presented in 'Imagine the possibilities: Information without overload', *Logique et Analyse* 49 (2006), 345–71.

My account of the content of informative logical deductions in §8.2

first appeared in 'The content of deduction', *Journal of Philosophical Logic* 42 (2013), 317–34. The account of trivial consequence in §8.3 and the formal results in §8.5 first appeared in 'The problem of rational knowledge', forthcoming in *Erkenntnis*. My response to the objection that impossible-worlds accounts trivialise content, in §8.8, is taken from 'Are impossible worlds trivial?', forthcoming in V. Puncochar and P. Svarny (eds.), *The 2012 Logica Yearbook 2012*, London: College Publications. In all cases, I thank the relevant editors for their kind permission to use this material.

Many, many thanks also to Chris Woodard, my head of department at Nottingham, who allowed me to arrange my teaching so as to have time to draft the entire book in Autumn 2011; to Natasha Alechina and Brian Logan, for encouraging me to work on bounded rationality in my PhD thesis; to Eros Corazza, for encouraging me to think about attitude ascriptions; and to Peter Momtchiloff at OUP, who has been wonderfully encouraging throughout the production of this book.

Thanks above all to Anna, who kept the world around me turning whilst I wrote. 'Modern love walks beside me.'

Introduction

Impossible Thoughts

We think about impossible things all the time. We can think about alchemists trying to turn base metal to gold and about unfortunate mathematicians trying to square the circle. We can think about what those people tried to do and say, truly, that what they tried to do is impossible. We can ponder whether God exists and philosophers frequently debate whether there are such things as properties, numbers, sets, moral and aesthetic qualities and qualia. In such philosophical debates, when one side of the argument gets things wrong, it necessarily gets them wrong. If properties or numbers or sets exist, then they don't just happen to exist. They exist necessarily, and their non-existence is impossible. And if they fail to exist, then they necessarily fail to exist and so their existence is impossible. As we consider both sides of one of these philosophical arguments, we will at some point think about something that's impossible.

Sometimes, we're aware that what we're thinking about is impossible, as in when we think about turning base metal to gold, or about squaring the circle. But often, we're unaware that what we're thinking about is impossible. From the point of view of the person thinking about these things, thinking about some impossible situation need not be very different than thinking about a possible situation. Having forgotten most of our school chemistry, we might wonder whether table salt is NaCl or SiO_2 and whether gold has atomic number 72 or 79. We consider each option in turn, racking our memory for a clue.

Many philosophers, following Saul Kripke's influential *Naming and Necessity* (1980), hold that statements such as 'table salt is NaCl' and 'gold has atomic number 79' are necessarily true. So one of the options we considered in each case was an impossible option. Most theists hold not only that God exists, but that God exists of necessity: he couldn't have failed to exist. Most atheists hold not only that God doesn't exist, but also that it's a necessary fact that God doesn't exist. So theists and atheists can agree on one thing: whoever is right about God's existence or non-existence hits on a necessary truth. Whoever's wrong, by contrast, hits on a necessary falsehood. So either the theists or the atheists believe something that is necessarily false. Unwittingly, they have impossible beliefs. Impossible thoughts such as these do not jump out at us as impossible. Impossible thoughts need not wear their impossibility on their sleeve, as '1 + 1 = 3' does. Thinking about the impossible is often a mundane, everyday fact of life.

We can take a variety of attitudes to impossible contents. Alchemists believed that base metal can become gold; they desired that the transformation take place; they hoped that such-and-such methods would make the transformation. These beliefs, desires and hopes have a certain content: they are about certain states of affairs. Those states of affairs turn out to be impossible: they could not possibly exist. So what the alchemists' beliefs, desires and hopes were about is impossible. I'll call such contents *impossible thoughts*. By this, I don't mean that those contents are impossible to think; for clearly, the alchemists thought them. Rather, I mean what those thoughts are about could not possibly have been the case. When we entertain an impossible thought, we think about something that could not possibly have been the case. This book is concerned with explaining impossible thoughts.

We have impossible thoughts. Such thoughts are often meaningful, and they can be important to our lives. Committed alchemists didn't devote their lives to nothing: they devoted their lives to something that turned about to be impossible. A mathematician might devote years of his life to proving some hypothesis which later turns out to be unprovable. And even in less stark cases, impossible thoughts are, by any common standard, perfectly meaningful. We can tell good stories about alchemists, or about attempts to square the circle. Those stories can be pretty funny. They can convey the folly of such attempts.

Against the Impossible

Impossible thoughts might appear nothing more than a quirky feature of the way we can meaningfully represent the world around us. It may come as something of a surprise, therefore, to learn that just about every major philosophical theory of content and meaning is unable to account for impossible thoughts. Moreover, a wide variety of philosophical views converge in a kind of pressure group against the existence of impossible thoughts.

First, many philosophers hold views of psychological attitudes, including belief and desire, on which such attitudes cannot be about (or cannot represent) impossible situations. On these views, one cannot believe, or desire, the impossible. This philosophical view is supported by most logics of belief and desire, which make it a matter of logic that one cannot believe or desire the impossible. One might hold this view because one holds that attitudes such as belief and desire are rational attitudes and that rationality rules out the impossible. But one might hold the view for independent reasons. One might hold that a state of belief amounts to a way of ruling out various possible situations. On this view, impossible situations are never candidates for being ruled in or ruled out and so contribute nothing to a state of belief.

Second, many hold that, if we attempt to describe in words or thought some impossible situation, that description has no content. 'Content' here is an elusive notion, but the idea, roughly, is that when one asserts a sentence such as 'there is a round square', one literally says nothing. This is not quite to say that 'there is a round square' expresses no proposition at all. Since it would be false to say that there is a round square, that assertion must express a proposition. But, according to many philosophers, the proposition it expresses is in some way empty, in a way that genuine propositions are not.

Third, many philosophers hold that it is uninformative to think or reason about impossibilities, or to discover that such-and-such is in fact impossible, particularly where the impossibilities in question are logical impossibilities. On this view, if it is a logical truth that A, and hence a logical truth that '$\neg A$' ('not-A') is false, then learning that '$\neg A$' is false is uninformative. It contributes nothing to our cognitive information.

Fourth, many philosophical accounts of meaning rule that descriptions of impossible situations are not even meaningful. Broadly speaking, we can focus on *truth-conditional accounts* and *use theories* of meaning. On the former, a sentence's meaning is given (again, speaking very roughly) by specifying the possible situations under which it would be true. But a description of an impossible situation would not be true in any possible situation and hence it has no meaning (or perhaps, its meaning is empty). On the use theory of meaning, a sentence's meaning is given by the rules governing its use, or governing the situations in which the sentence would or would not be assertible. In the specific case of logical vocabulary, these rules are just the relevant proof rules. But proof rules, if they are powerful enough, rule out logical impossibilities. They rule that there are no situations in which a description of a logically impossible situation is assertible, and so that description is judged to be meaningless (or at least, that its meaning is empty).

Impossibility and Necessity

There is a flip-side to these stances, concerning what is necessary. If one cannot believe what cannot be, the flip-side is that one must believe whatever has to be. If rationality forbids belief in the impossible, it also mandates belief in the necessary. If belief states amount to a way of ruling out various possibilities, then whatever is necessary is never ruled out (since it holds in all possible scenarios) and so must always be believed. Just as various views consider descriptions of the impossible to have no genuine content (or only a trivial content), they also view descriptions of the necessary to have no genuine content (or only a trivial content). If so, then one cannot gain or lose beliefs about impossibilities or necessities. Learning that such-and-such is logically necessary is deemed uninformative and cognitively insignificant, on these views.

These views form the orthodoxy in those areas of epistemology and philosophy of language concerned with belief, information and content. If these views were correct, we could not learn anything, or gain new information, through logical or mathematical reasoning, or through philosophical argument (at least, in those typical cases when philosophers argue about views which, if correct, are necessarily so). Such reasoning and argumentation would never genuinely alter our beliefs. But these conclusions are incorrect. We do gain new information, new beliefs and, sometimes, fresh knowledge through logic, mathematics and philosophy. Consequently, we require an account of how this can be the case, given that so much prior philosophy argues that it cannot be so. We require accounts of attitudes such as belief, of content, of information and cognitive significance, and of meaning which allow space for the impossible.

Impossible Content

To help us be clear on what I mean by 'impossible thoughts', let's fix on an example description of an impossible situation:

(1) it is both snowing and not snowing here right now.

The described situation is metaphysically impossible. Or rather, to avoid giving the impression that there's such a situation out there somewhere with the property *being impossible* (there isn't), I should say: it is metaphysically impossible for (1) to be true. It might be that it is snowing here but not snowing over there, or that it is snowing on-and-off hereabouts, or that it is indeterminate whether it is snowing here at present. But that's not what is at issue here. It can't be the case that, at precisely the same time, in precisely the same place and in precisely the same way, it's both snowing and not snowing. Now suppose someone argues as follows:

> Thinking impossible thoughts isn't mysterious at all! Take the
> sentence (1). That's impossible: the sentence can't possibly be
> true. But we can utter the sentence out load, or say it silently
> in our own minds. When we do that, we have an impossible
> thought. Simple!

It's true that we can interact meaningfully with sentences describing
impossible situations, such as (1). If they weren't meaningful, we
couldn't truthfully say that such sentences describe impossible
situations. But thinking that such-and-such does not amount to
uttering the sentence 'such-and-such'.

Take Bob, who's learning French for the first time. He begins by
learning how to pronounce French words, without understanding
what they mean. So he can utter 'il est neige et ne neige pas ici
maintenant'. But his utterance isn't accompanied by the thought that
French speakers typically express using that sentence, or that English
speakers typically express with (1). He doesn't think that it is both
snowing and not snowing right now. There's more to thinking a
thought than merely saying the corresponding sentence, either out
loud or silently to yourself. So the fact that we can utter sentences
like (1) doesn't make any progress on the question of impossible
thoughts.

The problems I am concerned with are problems of *impossible
contents*. I am concerned with what is said or thought, rather
than with the particular form of the speech-act or thought episode.
This notion of content will be important throughout this book.
Impossible contents, such as the content *that it is both snowing
and not snowing right now*, do not correspond to any possible
situation. One philosophical problem raised by impossible contents
is to say what these contents are. Contents play a central role in the
philosophies of language and mind, and so a general answer to the
question, 'what are contents?' is central to both areas of philosophy.
As I said above, the most popular theories of content in general do
not leave room for impossible contents. It is not merely that they do
not tell us about the nature of impossible contents. The situation is
not that they give us an answer to the question 'what is the nature of

the content *that A*' when '*A*' describes a possible situation, but say nothing when '*A*' describes an impossible situation. Rather, in these cases, the theories tell us that there is no content associated with '*A*' when '*A*' describes an impossible situation. These theories explicitly rule out impossible contents.

As well as giving an answer to the question of what contents are (in a way that makes room for impossible contents), we need to tell a story about the normative relations we bear to those contents. One may know, believe, suppose, hope or fear that such-and-such. These are relations to a content (*that such-and-such*). When we restrict our attention to possible contents (that is, to contents which describe possible situations), telling this story is a matter of describing the role played by each of those relations. Plausibly, a mental state is a belief state (rather than merely a state of assumption, say) because of the relations that type of state has to one's actions (including the assertions one is disposed to make). Typically, one's beliefs (together with one's desires) lead to appropriate actions in a way that one's hypothetical assumptions do not.

When we widen our gaze to include impossible as well as possible contents, however, the story becomes much more complicated. For then it seems that there are contents (or putative contents) which cannot be believed, or assumed. Take our example from above, 'it is both snowing and not snowing here right now'. This sentence is perfectly meaningful, for both of its conjuncts are meaningful, and a sentence '*A* ∧ *B*' is meaningful whenever its conjuncts '*A*' and '*B*' are individually meaningful. But one cannot literally believe that it is both snowing and not snowing in one and the same place and time. You can't even conceive what it would be like for that content to be true. Beyond saying the sentence 'it's both snowing and not snowing', there is no access to that content. Or so I will claim in chapter 6. For the time being, a weaker claim will be enough: there is a clear epistemic difference between (1) and the following statement:

(2) There are three integers x, y and z and an integer $n > 2$ such that $x^n + y^n = z^n$.

Both statements describe (metaphysically and mathematically) impossible situations, and both are *a priori* falsehoods. That is, in each case, we can discover their falsehood via *a priori* reasoning alone. But the clear difference is that (1) is a trivial falsehood, whereas (2) is non-trivial in the extreme. 'Trivial' here doesn't mean '*a priori* truth/falsehood'. It relates to the *a priori* obviousness of the claim in question. (Just what this 'obviousness' amounts to is a thorny issue. I'll delay the question until chapters 6 and 7.)

Epistemic Possibility

Being an obvious or trivial truth is not an all-or-nothing matter: there are shades of grey in between the obvious and the non-obvious *a priori* truths (and falsehoods). But there are clear cases too: (1) is a clear case of a trivial falsehood, whereas (2) is a clear case of a non-trivial falsehood. When it is not *a priori* obvious or trivial that a statement is true (or that it is false), I'll say that it describes a situation which is an *epistemic possibility*. Or, to avoid the implication that there are such metaphysically impossible but epistemically possible situations out there somewhere (there aren't), we can say that in such cases, it is epistemically possible that such-and-such. In this sense, (2) represents an epistemic possibility, whereas (1) does not. The concept of epistemic possibility is meant to capture an epistemic kind of openness. A shrug of the shoulders and an 'I don't know' indicates an attitude of epistemic possibility towards a range of answers. Since we don't always know precisely what is and what isn't genuinely (metaphysically or logically) possible, there are many cases in which it is epistemically possible, but metaphysically or logically impossible, that such-and-such.

As I find out more and more about the world, many things that were once epistemic possibilities for me cease to be. And if you know more than me about trees, then it might be epistemically possible for me but not for you that this tree is an elm. This is a relative sense of 'epistemic possibility', which differs from time to time and from agent to agent. This relative notion is important in the analysis of states of knowledge (§1.2). But whether a truth (or falsehood) is trivial doesn't change in precisely this way. (A truth or falsehood may become obvious or trivial given some additional information. But that doesn't make that truth or falsehood obvious or trivial in itself.) It is useful to have at our disposal a non-relative notion of epistemic possibility, and then think of relative epistemic possibility as a narrowing-down of the non-relative notion.

Hyperintensionality

There are impossible contents, expressed by meaningful descriptions of impossible situations, many of which are the objects of normative epistemic relations such as *knowing* and *believing*. Some of these impossible contents are trivial (such as the content of (1)), whereas others are not (such as the content of (2)). That is the message so far.

Triviality and non-triviality are properties of contents. We can stand in epistemic relations to non-trivial impossibilities, but (perhaps) not to trivial impossibilities. Sentences with non-trivial contents describe epistemic possibilities (for some agents), whereas sentences with trivial contents do not describe epistemic possibilities (for any agent). So clearly, not all impossible contents are on a par. There are many distinct impossible contents, arranged on a gradual scale from the trivial to the highly non-trivial. The same goes for necessary contents, which correspond to situations which have to be the case. Some necessary contents are trivially necessary, such as the negation of (1). But others are highly non-trivial, such as the negation of (2), Fermat's Last Theorem. There are many distinct necessary contents, arranged on a gradual scale from the trivial to the highly non-trivial.

When a concept draws a distinction between (metaphysically or logically) equivalent contents, that concept is *hyperintensional* (§2.3). This will be a key concept in this book. Typically, philosophical theories of meaning and content (as well as the formal semantics accompanying them) are *intensional*, meaning that they can draw distinctions between contents which in fact have the same truth-value, but not *hyper*intensional. The first problem to be addressed, therefore, is the problem of how to theorise about and model hyperintensional concepts. I'll discuss and evaluate the options in chapters 3–5.

Normative Relations

The second and perhaps harder problem we must face is to reconcile hyperintensional contents with the normative principles governing epistemic concepts. Impossible contents (as well as possible contents) must respect the meanings of logical inference rules, in some way or other. If someone asserts that it's hot and stuffy in here, she thereby asserts that it's hot in here. She asserts both contents with the one speech-act, uttering 'it's hot and stuffy in here'. So there clearly has to be a relation between the content *that it's hot and stuffy in here* and the content *that it's hot in here*. The same goes for impossible contents. The content *that it's hot in here and Fermat's Last Theorem is false* is clearly related to the content *that it's hot in here* by the logical rules for 'and'.

At first, this relationship looks to be one of logical entailment, from the content *that A ∧ B* to *that A*. But this idea does not respect the hyperintensionality of contents. The content *that it's hot in here and Fermat's Last Theorem is false* entails every content (for it is an impossible content: Fermat's Last Theorem is necessarily true). Yet one who asserts that content does not thereby assert everything. So the normative relationship between logically related contents is not logical entailment.

On reflection, it cannot be some non-classical entailment relation either. A paraconsistent entailment relation is one on which contradictions do not entail everything. So a paraconsistent consequence relation might seem a promising way to cash out the normative connections between contents. But not so. As I discuss in §6.2, models of paraconsistent logics are either classical or trivially impossible (explicitly saying that some 'A' is both true and false). They do not describe genuine epistemic possibilities, for no epistemic possibility is trivially *a priori* impossible. So contents should not be analysed in terms of models of paraconsistent logics, and hence the normative connections between contents are not captured by paraconsistent consequence. Other proposals based on non-classical logics fail in other ways (§6.3).

The Problem of Bounded Rationality

The problems of hyperintensionality come to a head in what I will call the *problem of bounded rationality*. The problem is in essence a conflict between normative principles linking logically-related contents, on the one hand, and the empirical fact that we are cognitively bounded agents, with finite memory and reasoning ability, on the other. It seems that, in order to count as being rational, (i) rational agents must know the trivial consequences of what they know but, as an empirical fact, (ii) they do not know all logical consequences of what they know.

The problem is that (i) and (ii) are incompatible. Any (first-order) logical consequence of a set of premises is derivable from those premises via a chain of trivial inferences and so, if one does not know some logical consequence of what one knows, then one must fail to know some trivial consequence of what one knows. But that would seem to make one irrational. Real-world agents such as you and I are not logically ideal, but neither are we wholly irrational. We have *bounded rationality*. The problem is to explain how there can be such a phenomenon as bounded rationality, in light of points (i) and (ii) above.

Here is a concrete example of the problem. Consider an agent about to perform a logical deduction, to find out whether '*A*' follows from premises she already knows. (Let's suppose it does, but non-trivially.) She sets about performing trivial inference steps, inferring '*B* ∧ *C*' from '*B*' and '*C*', inferring '*D*' from '*E* → *D*' and '*E*', and so on. Because each of these inferences is trivial, none of them provides her with any new information and hence none of them adds to what she knows. Eventually, her deductions arrive at '*A*', at which point she comes to believe and (let us suppose) thereby comes to know that *A*. Since she didn't know that *A* before, her deductions furnished her with fresh knowledge. But how can this be, if each step on the way was trivial, leading to no knowledge gains?

This problem has been widely overlooked both by accounts of content and by technical responses to the *logical omniscience* problem. (Stalnaker (2006, 1991, 1999, 1984) and Lewis (1982, 1986) are notable exceptions. I discuss (and reject) their responses to the problem in §§2.4–2.6.) The logical omniscience problem is that, in standard logics of knowledge, agents are modelled as knowing all consequences of what they know, including all tautologies. Duc (1995, 1997), Fagin et al. (1990), Jago (2006b), Stalnaker (1991, 1999) and Vardi (1986) discuss the issue in detail.

In the vast technical literature on the problem, many approaches (including Duc 1995, 1997, Fagin et al. 1990, and Vardi 1986) adopt some non-classical logic or other and let what worlds represent be closed under the corresponding consequence relations. But this doesn't address the full problem of bounded rationality. (I'll say more on this point in chapter 6.)

Other responses to the logical omniscience problem adopt a 'sentential' approach, on which knowledge or belief states are merely boxes containing object-language sentences. (I discuss approaches along these lines in §2.7 and in more detail in Jago 2006b.) Again, such approaches do not address the normative component of the problem of bounded rationality. Avoiding logical omniscience is but one half (and by far the easier half) of the problem. A full solution must show how logically non-omniscient agents are nevertheless rational. By the same token, a full solution must maintain normative links between logically-related contents, such that trivial contents are ruled out of play for epistemic purposes, without thereby conflating all equivalent contents.

I'll say more on logical omniscience in §2.1 and §2.2. For a general overview of the problem, see Jago 2006b or Stalnaker 1991, 1999.

Aims

My aim in this book is to provide a full discussion of and solution to the problem of bounded rationality. I'll give a detailed analysis of the concept of hyperintensionality and develop a theory in terms of possible and impossible worlds. The specific aims of the book are to provide:

1. An account of the knowledge and belief states of rational but non-ideal agents, such as you and I, who do not know or believe all consequences of what they know or believe.

2. An account of how engaging in deductive reasoning can be a cognitively significant procedure, capable of furnishing us with new information.

3. A metaphysical account of impossible worlds, which is compatible with the actualist notion that everything that exists actually exists.

Outline of the Book

The Possible Worlds Approach

I begin the book with a discussion of *possible worlds semantics*, as this establishes the key concepts required for the remainder of the book. As I show in chapter 1, possible worlds semantics can be used to analyse concepts of knowledge and belief (§1.2), propositions and content (§1.3), and information and cognitive significance (§1.4). It is one of philosophy's success stories, having been adopted by linguists, computer scientists, game theorists and artificial intelligence researchers. But it is also the main offender in treating impossible thoughts as being contentless and in treating agents as being unable to believe the impossible.

In chapter 2, I outline how the possible worlds semantics is unable to provide fine-grained hyperintensional contents. In the case of accounts of knowledge and belief, the possible worlds semantics treats agents as being logically omniscient (§2.1): as knowing all consequences of what they know and believing all consequences of what they believe. In the case of the concept of *informativeness*, the possible worlds semantics treats all necessary truths as being wholly uninformative. For if no logical truth (and more generally, no consequence of what one knows) can ever be learned as new knowledge, then all logical truths are uninformative.

Because the possible worlds semantics is otherwise so successful, it is very tempting to try to overlook these defects. Some philosophers, most notably Stalnaker (1984) and Lewis (1982, 1986), argue that the deliverances of the possible worlds semantics are in essence correct. Logically equivalent contents are identical and impossible contents do not exist (§2.4). They admit that we typically ascribe inconsistent beliefs to agents and they attempt to explain how this can be, given their acceptance of the possible worlds account of content. I'll argue that these approaches do not work as intended (§2.5 and §2.6). Contents are genuinely hyperintensional. We then have a choice: either abandon the possible worlds approach entirely, or try to modify it to incorporate hyperintensionality, whilst preserving its best features. In §2.7, I argue for the latter option.

The two main ways to modify the possible worlds approach are:

(A) add structure; and

(B) add impossible worlds.

I discuss option (A) in chapter 3. Equivalent sentences (which express the same possible-worlds content) may nevertheless differ in their syntactic structure. The idea behind option (A) is to capture those syntactic structures at the level of content. This allows equivalent contents to remain distinct (§3.1). I'll argue that, whilst this approach delivers hyperintensional contents, it does not deliver all the fine-grained contents we require (§3.2). There are cases of logically equivalent sentences with identical syntactical structure, which should nevertheless be assigned distinct contents. I also pose an independent problem, concerning how this *structuralist* account deals with logical connectives (§3.3 and §3.4). So I reject option (A).

Option (B) adopts worlds which represent states of affairs in a strictly more fine-grained way than possible worlds. If '*A*' and '*B*' are logically equivalent then a possible world *w* represents that *A* if and only if it represents that *B*. Impossible worlds break this rule. By allowing contents to consist of both possible and impossible worlds, we can pull apart logically equivalent contents. This option suffices for all our hyperintensional needs. But for it to be acceptable, we need to say what impossible worlds (and worlds in general, for that matter) are.

Impossible Worlds

Semantics rests on the basis of metaphysics. If we are going to use worlds which represent in *these* ways, but not in *those* ways, then we'd better say what those worlds are and how they go about representing. To understand the semantic story fully, we first need a metaphysical story in place. Chapters 4 and 5 tell this story about worlds in general and impossible worlds in particular.

Chapter 4 is concerned with the question of what kind of entity possible and impossible worlds are. Impossible worlds are not worlds which themselves could not exist. Rather, they are worlds which represent impossible states of affairs as obtaining. Rather like an Escher drawing, they say that such-and-such is the case, where such-and-such is impossible (§4.1). In general, worlds other than our own might be the same kind of entity as our own, differing only in particular matters of fact. Or they might be non-existent entities which somehow have being but lack existence. Or they might be abstract entities which genuinely exist, but are not of a kind with the world around us (§4.2). It may be that both possible and impossible worlds (other than our own) fall into the same ontological category, an option Berto (2010) calls the *parity thesis*, or it may be that impossible worlds are a different kind of entity to possible worlds.

Having dismissed the Meinongian view that there are beings which lack existence, I consider the Lewisian view that non-actual worlds are metaphysically of a kind with our own. I argue that impossible worlds cannot be like this (§4.3). Impossible worlds must be abstract entities of some kind. Such worlds are typically called *ersatz* worlds. So we should either accept the parity thesis and take all non-actual worlds to be ersatz worlds, or else with Berto (2010) adopt a hybrid view, on which all and only the possible worlds are metaphysically of a kind with our own (§4.4). The latter position invokes a Lewisian conception of possible worlds. In §4.5, I argue against the Lewisian position, and hence against the hybrid view of worlds. I conclude that all worlds other than our own are ersatz abstract entities. This is rather reassuring, since it does not require us to believe in the existence of non-actual entities. All that exists are the inhabitants of our own world (including the set-theoretic entities, of course).

We then face the task of saying what these ersatz worlds are and, perhaps more importantly, how they represent possible and impossible states of affairs. My approach is that non-actual worlds are, at bottom, re-arrangements of actually existing entities. The re-arrangements are set-theoretic structures resembling sentences in their structure, in which the 'words' are actually existing entities (§5.1). This gives us an easy job of interpreting the language. Worlds are then built from sentences of this *worldmaking* language.

There is a serious problem for this approach and for all approaches which use ersatz worlds: how can such worlds represent non-actual entities? Those entities do not exist, so they have no names in the worldmaking language. They can be described, using the worldmaking language's equivalent of definite descriptions. But, as Lewis (1986) argues, this approach is at risk of conflating possibilities which should remain distinct (§5.2). Melia (2001) and Sider (2002) have interesting responses, but I argue that neither is successful. The way to avoid the problem, in my view, is to look to the ontological grounds for absences in our world. When such-and-such doesn't exist, there is some particular ontological ground for this. We can think of this ground as the state of affairs *that such-and-such doesn't exist*, and we can use that state of affairs to represent such-and-such in our worldmaking language (§5.3). This approach is somewhat unpopular and requires a careful defence. But, I argue, there are strong independent reasons for accepting an ontology like this (§5.4).

Given this approach, the problem of representing impossible states of affairs is not much more difficult than representing merely possible states of affairs. As pointed out above, sentences describing logical impossibilities are relatively unproblematic. In §5.5, I discuss ways to represent merely possible particulars, impossible particulars and fictional characters. The road is then open to constructing all the possible and impossible worlds we need to build fine-grained contents (§5.6).

Bounded Rationality and Content

With the metaphysical basis laid down, the task is then to construct fine-grained contents from ersatz worlds. This is not a simple task, because of the problem of bounded rationality. Those contents must respect normative logical connections, whilst at the same time avoiding logical idealisation. We want to use these contents to model agents who, as Duc (1995, 1997) puts it, are neither logically omniscient nor logically ignorant. I discuss the problem of bounded rationality in more detail in chapter 6 and argue that a number of approaches based on non-classical logics do not help (§6.2 and §6.3).

I argue that the problem is intimately related to the *sorites paradox* (§6.4). Losing just one hair doesn't make someone bald; earning one more penny doesn't make someone rich; and ageing by one second doesn't make someone old. But take a clear case of a hirsute poor young person who gradually loses his hair whilst becoming rich and old, hair by hair, penny by penny and second by second. It cannot be that losing just one hair made no difference to his baldness, or gaining one penny made no difference to his wealth. Each step seems to make no difference, for it seems absurd to think that there is a precise minimum number of hairs one needs to have without being bald, or a precise minimum number of pennies one must own to be rich. But the steps taken together make all the difference. This is the sorites paradox, and the problem of vagueness.

The case is very similar with deductive reasoning and the information it conveys to us. Each little step of inference we make in the deduction is trivial and doesn't convey to us any genuinely new information, but the deduction as a whole (which is nothing more than a series of trivial steps) can convey new information (§6.4).

Drawing this analogy between the problem of bounded rationality and the sorites paradox does not solve the former problem. But it does open the road to a solution. What a full solution needs is a way of looking at contents in a step-by-step way, in parallel to the step-by-step reasoning of the sorites paradox. My approach is, firstly, to analyse contents in terms of epistemically possible worlds (§7.1). These include some impossible worlds (since some logical or metaphysical impossibilities are nevertheless epistemic possibilities), but no trivially impossible ones. The epistemically possible worlds are the representations which cannot easily be ruled out *a priori*.

The second step is to impose a structure on the entire space of ersatz worlds, corresponding to possible proofs in the worldmaking language. This structure imposes normative logical relations between worlds. This provides us with a way to differentiate between the trivial and the non-trivial worlds, that is, between those that can easily be ruled out *a priori*, and those than cannot (§7.2 and §7.4). There is vagueness here and so the class of worlds which count as epistemically possible has vague boundaries. I call the resulting structure *epistemic space*.

There is a serious objection to this kind of approach, recently pointed out by J. C. Bjerring (2010; 2012), which threatens to collapse the approach so that all worlds are either logically possible or else trivially impossible (and hence not epistemically impossible). I respond to the worry in §7.3. §7.5 investigates the challenge from *dialetheists*, who hold that some explicit contradictions are in fact true (and hence are not trivially impossible). Even if they are wrong, surely they can genuinely believe their own view? I argue that their beliefs are indeed contentful and that this fact poses no threat to my account.

In the final chapter, I put the epistemic space developed in chapter 7 to use. Simple epistemic contents can be constructed as regions of epistemic space (§8.1). These can be used to give an account of how valid deductions are informative (§8.2). The account tells us how deductions can be informative (by ruling out would-be possibilities) and what their contents are (regions of epistemic space).

The most challenging notion of content to develop is an account of epistemic and doxastic states. The problem concerns *epistemic oversights*: cases in which an agent does not know some trivial consequence of what she knows (or does not believe some trivial consequence of what she believes). It seems that an agent suffering from epistemic oversights must be irrational; and yet an agent with no epistemic oversights would be logically omniscient (for she would never fail to know any consequence of what she knows). So what of rational but logically non-omniscient real-world agents such as you and I?

My approach in §8.4 is again to draw an analogy with the sorites paradox. *Tolerance principles* ('losing one more hair can't make you bald', for example) seem to be in some way rationally related to vague predicates like 'bald'. Yet tolerance principles generate the sorites paradox and so must be rejected. The puzzle of vagueness, at heart, is to explain how we can rationally reject tolerance principles. The same goes for the problem of bounded rationality.

The solution in both cases, I argue, is that we can never rationally assert that such-and-such is an epistemic oversight (or that such-and-such is a counterexample to a tolerance principle). Such cases are always indeterminate cases and as such do not rationally support assertions about them in the way that clear cases do. I develop this into a formal account of epistemic states in which there are no determinate epistemic oversights: it is never the case that an agent determinately fails to know some trivial consequence of what she determinately knows. Epistemic oversights are elusive. This explains why we are tempted into the false picture on which rational agents must know whatever follows from what they know.

Notation

Throughout the book, I'll use standard logical notation (to the extent that such a thing exists!) with

$$ `\neg` \quad `\wedge` \quad `\vee` \quad `\rightarrow` \quad `\exists` \quad `\forall` $$

being the symbols for *negation* ('not'), *conjunction* ('and'), *disjunction* ('or'), *implication* ('if ... then'), and *existential* and *universal* *quantification* ('there exists' and 'for all'), respectively. The operators 'K_i' and 'B_i' abbreviate 'agent i knows that' and 'agent i believes that'. Other notation will be explained along the way as it is introduced.

I'll use the italic letters 'A', 'B', 'C' and so on as placeholders for English sentences. When I write 'blah blah blah A', you can insert any English declarative sentence you like in place of the 'A': what I say should hold for any choice of sentence in place of 'A'. For the special case of logically simple sentences (i.e., those not containing any logical vocabulary), I'll use 'p', 'q' and 'r'.

Since I'll frequently be talking about sentences, I'll employ the convention that sentences in single quotation marks are mentioned, rather than used (i.e., I'm talking about those quoted sentences, rather than asserting their content). When necessary, the single quote marks will also act as the Quine-quotes. When it's obvious that sentences are being mentioned rather than used (for example, when discussing deductive relationships between sentences), I'll drop the quote-marks: I'll write '$A \vdash B$' rather than "'A' $\vdash$ 'B'". (This is a logician's convention, often used but rarely mentioned.)

It is also useful to have some notation for the proposition *that A* (for any sentence 'A'). Some authors (e.g. Horwich 1990) use angle-brackets '$\langle \cdot \rangle$' to denote propositions. This is somewhat unfortunate, since that notation is already used in mathematics to denote ordered n-tuples (sequences). To avoid confusion, I will write '$[\![A]\!]$' for the proposition *that A*.

1

The Possible Worlds Approach

In this chapter, I introduce possible worlds semantics, which will serve as the background to the discussion in the rest of the book. I show how possible worlds semantics can be used to analyse concepts of knowledge, belief, information and cognitive significance, propositions and content in general.

1.1 Possible Worlds Semantics

When you gain a new piece of knowledge, or form a new belief, you thereby rule out a bunch of possible scenarios. Before gaining that knowledge or forming that belief, those scenarios were ways the world could be, as far as you were concerned. Then, when you gain the new piece of knowledge or form your new belief, they cease to be ways the world could be, as far as you're concerned. Suppose you consult the UK met office website and discover that it rarely rains in Cambridge, something you previously didn't know. You then form the belief that it rarely rains there and, let's suppose, this belief counts as knowledge. Prior to consulting the met office, you had no idea about Cambridge's average rainfall. As far as you were concerned, it might rain there all the time, as it does in Manchester. But now you know better: Cambridge is much drier than Manchester.

In your previous state, scenarios in which Cambridge's climate is wetter than Manchester's were *epistemic possibilities* for you. If asked whether Cambridge is as those scenarios say it is, you might have said 'it might be, for all I know'. This shrugging, non-committal attitude towards a scenario is what I mean by saying that the scenario is epistemically possible for you at that time. The epistemically possible scenarios are the ones that represent a way the world might well be, for all you know.

Now that you know that it rarely rains in Cambridge, however, those scenarios in which Cambridge is always wet are no longer epistemically possible for you. In gaining your new piece of knowledge, you ruled out those scenarios as ways the world might be. Gaining new knowledge goes hand-in-hand with ruling out various scenarios as ways the world might be, as far as you're concerned.

The possible worlds approach to knowledge takes this idea as its theoretical starting point and analyses states of knowledge in terms of scenarios or *possible worlds*. (Just what these scenarios or possible worlds are needn't detain us yet. Think of them as representations of ways the world could be.) In the example, your knowledge before consulting the met office is analysed as a large bunch of scenarios, including scenarios in which is always rains in Cambridge as well as scenarios in which it rarely rains there. When you come to know that it rarely rains there, your new state of knowledge is analysed as being very much like the previous state, except with those scenarios in which it always rains in Cambridge thrown out.

In the latter state of knowledge, all scenarios represent that it rarely rains in Cambridge. This is what it is for you to know that it rarely rains there, according to the possible worlds account of knowledge: all the scenarios epistemically possible for you represent that it rarely rains in Cambridge. In general, for an agent to know that A is for all that agent's epistemically possible scenarios to represent that A. We can tell a similar story for an agent's belief states. This is our first theoretical use for scenarios: analysing states of knowledge and belief. I'll give the details of this approach in §1.2.

Because you learned something new in consulting the met office website, the website was informative for you. You learned from it that it rarely rains in Cambridge. What you learned can be viewed as the difference between your states of knowledge before and after consulting the met office. On the possible worlds approach, this difference is a difference between two sets of scenarios, with a larger one giving way to a smaller one. This narrowing down of the set of epistemically possible scenarios constitutes learning, and what you learn can be viewed in terms of the way in which the set of scenarios is narrowed. So we can view information as a way of narrowing down a set of scenarios. The information *that in rarely rains in Cambridge* narrows down any set of scenarios by throwing out all those scenarios in which it does not rarely rain in Cambridge. More simply, we can view that information itself as a set of scenarios. That information narrows down a set X of scenarios by throwing out scenarios in X which are not in the information. This is a second theoretical use for possible worlds: analysing the information an agent receives. I'll go into the details of the idea in §1.4.

In conceptualising the information *that it rarely rains in Cambridge* as a set of scenarios, we detach that information from the English sentence 'it rarely rains in Cambridge', or from the particular brain activity involved in thinking that it rarely rains in Cambridge. That information is the content of that English sentence (and of the synonymous French 'il pleut rarement à Cambridge' and German 'es regnet selten in Cambridge'). It is what one says, or expresses, in uttering one of those sentences. Philosophers typically call the entities expressed by utterances of declarative sentences *propositions*. So here is a third theoretical use for possible worlds: analysing the content of sentences and accounting for what philosophers may mean by 'proposition'. The details will appear in §1.3.

A fourth (and perhaps the most fundamental) application of possible worlds is to analyse modal notions, including possibility and necessity. What is possible is whatever is true according to some possible world, and what is necessary is whatever is true according to all possible worlds. Other modal notions, including entailment and consistency, can then be analysed accordingly.

For the present, I'll think of possible worlds merely as representations of ways our universe could have been. Precisely what they are isn't too important right now: I'll discuss the issue at length in chapters 4 and 5. What is important here is the logical properties of those possible worlds. Because they represent ways the universe could have been, a possible world w will obey the following conditions:

(i) w represents that $\neg A$ if and only if it does not represent that A;

(ii) w represents that $A \wedge B$ if and only if it represents both that A and that B;

(iii) w represents that $A \vee B$ if and only if it represents either that A or that B; and

(iv) w represents that $A \to B$ if and only if it represents either that $\neg A$ or that B.

In summary, possible worlds semantics seeks to analyse philosophically interesting notions such as possibility and necessity, knowledge and belief, information, content and proposition. Possibility and necessity aside, these notions will play a large part in what follows. §§1.2–1.4 give a more detailed overview of the possible worlds approach in these areas. This will serve as background for the rest of the book and will provide motivation for adopting the possible worlds approach. (If you're already familiar with these approaches, you might want to skip these sections and jump straight to chapter 2.)

1.2   Knowledge and Belief

I will begin by setting out the details of the possible worlds analysis of knowledge and belief states (and the intimately related semantics for 'knows' and 'believes'), as this will introduce the concepts that are important in subsequent sections. I'll set out the semantics informally in this section; the formal details can be found in the appendix.

In §1.1, I described a change in an agent's state of knowledge in terms of her ruling out certain possible worlds. When she gains a new piece of knowledge, worlds that were epistemically possible for that agent are ruled out and no longer treated as being epistemically possible for her. The possible worlds analysis of an agent's state of knowledge (at a time) treats that state as a set of possible worlds, thought of as those that capture the epistemic possibilities for the agent at that time. The semantics for 'knows' is given in terms of this set of worlds. 'Agent i knows that A' is deemed true if and only if all worlds that are epistemic possibilities for that agent represent that A.

This is the basic idea behind the semantics. Possible worlds semantics is not concerned only with what is in fact true now, but also with what was and will be true at other times, and with what would have been true had things been different. So we will not restrict our attention to the worlds that are in fact epistemic possibilities for the agent in question right now. We think in terms of a space of possible worlds, one of which is (or which represents) our world (the totality of all stuff around us). For each world w in the space, we fix a set of worlds that are epistemically possible for our agent *relative to* w. We do this in terms of a relation R of *epistemic accessibility*: Rwu says that world u is epistemically accessible (for our agent) from world w. The agent's state of knowledge at world w is then a matter of what the worlds u accessible from w represent: the agent knows that A, according to world w, if and only if all worlds u accessible from w represent that A.

One of the great features of this relational approach (in terms of the epistemic accessibility relation R) is that it is simple to extend to more than one agent. Suppose we have n agents which, for simplicity, I'll refer to by number: $1, \ldots, n$. Then we introduce n epistemic accessibility relations, $R_1, \ldots, R_n$, and analyse the knowledge of agent i in terms of R_i: agent i knows that A, according to world w, if and only if all worlds u such that $R_i wu$ represent that A.

In informal terms, the possible worlds semantics for knowledge (which originated with Hintikka (1962)) then goes as follows. (I give the formal details in the appendix.) The semantics interprets a language containing knowledge and belief operators 'K_i' and 'B_i' for each agent i, with '$K_i A$' and '$B_i A$' read as 'agent i knows that

A' and 'agent i believes that A', respectively. The semantics for this language is given by *models*, which consist of a set of possible worlds with epistemic accessibility relations $R_i, \ldots, R_n$ between them. The characteristic clause of the possible worlds semantics for knowledge (in addition to clauses (i)–(iv) from §1.1) is:

(v) w represents that $K_i A$ if and only if, for all worlds u such that $R_i wu$, u represents that A.

We can model belief, as well as knowledge, by expanding the model with doxastic accessibility relations $R_1^\delta, \ldots, R_n^\delta$: see the appendix for the details.

The possible worlds semantics does not seek to give a philosophical definition of knowledge in the sense of a set of necessary and sufficient conditions. (Historically, the project of developing modal epistemic logic and its semantics was carried out independently of but contemporaneously with attempts to solve the Gettier problem, which shows that truth, justification and belief are not jointly sufficient for knowledge (Gettier 1963).) Increasing numbers of philosophers hold that the aim of theorising about knowledge is not to provide a definition of 'knows' but instead to investigate features of knowledge and its relations to other concepts. Williamson (2000a), for instance, holds that knowledge is a basic mental state, yet one about which we can say plenty.

One way to investigate such conceptually basic states is by investigating its logical properties. We do this by building logical models, finding out what they entail and testing how these map on to our concept of knowledge. The possible worlds semantics plays a leading role in this philosophical approach to knowledge. Indeed, there are several prominent philosophical accounts of knowledge which draw on the possible worlds semantics. One is the *relevant alternatives* approach, which treats knowledge as 'an evidential state in which all relevant alternatives (to what is known) are eliminated' (Dretske 1981, 367). Lewis (1996) presents the most sophisticated version of a relevant alternatives theory, on which knowledge amounts to what is true in every uneliminated possibility.

The parallel between *uneliminated possibility* and *accessible possible world* is then explicit.

Another approach which draws on the possible worlds semantics approach is *epistemic contextualism* (Cohen 1998; DeRose 1992, 1995; Lewis 1996). This approach emphasises how context (in particular, the context of the attributer) can affect the truth of an attribution 'agent i knows that A' by varying the evidential standards in play. The idea is that in everyday contexts, evidential standards are low and hence an assertion 'agent i knows that A' may be true, whereas it might not be when the stakes are higher. In particular, anti-skeptical assertions such as 'I know that I have two hands' are typically true in everyday contexts but false in epistemology seminars (when skeptical scenarios are raised to salience), according to the contextualist. In Lewis's hands, context plays a role in restricting the domain of quantification of 'all relevant alternatives' (Lewis 1996). In terms of the possible worlds semantics, we can think of the role of context as varying the epistemic accessibility relations R_i. This form of contextualism is very natural, given the possible worlds semantics clause for '$K_i A$' and the fact that, quite generally, (natural language) quantifiers are subject to contextual domain restriction.

In summary, the possible worlds semantics is well-motivated, intuitive and elegant, and it receives support from various philosophical approaches to knowledge.

1.3 Propositions and Content

I now turn to issues surrounding the content of a sentence or utterance, and how a possible worlds approach addresses some of these philosophical problems. Philosophers often talk about the things we say, or believe, or think, or mean. These things are often called 'propositions'. A proposition is what one believes, or thinks, or means when one believes, thinks, or means something. Talk about propositions is ubiquitous when philosophers turn their gaze to language, meaning and thought. Having well-behaved propositions at one's disposal is of great theoretical benefit to metaphysicians and philosophers of language and mind. I'll briefly go over a few of the philosophical uses to which propositions have been put, to highlight why it's useful to have propositions around.

Philosophers often think of propositions as the things that are (in the first instance) true or false (the 'primary' bearers of truth and falsity). By saying that propositions are the primary bearers of truth or falsity, one is saying that the truth or falsity of an utterance or belief depends on the truth or falsity of the proposition expressed by that utterance or the proposition believed. We can distinguish between a specific act of believing (a specific mental state or event) and what is thereby believed. Whether that belief is true or false depends only on what is believed. It does not depend, for example, on the particular neural realisation of that mental state or event (unless the belief happens to be one about its own particular realisation, in which case, this is reflected in the proposition that captures what is believed). Assuming that what is believed is a proposition, we can explain the truth or falsity of a particular belief in terms of the truth or falsity of the proposition believed.

The story is similar in the case of the truth or falsity of particular utterances. In general, the truth or falsity of an utterance depends only on the content of what is uttered (or *what is said* in making that utterance) and how the world is. The magnitude of the sound waves produced by the utterer, or the particular timbre of her voice, is irrelevant. What is said in making the utterance is a proposition. So again, we explain the truth or falsity of a particular utterance in terms of the truth or falsity of the proposition thereby expressed.

If one takes propositions to be the primary bearers of truth and falsity, then it is also an attractive option to take propositions to be the bearers of the alethic modal properties *being possible* and *being necessary*. In saying that *being necessary* applies to the proposition *that A*, we are saying that that proposition is *necessarily true* (and not that the proposition necessarily exists, although that might also be true). The reason for thinking that the alethic modal properties attach to propositions and not states of affairs (for instance) is that we want to be able to talk about what is necessarily or contingently not the case (e.g., the existence of round squares, or a female American president in 2012). Yet there exist no states of affairs (or at least, no actual states of affairs) to bear these alethic modal properties. What do exist, however, are the necessarily/contingently false propositions *that there are round squares* and *that there is a female American president in 2012*.

Propositions are also frequently taken to be the objects of belief, desire and other psychological (or 'propositional') attitudes. Beliefs are in some sense shareable: Anna can believe what Bill believes. But Anna's and Bill's shared belief will not be realised in the same way. (For one thing, Anna's and Bill's brains are in different places.) Anna can also doubt or disbelieve what Bill believes, and her doubt or disbelief will be a different sort of disposition from Bill's belief. So philosophers tend to distinguish between the specific mental state or event token and its content (what is thereby believed, desired or feared) and identify the latter with a proposition.

In an even more obvious sense, assertions are shareable: Anna can assert what Bill asserts; she can also accept what Bill asserts and thereby make it part of the common ground, or challenge what Bill asserts and thereby make it a topic for debate. Notice that uttering the same words is neither necessary nor sufficient for asserting the same thing. If both Anna and Bill utter the words 'I am terrified of snakes' (in a suitably assertoric tone), each of them conveys different information. Anna's utterance is an assertion that Anna is terrified of snakes, whereas Bill's utterance is an assertion that Bill is terrified of snakes. What each speaker says (or what the utterance expresses) differs from speaker to speaker.

Conversely, different strings of words can be used to assert the same thing. As Frege noted,

> If someone wants to say the same today as he expressed yesterday using the word "today", he must replace this word with "yesterday". (Frege 1956, 296)

Utterances of 'today was fun' and 'yesterday was fun', if the latter is made a day after the former, express the same information. In at least one good sense of 'saying the same thing', the speakers of those utterances say the same thing as one another.

In these ways, it's good to have propositions around. But what are propositions? Should they even be treated as things at all? Some arguments against the existence of propositions, most notably the ones advanced by Quine (1951, 1960, 1969), appeal to general skeptical principles. Nominalists ask: why believe in spooky, abstract propositions when we can get by with eternal sentences (or perhaps even token utterances of sentences)? Skeptics about intensional phenomena ask: can we really make sense of *analyticity*, *synonymy*, *meaning* or *proposition*? (Here, 'intensional' indicates a linguistic context in which one cannot infer from '...a...' and '$a = b$' to '...b ...'.) Defenders of the slogan 'no entity without identity' insist that until we have a method for discovering when two sentences express the same proposition, we have no business talking about propositions at all.

The possible worlds approach to propositions takes propositions to be sets of possible worlds. The proposition *that* A is the set of all possible worlds which represent that A (Stalnaker 1976b). Questions about the existence of propositions then become questions about the existence of possible worlds and sets. So for the proponent of possible worlds semantics, who already believes in possible worlds (and presumably, also in sets), propositions are no addition to her ontology.

Moreover, there are good, independent reasons to believe in the existence of both possible worlds and sets. Belief in sets is justified by taking our best scientific (including mathematical) theories at face value. Our best mathematical theories quantify over sets; indeed, mathematics is most elegant when formulated with set theory at its core. Belief in possible worlds is justified by our best linguistic theories (and by formal semantics in particular), which make heavy use of possible worlds. Possible worlds are also essential to our best theories of possibility and necessity (§1.1).

In claiming that belief in possible worlds is justified, I am not assuming that we should believe in other worlds of the same kind as our own. Formal semantic theories (which justify belief in possible worlds) quantify over entities with such-and-such logical properties, but they do not require them to be concrete spatiotemporal entities. The thesis that there are concrete, spatiotemporally located worlds other than our own (that is, outside our own universe and spatiotemporally disconnected from it) goes greatly against common sense; it is a high price to pay. David Lewis, the principle defender of this thesis, argues that the price is worth it (Lewis 1973, 1986). Most other philosophers disagree (see §4.2 and §4.5).

This debate is not my present concern, for we can believe in possible worlds without accepting Lewis's thesis. Many philosophers, including Adams (1974, 1981), Melia (2001), Skyrms (1981), Sider (2002) and Stalnaker (1976a), hold that possible worlds are set-theoretic constructions out of actually existing entities: see §4.2 and §5.1. (Indeed, Hintikka (1962) originally defined his 'alternatives' (which play the role of possible worlds) as downward closed sets of sentences.) If so, then we will agree that those worlds exist if we agree that sets and the relevant actual entities exist. For example, if we think of possible worlds as sets of sentences (as Adams (1974, 1981) does) and sentences as set-theoretic constructions out of English words, then it is very difficult to deny the existence of possible worlds.

What of the worry mentioned above, concerning identity conditions for propositions (i.e., the conditions under which the proposition *that A* is identical to the proposition *that B*)? If we take propositions to be sets of possible worlds, we have a ready-made answer to this question. The proposition *that A* is identical to the proposition *that B* just in case every possible world that represents that *A* also represents that *B* and vice versa. In particular, the account comes with a ready-made story about the identity conditions for logically complex propositions. Writing '$[\![A]\!]$' to denote the proposition *that A* and X^c for the set-theoretic complement of X (i.e., all those things in the domain but not in X), we have the following identities:

$$[\![A \wedge B]\!] = [\![A]\!] \cap [\![B]\!] \qquad\qquad [\![A \vee B]\!] = [\![A]\!] \cup [\![B]\!]$$

$$[\![\neg A]\!] = [\![A]\!]^c \qquad\qquad [\![A \rightarrow B]\!] = [\![A]\!]^c \cup [\![B]\!]$$

If possible worlds are themselves extensional entities, as they are if they are constructed set-theoretically from actual entities (and as Lewis's worlds are), then propositions qua sets of possible worlds are extensional entities. If $[\![A]\!]$ and $[\![B]\!]$ are sets-of-worlds propositions with the same members, then they are the same proposition. Indeed, it is a consequence of the account that necessarily or logically equivalent propositions are identical. (This is Stalnaker's principle (I) (1976a, 9).) Hence on this account, necessarily or logically equivalent sentences never differ with one another on which proposition they express. This feature of the account will be important in the discussion below, in §2.1.

An interesting question is how this possible worlds approach to content fits in with the possible worlds approach to knowledge and belief. When describing the former approach in §1.2, I did not mention 'proposition' and did not take either *knowledge* or *belief* to be a relation between an agent and a proposition. So this approach might seem in tension with the idea that propositions are the objects of knowledge and belief. Yet the two approaches are not in tension with one another. Far from it: they mesh with one another very easily.

The possible worlds approach to knowledge and belief deals in the first instance with an agent's total epistemic and doxastic states, rather than with individual pieces of knowledge or with individual beliefs (Lewis 1986, 32). It takes these holistic states to be the more important theoretical notion, even though we attribute knowledge and belief to an agent in a piecemeal way. (We use individual English sentences to attribute knowledge and belief, of course. But this does not show that knowledge or belief itself is had in a piecemeal way. Stalnaker (1984, 64) argues that thinking of belief in a piecemeal way is misleading.)

The piecemeal notion of knowledge, as a relation between an agent and a particular proposition, is simply one of inclusion of the agent's epistemic state in the proposition in question. More precisely, agent i stands in the *knowledge* relation to proposition $[\![A]\!]$ at world w if and only if, for every world u epistemically accessible from w for agent i (that is, all u such that $R_i wu$), $u \in [\![A]\!]$. Similarly, agent i stands in the *belief* relation to proposition $[\![A]\!]$ at world w if and only if, for all worlds u, $R_i^\delta wu$ only if $u \in [\![A]\!]$. Thus the possible worlds approach to knowledge and belief meshes very well with the account of propositions as sets of possible worlds.

In summary, if we already accept the existence of possible worlds (and sets), then treating propositions as sets of possible worlds furnishes us with propositions at no extra cost to our ontology. As in the case of the approach to knowledge and belief, the possible worlds approach to propositions is well-motivated, intuitive and elegant.

1.4   Information and Cognitive Significance

Statements that express a genuine content can be informative. We can think of that content itself as carrying information. An agent learns that A when she rejects all non-A worlds from her epistemic state. We can think of this information gain dynamically, in terms of the content *that A* restricting the agents's epistemic accessibility relations. The content (set of possible worlds) $[\![A]\!]$ restricts agent i's epistemic state at world w when $R_i wu$ holds only if $u \in [\![A]\!]$. Thus, we can think of a content qua set of worlds as an entity which carries information. When the content *that A* restricts agent i's epistemic state (i.e., if R_i is genuinely narrowed), agent i gains that information and thereby comes to know that A. The content itself is informative, in the sense that some agent could move from ignorance to knowledge that A. This is the general stance that the possible worlds approach takes to information and informativeness.

There is a particular puzzle about information, concerning true identity statements, on which the possible worlds account can shed light. In this section, I'll discuss the puzzle and how the possible worlds semantics views the situation. Frege (1892) directs our attention to the puzzle as follows. Suppose it's 1972 and we're going to see the Ziggy Stardust tour. We're young, impressionable and pretty confused about who we're going to see. We know it's Ziggy Stardust, but unsure who Ziggy is. You say to me,

(1.1) David Bowie is Ziggy Stardust

Since I trust your superior musical knowledge, I believe you and so I come to learn something: I learn *that Ziggy is Bowie.* (I'm treating 'Ziggy Stardust' as another name for David Bowie, rather than as a name of a fictional character, played by David Bowie. Nothing hangs on this: it's just an example!) Suddenly, so much becomes clear: *that's* why Ziggy's voice sounds so much like Bowie's, now that I think about it!

Sentence (1.1) has the form '$a = b$'. When such identity statements are true, we can (in extensional contexts, such as identity statements) replace the name 'b' in a sentence '... b ...' with 'a' without affecting the truth of the sentence. If we do this with (1.1), we get

(1.2) David Bowie is David Bowie

Now here's the puzzle: (1.1) is informative (for it conveyed new information to me), whereas (1.2) is not (for it cannot convey new information to any agent). (1.2) is a trivial logical truth. We can discover its truth merely by reflecting on the form of the sentence. (1.1) by contrast is not trivial. To discover its truth, one has to find out by looking at the world or asking someone who knows. In Frege's terminology, (1.1) is *cognitively significant* whereas (1.2) is not.

Frege takes this to show that, since (1.1) is true just in case (1.2) is, there must be more to the meaning of (1.1) than just its truth-condition. Frege's solution (1892) is that names have a sense (*sinn*) as well as a reference (*bedeutung*). The sense of a name is the way we think about the name's referent. Frege gives the example of the planet Venus, referred to both as 'the morning star' and 'the evening star'. (Both 'the morning star' and 'the evening star' seem to function as names, despite having the form of definite descriptions.

Since both refer to Venus, which isn't a star, they cannot be simple descriptions. We might call them *description-names* (Corazza 2002).) 'The morning star' is associated with a sense which we might express via the description 'the bright light in the sky seen in the northern hemisphere in the morning', whereas 'the evening star' is associated with a different sense, which we might express via the description 'the bright light in the sky seen in the northern hemisphere in the evening'. Similarly, whilst the reference of both 'Ziggy Stardust' and 'David Bowie' is David Bowie, each name is associated with a different sense.

Frege uses these differences in sense to explain the difference in cognitive significance between (1.1) and (1.2), and between 'the morning star is the evening star' and 'the morning star is the morning star'. In general, the terms flanking '=' in an identity statement of the form '$a = a$' are associated with the same sense, and this is why '$a = a$' is trivial. But when the terms flanking '=' in an identity statement of the form '$a = b$' are associated with different senses, as in the case of (1.1), '$a = b$' is cognitively significant and hence may be informative to some agent.

Frege tells us that the sense associated with a name is a way of thinking about the name's referent, or that referent's 'mode of presentation'. But this doesn't go very far towards telling us what senses are. Consequently, one might (justifiably) feel suspicious about Fregean senses, for much the reasons discussed in the case of propositions in §1.3. If we can give a theory of senses in the same way that we gave a theory of propositions, however, this will go a long way to alleviating these worries.

The development of formal accounts of Fregean senses began with Church (1951, 1973, 1974) and Carnap (1947). Church investigated the logic of senses in an axiomatic way, and this saw the start of *intensional logic* (in contrast to Frege's (1879; 1884; 1893; 1903) and Whitehead and Russell's (1910; 1912; 1913) extensional logics.) Carnap, by contrast, pursued a semantic approach in terms of 'state-descriptions', a forerunner of possible worlds semantics. Carnap was influenced by Wittgenstein's theory of meaning in the *Tractatus* (Wittgenstein 1922). Wittgenstein recognised that statements describe states of affairs (1922, §4.023) and, since there are false statements, some of these states of affairs are not the ones that actually exist. So to understand what a statement means, we must consider all possible states of affairs, existing in 'logical space' (1922, §2.11). The meaning of a statement is then a way of dividing these possible states of affairs into two classes: those that agree with the statement and those that disagree with it.

Carnap takes the idea of presenting possible states of affairs in logical space. He uses *state-descriptions*, which we can think of as linguistic descriptions of possible worlds. Carnap's approach associates an extension to each term (a name, description or predicate) at each state-description. The extension of a predicate '*F*' at a state-description *s* is the set of things that satisfy '*F*', according to *s*. The extension of a name or description '*a*' at *s* is the thing picked out by '*a*' at *s*. The *intension* of a term is then a function from state-descriptions to extensions. Thus, the intension of a name '*a*' (which Carnap calls an *individual concept*) is a function from state-descriptions to referents.

Carnap's account is a precursor to possible worlds semantics. We can improve on Carnap's semantics by replacing his state-descriptions with possible worlds (so that the choice of object language does not affect what is treated as being possible or necessary, as it does on Carnap's account). We can interpret Fregean senses as Carnap's intensions, now thought of as functions from possible worlds to extensions. This result delivers the Fregean theory about the cognitive significance of an identity statement '$a = b$', provided that '*a*' and '*b*' are assigned different intensions.

(Against this view, Kripke (1980) argues that proper names and natural kind terms are *rigid designators*, denoting the same entity in all possible worlds. If Kripke is right, then true identity statements involving such terms are always necessary truths and so we cannot use (metaphysically) possible worlds to explain the informativeness of '$a = b$' in the way just described. I return to the point in §8.6.)

In summary, just as sets of possible worlds provide us with a clear account of what propositions are, functions on possible worlds (in the form of intensions) provide us with a clear account of what Fregean senses are. The possible worlds semantics thus provides us with a way of understanding cognitive significance and informativeness. In fact, there is a very close relationship between the possible worlds accounts of propositions, on the one hand, and senses, on the other. To see why, we need to return to Frege's philosophy of language. For Frege, sentences as a whole (as well as the subsentential components that make them up) have both a sense and a reference. The sense of a sentence for Frege is the thought it expresses; the reference of a sentence is its truth-value.

Transposing this idea into Carnap's theory, the extension of a sentence at a world is its truth-value at that world and hence the intension of a sentence is a function from possible worlds to truth-values. The intension of a sentence thus divides all possible worlds into two classes, those for which the extension of the sentence is true and those for which it is false, just as on Wittgenstein's account. Mathematically, this function is equivalent to a set of worlds. (To see why, let $|A|$ be the set of worlds according to which 'A' is true. The characteristic function for $|A|$ maps each world to either *true* or *false*. This function is none other than the intension of 'A'. Since sets can (without loss of information) be replaced with their characteristic function, intensions of sentences are equivalent to sets of worlds.) Hence by treating Fregean senses as intensions, Fregean thoughts are treated as sets of possible worlds, that is, as possible-world propositions. This is a good result, since Fregeans identify propositions qua objects of knowledge and belief with Fregean thoughts.

This last point alerts us to a further relationship between the Fregean theory and possible worlds semantics. Frege takes senses (in this case, thoughts) to be the objects of knowledge and belief in a very literal way. To understand why, we need to look at a further puzzle to which Frege draws our attention. Suppose Bill is at the Ziggy Stardust concert, watching Ziggy sing. He knows it's Ziggy singing, but doesn't know that Ziggy is David Bowie. Thus the following are true:

(1.3) Bill knows that Ziggy is singing

(1.4) Bill doesn't know that Bowie is singing

Since both are true and Ziggy is Bowie, the inference from (1.3) and (1.1) to 'Bill knows that Bowie is singing', which seems to be a simple substitution of co-referring names, must be invalid. We need some explanation of how this can be. Frege's explanation is that terms within the scope of the 'knows that' operator do not refer to their ordinary referent; rather, they switch reference to their ordinary sense. Thus, in (1.3), 'Ziggy' refers not to Bowie, but to the sense ordinarily associated with 'Ziggy'. Similarly, 'Bowie' in (1.4) refers not to Bowie, but to the sense ordinarily associated with 'Bowie'. Hence the referent of 'Ziggy' in (1.3) is not the referent of 'Bowie' in (1.2), on Frege's view. This blocks the substitution inference from (1.3) and (1.1) to 'Bill knows that Bowie is singing', as required.

More generally, the extension of a sentence embedded within a knowledge or belief operator is not a truth-value but rather the thought usually associated with that sentence, according to Frege. In this way, senses are the objects of knowledge and belief on the Fregean view. The belief that A and the belief that B are the same belief if and only if the sense ordinarily associated with 'A' is identical to the sense ordinarily associated with 'B'. In short, the Fregean account individuates epistemic and doxastic states in terms of senses (thoughts).

Transposing this to the possible worlds account, we get that epistemic and doxastic states are individuated in terms of functions on possible worlds. This is equivalent to saying that such states are individuated by sets of possible worlds. This result meshes very neatly with the possible worlds semantics for knowledge and belief from §1.2, which defines an agent's epistemic and doxastic states in terms of sets of possible worlds, via the accessibility relations R_i and R_i^δ. (Unlike the Fregean account, however, the possible worlds approach does not entail that the reference of a name switches from its ordinary referent to its ordinary sense when embedded within 'knows that' or 'believes that'. I return to this point in §8.6.)

In short, the possible worlds semantics explains Frege's puzzles of cognitive significance and knowledge. It also provides the means to interpret Fregean senses in a clear way. This is a very brief overview of how possible worlds semantics can deal with notions of information. Much more sophisticated models have been developed, which allow us to reason about how an agent's actions (including her reasoning) affect the information she has. van Benthem and Martinez (2008) and van Benthem (2011) give overviews of the recent literature.

Chapter Summary

In this chapter, I have presented the possible worlds account of knowledge and belief (§1.2) and propositions (§1.3). Given acceptance of possible worlds, this account gives us a clear account of what propositions are and demystifies content in general. Similarly, the possible worlds approach provides an interpretation of Fregean senses as intensions and explains how true identity statements can be informative (§1.4). Of course, like any good philosophical theory, there is a serious problem with the possible worlds approach. This will be the subject of the next chapter.

2

Hyperintensionality

In this chapter, I will introduce a number of related problems for the possible worlds approach to analysing knowledge, belief, information and content. The problems, at heart, are that these notions require distinctions to be made between logically equivalent contents. They are hyperintensional notions, but the possible worlds semantics does not deliver a hyperintensional account. I'll discuss attempts to explain away the apparent counterexamples to the possible worlds account. These are unsuccessful and so the possible worlds approach must either be amended or rejected entirely.

2.1 The Problem of Logical Omniscience

I will begin by discussing a deep problem that arises for the possible worlds account of knowledge, the problem of *logical omniscience*. I'll then go on to show how similar problems affect the possible worlds accounts of belief, information and content (§2.2).

Here is how the problem arises in the case of knowledge. Suppose for some set of sentences Γ, agent *i* at world *w* knows that *B* for each '*B*' ∈ Γ, and suppose that Γ logically entails '*A*'. Then, on the possible worlds approach, every world *u* epistemically accessible for *i* from *w* represents that *B* for each '*B*' ∈ Γ. Since Γ logically entails '*A*', each of these worlds also represents that *A* and hence *i* knows that *A* at *w*, according to the possible worlds account. In short, all agents know all consequences of what they know, according to the possible worlds account (Hintikka 1962). Moreover, since this is the case for all worlds w, it is on the possible worlds account a necessary truth that agents know all consequences of what they know. As a particular instance of the problem, agents are viewed as knowing that A whenever 'A' is a logical truth. This is because each logical truth follows from any set of premises (including the empty set): logical truths are true according to all possible worlds, and hence are always known by all agents, on the view. The same goes for all truths of mathematics. Since they are true according to all possible worlds, the possible worlds account says that every agent automatically knows every mathematical truth, regardless of how complex it is. An agent who knew all logical consequences of her knowledge would be logically omniscient. It is clearly not the case, however, that real-world agents such as you and I know all consequences of what they know. The problem of logical omniscience is that the possible worlds semantics incorrectly treats all agents as being logically omniscient.

To see that real-world epistemic agents are not logically omniscient, just consider any currently unproven mathematical hypothesis. Let's take Goldbach's conjuncture, which says that every integer $n > 2$ is the sum of two primes, as our example. If true, then it is true according to all possible worlds and hence it is known to be true by all agents, on the possible worlds account. If on the other hand it is false, then it is false according to all possible worlds and hence it is known to be false by all agents, on the possible worlds account. Either way, the possible worlds account entails that we all know whether Goldbach's conjecture is true.

Yet Goldbach's conjecture is one of the oldest unsolved problems in number theory. It is an open question whether it is true or false. It is easily stated and understood by those with a little high-school mathematics. Suppose we explain what the conjecture says to someone who hasn't heard it before, and ask her to consider it for a while. If she is sincere, it is overwhelmingly likely that she will claim not to know whether the conjecture is true or false.

Here is another route to the conclusion that we do not automatically know all consequences of what we know. Suppose you and I play a game of chess (with no time controls) in which a draw counts as a win for black. This guarantees the game will have a winner. It is then a surprising mathematical fact that, at any stage of the game, one of us has a *winning strategy*: there exists a strategy for one of us (that is, a function from the game's previous moves to that player's next move) that is mathematically guaranteed to win, regardless of how the other player plays.

Suppose that at one stage of the game s, σ is a winning strategy for me and σs tells me to move my queen to e7. This means that it is a mathematical fact that, if I do move my queen to e7 and continue to follow the recommendations of strategy σ, I am guaranteed to win. But as it is, I don't move my queen to e7 and I go on to lose the game. Had I known that Qe7 was the start of a winning strategy, I would have made that move. So I didn't know that σ is a winning strategy, even though σ's being so was entailed by my knowledge of the game. More generally, if I know all consequences of what I know and I play an even number of guaranteed-winner chess games, alternating between white and black each game, then I know how to win at least 50% of the games. This is regardless of who my opponent is! It's outlandish folly to think that I could beat Kasparov or Fischer in 50% of these games. I don't know those winning strategies, even though they are entailed by my knowledge of those games.

The fact that we do not know all consequences of what we know is central to this book and so I will give two more cases in support of the point. (If you're already convinced, feel free to skip ahead to §2.2.)

Early in the summer of 1902, the second volume of Frege's *Grundgesetze der Arithmetik* (Frege 1903) was in press. In the *Grundgesetze*, Frege sets down his logicist principles and attempts to derive arithmetic from the (supposedly) stable foundations of his logic. But Russell's famous letter to Frege of June 16 (Russell 1902/1967) pointed out that Frege's system was inconsistent. Basic Law V (the abstraction principle, stating that any concept determines a set) had allowed Russell to derive a contradiction similar to the one

Cesare Burali-Forti had discovered in 1897. Why would Frege have written the combined 565 pages of the *Grundgesetze*, if he knew at the outset that its core laws were contradictory? The only sensible interpretation of his actions is that, at the time of writing, he thought his system was consistent; he discovered the inconsistency only later, after reading Russell's letter. But then, since it is a mathematical truth that Frege's system is inconsistent, it cannot be the case that Frege knew all mathematical truths all along.

Here is one more case. Formal verification via model checking is a technique used in industry as a way of checking that certain properties hold of a system at the design stage. A formal model of the system is developed and used to check whether it satisfies a certain property, for example, that two users can never access the same account at the same time, or that the algorithm can never enter a cycle from which it will never exit. Even in seemingly simple systems, the number of possible states of the system can be enormous, which is why a formal tool for checking through all such states is required. It has often been the case that model checking has shown up unexpected flaws in the design, which then has to be rethought. Such examples highlight the value of model checking.

But if model checking a design has any value, it can only be because it allows us to find out whether the design satisfies a given property. That is, the value of model checking lies in providing us with knowledge. Yet the model checker itself does nothing but test logical consequences of the formal specification we give it. Since users do value model checking, it must be that those users did not know all logical consequences of their specification prior to running it through the model checker. This can only be the case if they are not logically omniscient.

I have been arguing that we do not know all consequences of what we know (and in particular, we do not know all logical truths). Real-world agents are not logically omniscient. In the next section, I turn to other epistemic concepts to which the possible worlds semantics has been applied: belief, information and cognitive significance, and content. We'll see that similar problems arise.

2.2   Related Problems

In this section, I show how similar problems arise for the possible worlds account of belief, information and content.

Belief

Just as the possible worlds approach to knowledge entails that agents automatically know all consequences of what they know, the possible worlds approach to belief entails that agents automatically believe all consequences of what they believe. The argument for this conclusion is just the same as in the case of knowledge. Whatever agent i believes at world w is true throughout all worlds u such that $R_i^\delta wu$. So any logical consequence of what i believes is also true at each such world and hence believed by i at w, according to the possible worlds account of belief.

All the cases I discussed above in arguing that agents are not logically omniscient also show that agents do not believe all consequences of what they believe. Frege did not believe his system to be inconsistent, for example. But there is an important additional reason for holding that agents do not believe all consequences of what they believe. Unlike knowledge, an agent's beliefs can be (and often are) contradictory (i.e., logically inconsistent with one another). Frege did not know that any concept determines a set, since this is false; but he did believe it. So, given Russell's reasoning, Frege's beliefs are mutually contradictory. But contradictions logically entail everything. So, if an agent has contradictory beliefs and also believes all logical consequences of what she believes, then she believes that pigs fly, that $0 = 1$, that Elvis lives, and any number of other absurdities. For any sentence 'A' you like, she believes that A. But clearly, no agent has beliefs like that. Indeed, I hold that it's impossible to have a belief state like that, for it would not count as a belief state at all. (I'll give an argument for that in chapter 6; see also §2.4.)

The possible worlds approach to belief clearly has a problem with inconsistent belief states. Indeed, it might seem that it cannot model inconsistent belief states at all, since contradictions are never true according to any possible world. But this is not quite right. On the possible worlds approach, belief is a matter of what is true according to all doxastically accessible worlds. If no worlds are doxastically accessible, therefore, this condition is trivially met, for all sentences 'A'. Hence if there are no worlds u such that $R_i^\delta wu$, then '$B_i A$' is true according to w, for every sentence 'A'. But if there are worlds u such that $R_i^\delta wu$, then the set of sentences 'A' such that '$B_i A$' is true according to w must be consistent. So on the possible worlds approach, each agent must either have an utterly consistent belief set, or else must believe everything.

Many of us have inconsistent beliefs at some time or other. One source of inconsistency is incorrectly believing something to be true, when in fact it is a logical or mathematical impossibility. Frege, in believing that every concept determines a set, had inconsistent beliefs in this way. But we can also fall into inconsistency by having beliefs, each of which is consistent when taken on its own, but which cannot all be true together. We each have a huge number of beliefs, only a very small subset of which we explicitly consider at any one time. It is not feasible to keep track of one's beliefs explicitly. This is why it is easy to come to believe something which contradicts something else one believes, if the latter is something one is not explicitly considering at that time.

Not only do we often have inconsistent belief states, we are sometimes justified in holding those beliefs. The overwhelming success of modern science (in comparison with competing means of investigating the world) justifies us in believing in our best scientific theories. Bill, a keen reader of popular science, reads about quantum mechanics and comes to believe in the theory as a whole. As a non-expert reader, he doesn't know all the details of the theory but, having read about its predictions being experimentally confirmed to a super-high level of accuracy, he comes to believe that quantum mechanics correctly describes the subatomic world. He also reads about general relativity and in a similar way comes to believe that general relativity correctly describes the structure of spacetime. However (and unbeknownst to Bill) quantum mechanics is inconsistent with general relativity at spacetime singularities. So Bill ends up with contradictory beliefs, even though he followed the good advice of believing in best science.

Informativeness

In §1.1, I described the information an agent gains from some source in terms of the difference between her epistemic state before and after gaining the information. (This applies to informative statements in general, not just about the informative identity statements from §1.4.) This section (which draws on Jago 2006a) considers the idea in more detail. On the possible worlds account, gaining information amounts to narrowing down the set of epistemically accessible worlds. As a consequence, logical and mathematical truths can never be informative, on the possible worlds account.

A logical or mathematical truth '*A*' is true at all worlds and hence narrowing down one's epistemic state to worlds which represent that *A* has no effect: no narrowing takes place. This is in line with the discussion of logical omniscience above. If all agents always automatically know that *A* (where '*A*' is any logical truth), then no agent can genuinely learn that *A* (i.e., move from a state of ignorance to a state of knowledge concerning whether *A*) and hence '*A*' is utterly uninformative. So the possible worlds approach must say that all logical and mathematical truths are utterly uninformative.

Wittgenstein (who, as we saw in §1.4, developed an account of meaning as a way of partitioning possible 'states' or worlds), agreed that logical truths are never informative. He held in the *Tractatus* that 'there can *never* be surprises in logic' (1922, §6.1251). Indeed, he held that logical truths are *sinnlos*, lacking any sense. They literally 'say nothing' (§6.11) and so 'theories which make a proposition of logic appear substantial are always false' (§6.111). Meaningful propositions, according to Wittgenstein, must form a 'logical picture' (§2.19) of the world, i.e., they must partition logical space into non-empty subspaces. Logical truths (and logical falsehoods) do not do this, since they are true (and false, respectively) according to all possible worlds.

But of course there are surprises in logic and mathematics, as a cursory leaf through the technical literature shows. As Dummett says, 'when we contemplate the wealth and complexity of number-theoretic theorems, ... we are struck by the difficulty of establishing them and *the surprises they yield* (Dummett 1978a, 297, my emphasis). Students who happily accept the truth-table for the material conditional '→' are surprised to learn that, for any sentences 'A' and 'B' whatsoever, in any situation either '$A \rightarrow B$' or '$B \rightarrow A$' will be true.

Even preeminent logicians are occasionally surprised by their results, as the reaction to early results in model theory shows. Löwenheim's theorem, stating that every satisfiable sentence (in a countable language) has a countable model, perplexed Skolem (who gave the first correct proof of it (Skolem 1922)). Skolem took the result to be paradoxical, for it entails that theories asserting the existence of an uncountable set, if consistent, have countable models. A natural way to explain what makes a given truth surprising is to appeal to its informativeness. If logical results were not informative, then they would never be surprising. So logical truths can be informative.

By way of anecdotal support from the experts in mathematical proof, here is Andrew Wiles, describing the subjective experience of working on his proof of Fermat's last theorem:

> You enter the first room of the mansion and it's completely dark. You stumble around bumping into the furniture but gradually you learn where each piece of furniture is. Finally, after six months or so, you find the light switch, you turn it on, and suddenly it's all illuminated. You can see exactly where you were. (Wiles 2000)

The lights come on and information rushes in. Of course, we shouldn't place too much emphasis on first-person phenomenological descriptions. Nevertheless, the best explanation of Wiles's phenomenology of becoming informed is that he was in fact informed: the process of constructing his proof provided him with genuine mathematical information.

Content

In §1.3, we saw that the possible worlds approach treats propositions as sets of possible worlds. As a consequence, logically equivalent propositions are identical to one another. This is Stalnaker's principle (I) (1976a, 9). But the principle is incorrect. We can bring out what's wrong with it by focusing on what a given proposition (or the sentence expressing it) is about, or by focusing on what makes a given proposition true.

One job of a proposition is to give the content of the sentence expressing it and, in particular, to specify what that sentence is about. Hence, if sentences 'A' and 'B' express the same proposition in a common context c then they should be about the very same things (in that context). As a consequence, the possible worlds approach entails that logically equivalent sentences are always about the very same things (in any context). But this is not so:

(2.1) Puss is crafty

is about Puss (and perhaps about *craftiness* too), but isn't about Rover. Likewise,

(2.2) Puss is crafty ∨ Puss isn't crafty

is about Puss (and perhaps about *craftiness* too), but isn't about Rover. Contrast this with

(2.3) Rover is snoring

which is about Rover (and perhaps about *snoring* too), but isn't about Puss. Likewise,

(2.4) Rover is snoring ∨ Rover isn't snoring

is about Rover (and perhaps about *snoring* too), but isn't about Puss.

Thus (2.2) and (2.4) are about completely different things. Yet (2.2) and (2.4) are logically equivalent, contradicting the consequence of the possible worlds approach. Similarly,

(2.5) Puss is crafty ∧ 1 = 1

is logically equivalent to (2.1) and so, on the possible worlds approach, (2.1) should be about precisely the same things as (2.5). But (2.5) is, in part, about the number 1, whereas (2.1) is not. Hence the possible worlds approach cannot be right.

We can make essentially the same point by focusing on the notion of what makes a proposition true or false. If Puss exists, then she is what makes the proposition

(2.6) ⟦Puss exists⟧

true. By that token, she is what makes the proposition

(2.7) ⟦Puss exists ∨ Puss doesn't exist⟧

true. Puss is (2.7)'s one and only (actual) *minimal* truthmaker: no proper part of Puss makes (2.7) true. By parallel reasoning, if Rover exists then the one and only (actual) minimal truthmaker for

(2.8) ⟦Rover exists ∨ Rover doesn't exist⟧

is Rover. Since Puss isn't Rover, (2.7) and (2.8) have different properties: one is minimally made true by Puss, the other by Rover. So (2.7) and (2.8) are not identical propositions. Yet they are logically equivalent. Hence propositions cannot be sets of possible worlds.

2.3   Intensionality and Beyond

The problem of logical omniscience, as well as its variants affecting the possible worlds approach to belief states, informativeness and content, all arise because the possible worlds approach is *intensional*.

An operator 'O' (a word or phrase which, when appended to a sentence results in a new sentence) is intensional if and only if 'OA' and 'OB' are materially equivalent whenever 'A' and 'B' are logically equivalent, but need not be when 'A' and 'B' are (merely) materially equivalent. Such operators (unlike extensional operators) can differentiate between sentences which happen to have the same truth-value, but are indifferent to logically equivalent sentences. Examples include 'it is necessary that', 'it is possible that' and 'it is a logical truth that'.

Operators which draw distinctions between logically equivalent cases, by contrast, are *hyperintensional* operators. For such operators 'O', 'OA' and 'OB' may fail to be materially equivalent even when 'A' and 'B' are logically equivalent. The possible worlds approach is intensional in the sense that it can define intensional operators, but cannot define hyperintensional operators.

We can put the problems pointed out in the previous two sections as follows: neither '*i* knows that', '*i* believes that' or 'it is informative that' are intensional operators. The concepts of knowledge, belief and information require us to make distinctions which are strictly more fine-grained than is possible within an intensional framework. They are hyperintensional concepts. To capture these hyperintensional concepts, our semantics must be able to draw distinctions between logically equivalent sentences.

Hyperintensionality is the key concept in this book and how to capture hyperintensionality is the main theoretical problem I will address in subsequent chapters. If we are to think meaningfully about impossible situations, thinking itself must draw hyperintensional distinctions. For we can think about some impossible situation, even some logically impossible situation, without thereby thinking about all logically impossible situations. All of those logically impossible situations are logically equivalent: purely as a matter of logic, they cannot obtain. Thinking about impossible situations is neither thinking about nothing nor thinking about everything. At least some impossible thoughts have content, expressing meaningful propositions. Moreover, not all impossible thoughts express the same proposition. To make sense of impossible thoughts, therefore, we need a hyperintensional account.

At this point, we have three options. We might claim that knowledge, belief, information and content are not hyperintensional concepts after all and hence that they are adequately captured by the possible worlds semantics (§§2.4–2.6). Alternatively, we might accept that knowledge, belief, information and content are hyperintensional and hence that we should abandon the possible worlds account in favour of a completely different approach (§2.7). Our third option is to accept that knowledge, belief, information and content are hyperintensional and consider ways to extend the possible worlds account to incorporate hyperintensionality.

To lay my cards on the table, I will adopt the third approach. Knowledge, belief, information and content are genuinely hyperintensional concepts; attempts to show otherwise fail. But rejecting the possible worlds approach entirely on this basis is throwing out the baby with the bathwater. The best option is to preserve the benefits of the possible worlds approach, whilst incorporating hyperintensionality. But this is jumping the gun. We must first establish that knowledge, belief, information and content are genuinely hyperintensional concepts, in the face of philosophical arguments to the contrary. It is to these arguments that I now turn.

2.4 Rational Attitudes

Stalnaker (1984) and Lewis (1982, 1986) maintain that the possible worlds analysis of knowledge, belief and content is (broadly) correct. They each give a positive argument in favour of the analysis, which begins with considerations on the nature of these concepts and concludes that knowledge and belief states are to be analysed in terms of sets of possible worlds. They acknowledge the weight of the objections that we do not know all consequences of what we know, that logical reasoning can be informative and so on. Accordingly, they add to the possible worlds account in a number of ways, in an attempt to avoid the worst of these objections. In this section, I will begin to address these arguments, focusing on Stalnaker's account of belief.

Stalnaker begins his account of belief states by giving an 'impressionistic picture of the nature of human activities which involve mental representation' (Stalnaker 1984, 4). On this picture,

> Rational creatures are essentially agents. Representational mental states should be understood primarily in terms of the role that they play in the characterization and explanation of action. What is essential to rational action is that the agent be confronted, or conceive of himself as confronted, with a range of alternative possible outcomes of some alternative possible actions. The agent has attitudes, pro and con, toward the different possible outcomes, and beliefs about the contribution which the alternative actions would make to determining the outcome. One explains why an agent tends to act in the way he does in terms of such beliefs and attitudes. And, according to this picture, our conceptions of belief are conceptions of states which explain why a rational agent does what he does. (Stalnaker 1984, 4)

Stalnaker calls this a 'pragmatist' account, since it holds that representational mental states 'must be explained ... in terms of their connections with the explanation of rational action' (1984, 4). By this, he does not intend a behaviouristic attempt to reduce unobserved inner states to patterns of behaviour (1984, 16). His approach attempts 'to explain the intentional in terms of the nonintentional' and not 'to explain the unobservable in terms of the observable' (1984, 16).

Belief, on Stalnaker's view, is a dispositional state of a rational agent and 'to believe that p is to be disposed to act in ways that would tend to satisfy one's desires, whatever they are, in a world in which p (together with one's other beliefs) were true' (1984, 15). Such dispositions play a role in causing the agent's behaviour, but they are also caused by states of the world (1984, 19). This is a *functionalist* account of belief (and other representational mental states).

The task is then to specify what the content of such dispositional states is. Stalnaker's idea is that we should 'assign to the *contents* of representations just the structure that is motivated by the pragmatic account of the functional role of representations' (1984, 23). This structure is a structure of alternative possibilities, for 'it is essential to the role of beliefs and desires in the explanation of action that the contents of those attitudes distinguish between the alternative possibilities' (1984, 23). It is this idea that links the functional account of belief to the possible worlds picture: the structure of content motivated by the functional account is precisely the structure of sets of possible worlds, according to Stalnaker. Hence, if the view is correct, contents should be identified with sets of possible worlds.

A consequence is that equivalent contents are identical. But now this is not merely a consequence of the possible worlds approach. It is also a consequence of (or at least motivated by) Stalnaker's far more general functional analysis of belief:

> Whatever propositions are taken to be, and however we make precise the propositional relations ... [which explain] belief and desire, it is clear from the general schemas for the definitions of those relations that the following will be true: if the relation holds between an individual and a proposition x, and if x is necessarily equivalent to proposition y, then the relation holds between the individual and y. (Stalnaker 1984, 24)

Stalnaker does not claim that this solves the problem of logical omniscience (or the associated problems). Rather, this shows that 'the possible worlds analysis of proposition ... [has] a deeper philosophical motivation than has sometimes been supposed' (1984, 24). The examples used to argue that agents are not logically omniscient 'are not just counterexamples to a particular analysis', that is, to the possible worlds semantics, 'but cases which are problematic in themselves' (1984, 24). They are problematic because 'we lack a satisfactory understanding, from any point of view, of what it is to believe that p while disbelieving that q, where the 'p' and the 'q' stand for necessarily equivalent expressions' (1984, 24).

The situation, according to Stalnaker, is that 'we have an argument to show that the identity conditions [on contents] are right, as well as examples that seem to show that they are wrong', and so 'the proper response is not so clear' (1984, 24). (Contrast this with the case in which we present a formal semantics 'to systematize brute intuitions about the structure and identity conditions for objects of belief' and yet find counterexamples. Then, 'the proper response would be to replace the technical apparatus with one that could make finer discriminations between the contents of attitudes and expressions' (Stalnaker 1984, 24).)

I do not intend to assess Stalnaker's functionalist account of belief, or whether it does indeed entail the possible worlds account of content, in detail. A functionalist account of belief looks to be in the right ballpark. The functionalist approach is the best way to account for the causal relations between belief, desire and action whilst also assigning to belief states the correct contents (problems of logical omniscience aside). And this approach certainly motivates an approach to content in terms of worlds, or alternative situations. Yet we can modify the possible worlds approach in a number of ways without having to surrender the functionalist account of belief. I consider two such ways in chapters 3 and 4.

Stalnaker, having motivated the possible worlds account of content, then sets about reconciling the account (as far as possible) with what seem to be clear facts about knowledge and belief attribution. For instance, we typically do not attribute knowledge or belief that A to an agent purely on the basis that 'A' is a necessary truth. Stalnaker acknowledges a broader problem, which is 'to explain how it is possible for the conclusion of a deductive argument to contain any information not already contained in the premises and, as a special case of this, how it is possible for a necessary truth to contain any information at all' (1984, 25). This is the problem of informativeness from §2.2.

Stalnaker has two complementary strategies for tackling these problems. The first strategy deals with agents who know (or believe) some premises but not the conclusion because they have not put the premises together into a single epistemic (or doxastic) state. The second strategy deals with the information gained in learning logical and mathematical truths. I'll discuss each in turn.

2.5 Fragments of Belief

In this section, I discuss the idea that an agent's beliefs might be divided into several fragments or clusters. The suggestion is to view the agent as having multiple belief states, one corresponding to each fragment (and similarly for her knowledge). Lewis (1982) and Fagin and Halpern (1988), as well as Stalnaker (1984), present versions of the idea. Lewis motivates his version of it as follows:

> I used to think that Nassau Street ran roughly east-west; that the railroad nearby ran roughly north-south; and that the two were roughly parallel. ... So each sentence in an inconsistent triple was true according to my beliefs, but not everything was true according to my beliefs. ... My system of beliefs was broken into (overlapping) fragments. Different fragments came into action in different situations, and the whole system of beliefs never manifested itself all at once. ... The inconsistent conjunction of all three did not belong to, was in no way implied by, and was not true according to, any one fragment. That is why it was not true according to my system of beliefs taken as a whole. (Lewis 1982, 436)

We can view each of Lewis's fragments as an individual belief state, so that an agent's total system of beliefs is divided into multiple (and perhaps overlapping) states. On Stalnaker's view, each of an agent's multiple belief states corresponds to a rational dispositional state:

> A person may be disposed, in one kind of context, or with respect to one kind of action, to behave in ways that are correctly explained by one belief state, and at the same time be disposed in another kind of context or with respect to another kind of action to behave in ways that would be explained by a different belief state. This need not be a matter of shifting from one state to another or vacillating between states; the agent might, at the

> same time, be in two stable belief states, be in two different dispositional states which are displayed in different kinds of situations. (Stalnaker 1984, 83)

An agent is then thought of as believing that A if and only if 'A' is true according to *at least one* of the agent's belief states. Then it may be the case that the agent believes that A, and believes that B, but does not believe that $A \wedge B$. This is the case when 'A' is true according to one of the agent's belief states, 'B' is true according to another, but both are true according to none of them. Since the fragments may contradict one another, as in Lewis's example, an agent may believe that A (in one fragment) and that $\neg A$ (in another fragment), without believing that $A \wedge \neg A$.

This opens the way for a possible worlds account of each of the agent's fragments of beliefs: each of the agent's individual belief states is represented as a set of accessible possible worlds. Each individual belief state is consistent (§2.2), even though the agent's beliefs in total need not be. Each belief state is closed under entailment: whatever is a consequence of what is true according to a belief state is also true according to that belief state. Yet the agent's beliefs in total are not closed under entailment: she may not believe all consequences of what she believes. In particular, she may have inconsistent beliefs and yet not believe everything.

Fagin and Halpern (1988) give a formal model of belief along these lines, which they call a model of 'local reasoning'. They think in terms of multiple 'frames of mind' of an agent and assign a belief state to each frame of mind of each agent. (Each frame of mind corresponds to one of Lewis's belief fragments.) Reasoning is 'local' to each frame of mind. A model for n agents is defined as a tuple

$$\mathcal{M} = \langle W, V, L_1 \dots L_n \rangle$$

where W is a set of worlds, V is a classical 2-valued valuation function and each L_i is a function of type

$$W \longrightarrow 2^{2^W}$$

assigning to each world a nonempty set of nonempty sets of worlds. If $L_i w = \{X_1, \ldots, X_k\}$, then each $X_{j \leq k}$ is the set of worlds that agent i considers possible from w when in state-of-mind j. In other words, each $X_{j \leq k}$ gives one of agent i's belief states. '$B_i A$' is interpreted as 'agent i believes A in some frame of mind':

$$w \Vdash B_i A \text{ iff for some } X \in L_i w \text{ and all } w' \in X, w' \Vdash A$$

A notion of implicit belief can also be defined within this framework by pooling information from an agent's various frames of mind. Agent i implicitly believes that A at w, $w \Vdash L_i A$, iff A is satisfied by all worlds considered possible from w in all frames of mind, i.e. in all worlds $w' \in \bigcap L_i w$:

$$w \Vdash L_i A \text{ iff, for all } w' \in \bigcap L_i w, w' \Vdash A$$

If an agent holds inconsistent beliefs at w (albeit in different fragments, or in different frames of mind), the intersection of the agent's belief states $\bigcap L_i w$ will be empty and thus the agent will implicitly believe everything. Yet the agent's explicit beliefs are not closed under entailment, as it is easy to verify. In particular, '$B_i A \wedge B_i \neg A$' is satisfiable, but '$B_i(A \wedge \neg A)$' is not satisfiable, on this semantics. Moreover, according to these models, an agent need not know all consequences of what she knows. It may be that agent i knows and hence believes that $A_1, \ldots, A_n$, and that 'A_1', $\ldots$, 'A_n' together entail 'B', yet i does not believe and hence does not know that B.

Despite not being closed under entailment, an agent's beliefs are closed under valid implication, on this semantics. If agent i believes that A and '$A \to B$' is valid, then that agent is modelled as believing that B. For if '$A \to B$' is valid, then it is true according to all of the agent's belief states. The agent has at least one belief state according to which 'A' is true, hence 'B' too is true according to that belief state, and so the agent believes that B. Thus '$B_i A \to B_i B$' is valid whenever '$A \to B$' is valid. As a consequence, the approach provides no way to avoid knowledge being closed under valid implication. For if agent i knows that A and '$A \rightarrow B$' is valid, then she is modelled as believing and hence (since entailment preserves knowledge from believed premises to believed conclusions) knowing that B.

This shows that the fragments of belief approach does not, on its own, solve the full problem of logical omniscience discussed in §2.1 and §2.2. But it is not supposed to; at least, not in isolation. Lewis (1982) uses the fragments of belief approach to show how we can reason about an agent's inconsistent beliefs without recourse to paraconsistent or relevant logic. Similarly, Stalnaker adopts the approach because he requires a possible worlds account on which an agent's beliefs are not closed under logical consequence. In these limited respects, I have no quarrel with the fragments of belief approach.

The fragments of belief approach does not do all the work Stalnaker requires of it, however. He wants to use it to explain how it is that we acquire the information conveyed in a statement about deductive relationships, such as 'the premises Γ entail the conclusion 'A''. The explanation afforded by the fragments of belief approach is that an agent can believe each premise in Γ and not the conclusion. An agent can have such beliefs when the premises Γ are split across her fragments of belief, so that no one fragment contains all of her beliefs in Γ.

It is implausible, however, that whenever an agent does not believe some consequence of what she believes, this is so because she hasn't put the relevant premises together. When an agent does put the premises 'A_1', . . . , 'A_n' $\in \Gamma$ together into a single fragment, she thereby comes to believe the conjunction of all of them and hence, on the fragments of belief account, automatically believes all consequences of Γ. The picture is that all the agent's deductive effort goes into combining the premises into a single belief state, that is, in the relatively trivial deductive move from the premises 'A_1', . . . , 'A_n' to '$A_1 \wedge \cdots \wedge A_n$'. If these are all the premises, the move from '$A_1 \wedge \cdots \wedge A_n$' to any logical consequence of Γ then comes for free.

This is implausible as a general explanation. It often happens that one does consider all the premises of a deduction at once (and perhaps even considers their conjunction) and yet cannot infer the conclusion. The information conveyed by a non-trivial valid deduction does not correspond to the move from individual premises to their conjunction, but rather in the deductive move from those premises (or their conjunction) to the conclusion. This notion is the target of Stalnaker's explanation, but it is precisely what the fragments of belief account leaves out.

2.6   The Metalinguistic Approach

I now turn to the second component of Stalnaker's solution to the problem of deduction. It is intended as an answer to the question, 'what is the nature of the information conveyed in a statement about deductive relationships?' (Stalnaker 1984, 85). As we saw in §2.1 and §2.2, logical truths are true in all possible worlds. So it is never informative, according the possible worlds account, to learn a logical truth. Similarly for meta-logical truths, such as 'the premises Γ entail the conclusion 'A''. If true, this is true in all possible worlds and hence learning that Γ entails 'A' is never informative, on the possible worlds account.

As Stalnaker acknowledges, we do learn something when we discover a deductive relationship. The fragments of belief approach, as Stalnaker uses it, is supposed to explain how we come by the information that Γ entails 'A'. The question now is, what is that information? Similarly for the case of logical truths, including those of the form '$A_1 \wedge \cdots \wedge A_n \to A$' that encode deductive relationships: just what is the information that they convey?

Stalnaker's answer is that in such cases, one learns which proposition the sentence in question expresses:

> Relative to any propositional expression one can determine two propositions: there is the proposition that is expressed, according to the standard rules, and there is the proposition

that relates the expression to what it expresses. If sentence S expresses (according to the standard rules) proposition p, then the second proposition in question is the proposition that S expresses p. In cases of ignorance of necessity and equivalence, I am suggesting, it is the second proposition that is the object of doubt and investigation. (Stalnaker 1984, 84–5)

On the possible worlds account, there is only one necessarily true proposition, namely the set of all possible worlds. Similarly, there is only one necessarily false proposition, namely the empty set. Stalnaker's idea is that 'the apparent failure to see that a proposition is necessarily true, or that propositions are necessarily equivalent, is to be explained as the failure to see what propositions are expressed by the expressions in question' (1984, 84). If 'A' is a necessary truth but it seems that I do not know that A, then what I do not know, according to Stalnaker, is that the sentence 'A' expresses the proposition *that* A, namely, the set of all possible worlds.

This is not a revision of the possible worlds account of content, or of what it is to know or believe that A. The claim is not that one does not know that A when one does not know which proposition 'A' expresses. If it is a necessary truth that A, then all agents always and automatically know that A, according to Stalnaker. Nor is the claim that one does not know that one knows that A in this case. For when it is a necessary truth that A, '$K_i A$' is true according to all worlds according to which i exists and hence according to all worlds epistemically accessible to agent i. So when it is a necessary truth that A, each agent knows that A, knows that she knows that A, knows that she knows that A and so on, for any number of iterations of 'knows that', on the possible worlds account.

Stalnaker's claim is that, even though one knows that A whenever it is necessarily true that A, one may not know that one's knowledge is expressed by the sentence 'A'. Similarly for the case of belief: one automatically believes every necessary truth, but one may not know (or believe) that 'A' expresses the proposition that A. In these cases, our agent 'will still believe that A, but will not himself put it that way' and, moreover, 'it may be misleading for others to put it that way in attributing the belief to him' (1984, 84). Stalnaker offers the following justification of this move:

> Because items of belief and doubt lack grammatical structure, while the formulations asserted and assented to by an agent in expressing his beliefs and doubts have such a structure, there is an inevitable gap between propositions and their expressions. Whenever the structure of sentences is complicated, there will be a nontrivial question about the relation between sentences and the propositions they express, and so there will be room for reasonable doubt about what proposition is expressed by a given sentence. (Stalnaker 1984, 84).

How plausible is this approach, as part of a systematic account of knowledge and belief ascriptions? There certainly do seem to be cases of the kind to which Stalnaker appeals, in which an agent i dissents from 'agent i believes that A' precisely because she does not grasp what the sentence 'A' expresses. Stalnaker offers the example '$(A \rightarrow ((B \rightarrow A) \rightarrow B)) \rightarrow (A \rightarrow B)$' (1984, 74). Consider that sentence for a moment: do you agree that you believe it is true? If you're like me, it took you a while to think through what that sentence means. It's plausible that, until you think it through and see that it's a tautology, you don't know what the sentence means. So, once you do grasp its meaning, you also realise that it is valid and hence believe that it is true. So in this case, Stalnaker's approach has some plausibility.

In general, however, the approach is not plausible. It is not plausible that, whenever an agent seems not to know (or not to believe) some necessary truth, then she must be ignorant of its meaning. In many cases, we can understand the question perfectly well and still not know the answer, even when the correct answer is a matter of logic (or mathematics). Many agents with high school mathematics can understand the statement that there are no three integers x, y and z such that, for any integer n greater than 2, $x^n + y^n = z^n$. Yet we want to deny that they thereby all know that Fermat's Last Theorem holds.

To resist this point, Stalnaker must insist that one of these agents does not fully grasp what the statement of the theorem means. But this is a hard doctrine to maintain. Our agent (let us suppose) understands the notation for variables ranging over integers; understands that they are universally quantified; understands the 'x^n' notation for exponentiation and the '+' and '=' symbols. So she must be unable to parse the way these symbols are syntactically combined. To be sure, there is complexity here. But there is hardly sufficient syntactic complexity to justify the difficulty agents might have in coming to know that Fermat's Last Theorem is true. Indeed, the structure of our previous example, '$(A \rightarrow ((B \rightarrow A) \rightarrow B)) \rightarrow (A \rightarrow B)$', seems harder to grasp than the statement of Fermat's last theorem. Yet the former can be checked for validity very quickly, whereas verifying Fermat's Last Theorem is non-trivial in the extreme.

Let us consider another example: our chess players from §2.1. Suppose that, at a particular stage of the game, white looks to be in serious trouble. Her defences are in disarray, her pawns doubled and blocking her bishops, her king in danger. She considers the game lost. Yet, let us suppose, she has a winning strategy σ available, beginning with queen to e7. This move looks to be a non-starter, since it loses her material immediately. To see that it forces a win takes serious in-depth analysis which is way beyond white's ability. (There clearly are such stages of games.) It is a mathematical truth that σ is a winning strategy, given the rules of the game and the current positions of the pieces. A list of the rules 'r' and a description of the current state of the game 's' necessarily entails that σ is a winning strategy. Hence white knows that 'r' and 's' entail that σ is a winning strategy, on the possible worlds approach. She also knows that, at the current state of the game, σ says to move the white queen to e7 (for again, this is a mathematical truth).

Yet from white's subjective perspective, her predicament remains. She acts as if the game is lost and were she asked, she would say the game is up. So we do not want to say that she knows that Qe7 will allow her to win. Hence she must either be ignorant of the meaning of "$r \wedge s$' entails 'σ is a winning strategy''', or else not know that

$r \wedge s$. As she does know the rules and the current position of the pieces, it must be that she does not know what "$r \wedge s$' entails 'σ is a winning strategy" means. But this is not a plausible explanation of her predicament. Her problem is that she cannot calculate possible sequences of moves deeply and quickly enough to spot that Qe7 sets her on a winning strategy. Hers is clearly not a linguistic problem.

Let us review the situation. Stalnaker presents two complementary approaches to the problem of logical omniscience (and the problem of deduction, of which he takes the logical omniscience problem to be a special case). The metalinguistic approach concerns the question, 'what is the nature of the information given by logical, mathematical and other necessary truths?' The answer Stalnaker gives is: it is information about which proposition the sentence in question expresses. The fragments of belief approach concerns the question, 'how does an agent come by this information?' The answer Stalnaker gives is: by combining premises from different fragments of her beliefs.

I have argued that neither approach is successful in answering the question it sets out to answer. It is implausible that logical and mathematical information is gained only in the process of combining premises. In general, the move from premises 'A_1',...,'A_n' to their conjunction '$A_1 \wedge \cdots \wedge A_n$' is (relatively) trivial and uninformative. The hard part of deduction, and the part which (in typical cases) is genuinely informative, is the move from the premises (either taken individually or conjoined) to the conclusion 'A'. Moreover, it is implausible that one learns nothing from such reasoning processes except the identity of the proposition expressed by "A_1',...,'A_n' entail 'A" or by '$A_1 \wedge \cdots \wedge A_n \rightarrow A$'. When a mathematician completes a complicated proof, she may gain deep mathematical knowledge, about the way numbers relate to one another, for instance. When a chess player reasons that such-and-such move forces a win, she learns how to win the game. Neither the mathematician's nor the chess player's new knowledge is merely linguistic, as Stalnaker would have us believe.

For these reasons, I reject Stalnaker's approach to the problems of logical omniscience and deduction. Knowledge, belief, information and content are genuinely hyperintensional notions. It is not the case that one automatically knows or believes every logical or mathematical truth. Such truths may well be informative and have a non-trivial content. They do not all share the same 'set-of-all-worlds' content. In the next section, I consider how we should proceed, given these conclusions.

2.7   Prospects

Stalnaker's valiant attempt to save the possible worlds approach to knowledge, belief, information and content from the challenge of hyperintensionality has failed. We must find an account which provides genuinely hyperintensional contents, so that logically equivalent sentences can be assigned distinct contents. Only in this way can we explain how impossible thoughts are often meaningful and contentful, and how there can be distinct impossible thoughts with distinct contents.

How then should we proceed in our search for these hyperintensional contents? One option is to abandon the possible worlds approach entirely and look elsewhere for inspiration. This isn't the approach I'll take, for two reasons. First, the problem of logical omniscience aside, the possible worlds approach is the best theory of content we have on offer. It offers the most comprehensive and systematic account of intensional notions. As always in science, the rational approach is to begin with our best theory and modify it so as to avoid phenomena which it does not currently accommodate. It is always better to preserve the best features of our current best account, if that is at all feasible.

Second, it is not clear that there is a rival account to the possible worlds approach when it comes to capturing hyperintensionality. To be sure, there is a 'sentential' or 'syntactic' approach in epistemic logic, which (trivially) avoids the logical omniscience problem. On this approach, knowledge ascriptions have subject-predicate form.

'Knows that' is treated as a binary predicate with the name of an agent as its first argument and a name for a sentence as its second. Thus 'agent i knows that A' is seen as having the form 'Knows(i, 'A')'. Quine and Ullian (1970, 12), Davidson (1968) and Loewer and Lepore (1989) provide philosophical support for this approach to knowledge ascriptions.

(There have been a wide variety of formal models of knowledge along these lines, offered by Eberle (1974), Moore and Hendrix (1979), Hayes and McCarthy (1969), des Rivieres and Levesque (1686), Morreau and Kraus (1998), Konolige (1986) and Grant et al. (2000). Some of these are discussed by Halpern and Moses (1990), Fagin et al. (1995, 314–316) and Jago (2006b).)

On this approach, the second argument of 'Knows(i, 'A')' is a name for the sentence 'A'. To see how this works, suppose we give the name 'Leslie' to the first sentence of the novel *The Go-Between*. Then the ascription 'Leo knows that the past is a foreign country' could be regimented as 'Knows(Leo, Leslie)'. Now, Leslie is equivalent to 'the past is a foreign country and there are no distinct integers x, y, z and integer $n > 2$ such that $x^n + y^n = z^n$'. Call the sentence just mentioned 'Fermat'. Clearly, 'Knows(Leo, Leslie)' does not entail 'Knows(Leo, Fermat)', even though Leslie and Fermat are equivalent sentences. So this approach to knowledge ascriptions does not suffer from the problem of logical omniscience.

This is an approach to knowledge (and belief) ascriptions only; it is not an approach to content. Indeed, it says nothing whatsoever about the content of knowledge or belief states. Moreover, it is not a genuinely hyperintensional account at all. It holds that knowledge and belief ascriptions have a certain logical form, which can be captured in standard first-order logic (so long as we have a quotation-forming or other sentence-naming device available). But standard first-order logic is extensional through and through. Quine, the arch-skeptic of the intensional, supports the first-order sentential approach to knowledge and belief ascriptions precisely because it treats them in an extensional way. No attempt is made by this approach to move beyond the ontology of sentences to their contents or meanings.

So this approach cannot help us one jot in explaining how many sentences describing the impossible are contentful and meaningful, or in explaining how we can think about those impossible situations.

One might look instead to *conceptual role semantics* to deliver a hyperintensional account of content. Conceptual role semantics identifies the meaning of a representation, such as a sentence or a particular mental state, with its conceptual role in the cognitive life of the agent in question (Field 1977; Harman 1987; Miller and Johnson-Laird 1976). One might then argue that, since there are equivalent sentences which nevertheless play a different role in an agent's cognitive life, we can use this approach to assign different contents to those sentences.

It is not obvious, however, that conceptual role semantics is best viewed as a theory of content in the same sense as the possible worlds approach I have described so far. A theory of content may be either a theory of what a particular content is, or a theory of how a particular representation gets to have a particular content. Possible worlds semantics is a theory of content in the former sense. It says: a content is a set of possible worlds. Conceptual role semantics is often taken to be (or perhaps, is best interpreted as) a theory of content in the latter sense. It says: a representation 'A' gets to have a particular proposition x as its content, for an agent i, in virtue of the cognitive role 'A' plays in i's mental life. Interpreted in this way, conceptual role semantics leaves it open just what the nature of that content x is.

Suppose instead that we do wish to interpret conceptual role semantics as a theory of what content is (in the sense that possible worlds semantics is a theory of what content is). Then the theory says: the content of a representation is the inferences the agent in question makes, or is disposed to make, with the representation in question. On this view, conceptual role semantics is a form of the *use theory* of meaning (Dummett 1978b, 1993; Horwich 1995, 2004; Wittgenstein 1953). The content of 'A' consists of sets of representations, those from which 'A' can be inferred and those that can be inferred from 'A'. In the case of logically complex sentences such as '$A \wedge B$' and

'$A \to B$', therefore, their contents are related to the contents of their sub-sentences 'A' and 'B' by the logical rules for reasoning with '$\wedge$' and '$\to$' sentences. In a natural deduction proof system, for example, the *introduction and elimination rules* for '$\wedge$' are:

$$\frac{A \wedge B}{A} \qquad \frac{A \wedge B}{B} \qquad \frac{A \quad B}{A \wedge B}$$

These say that we can always infer 'A' and 'B' from '$A \wedge B$', and we can always infer '$A \wedge B$' when we have both 'A' and 'B'.

(In this way, conceptual role semantics can be seen as a generalisation of proof-theoretic semantics. Proof-theoretic semantics began with Gentzen (1934) and was developed in the 1970s by Prawitz (1971, 1973) and Martin-Löf (1975). More recent contributions come from Dummett (1991) and Schroeder-Heister (1991).)

Now consider any logical truths 'A' and 'B'. We can infer 'A' from any set of premises Γ whatsoever; and similarly for 'B'. Moreover, from 'A' we can infer all other logical truths and nothing but logical truths. For if some 'C' provable from 'A' were not a logical truth, then there must be some model M on which 'C' is not true; but since 'A' is true on all models, M would be a counterexample to the entailment from 'A' to 'C'. Similarly for 'B': all and only the logical truths can be inferred from it. Hence 'A' and 'B' are assigned precisely the same content. Every logical truth is assigned the same content, on this approach.

More generally, suppose 'A' and 'B' are logically equivalent (they need not themselves be logical truths). Then any consequence of 'A' is a consequence of 'B' and vice versa, and for any set of premises Γ of which 'A' is a consequence, 'B' is also a consequence (and vice versa). So again, 'A' and 'B' are assigned precisely the same content, on this approach. Dealing with contents in this way does not provide us with a hyperintensional account. Contents are defined up to (proof-theoretical) equivalence: so long as the proof-rules of the system in question allow us to move between 'A' and 'B', the account of content cannot distinguish between the contents of 'A' and of 'B'.

I do not mean to dismiss proof-theoretic semantics, or conceptual-role semantics more generally. My point is that it does not easily deliver hyperintensional contents. The problem of hyperintensionality is a problem for any theory, not just for the possible worlds approach. As Stalnaker says, 'we lack a satisfactory understanding, from any point of view, of what it is to believe that A while disbelieving that B, where the 'A' and the 'B' stand for necessarily equivalent expressions' (Stalnaker 1984, 24).

Because the problem of hyperintensionality is a problem quite generally, it pays to approach it armed with our best intensional theory and see how that theory can be developed into a hyperintensional theory. That best intensional theory, in my view, is the possible worlds approach. It is one of philosophy's success stories. What started with Wittgenstein (1922) and Carnap (1947) as an approach in philosophical semantics, and was developed by Kripke (1959, 1963a,b), Hintikka (1962) and other philosophical logicians, has become one of the key theories in formal semantics and is now used widely in computer science, artificial intelligence and game theory. We should not abandon the benefits that the theory brings lightly.

The task, then, is to develop the possible worlds theory in a way that allows for hyperintensionality, whilst preserving (as far as possible) the benefits of the original approach. How can this be done? There are two general approaches which promise to deliver hyperintensional contents from the starting point of possible worlds theory:

APPROACH 1: ADD STRUCTURE. Whilst logically equivalent sentences are true according to precisely the same possible worlds, many such sentences differ in their syntactic structure. '$1 + 1 = 2$' differs in structure from '$e^{i\pi} = -1$', even though each is true according to all possible worlds. We can incorporate these structures in our account of content. This will allow us to assign distinct contents to logically equivalent sentences.

APPROACH 2: ADD MORE WORLDS. Whilst logically equivalent sentences are true according to precisely the same possible worlds, it may be that one but not the other is true according to worlds which look possible, but which in fact are not possible. These worlds are sometimes called *impossible worlds*. We can incorporate impossible (as well as possible) worlds in our account of content. If '*A*' and '*B*' are logically equivalent yet '*A*' but not '*B*' is true according to an impossible world *w*, then we can assign different contents qua sets of worlds (possible and impossible) to '*A*' and '*B*'.

I discuss the first, *structuralist*, approach in chapter 3. I will argue that it does not quite deliver the degree of hyperintensionality we require: it conflates contents when it should not. I discuss the second, *impossible worlds*, approach in chapter 4. I'll argue that this approach has the resources to deliver the hyperintensional contents we require. To develop the account, however, we need a theory of what impossible worlds are. I develop such an account in chapter 5. Chapters 6–8 then use the impossible worlds approach to develop an account of epistemic content, suitable for analysing concepts of knowledge, belief and information.

Chapter Summary

The problem of logical omniscience (§2.1) and related problems concerning belief, informativeness and content (§2.2) are serious worries for the possible worlds approach. The problem is that possible worlds deliver intensional contents, whereas concepts such as knowledge, belief and information are hyperintensional concepts (§2.3).

Stalnaker argues that the functionalist approach to belief states delivers a non-hyperintensional account (§2.4), and Stalnaker and Lewis show how to account for inconsistent, non-deductively-closed sets of beliefs within a possible worlds framework (§2.5). However, this is not an adequate response to Stalnaker's problem of capturing the content of a deduction (§2.5). Stalnaker claims, in addition, that the information gained from a valid deduction is linguistic knowledge, concerning which proposition the sentence in question expresses (§2.6). But this approach isn't tenable.

A genuinely hyperintensional account is required. I argued that, rather than abandoning the approach entirely, we should first investigate whether it can be developed into a hyperintensional account (§2.7). We can do this either by adding extra syntactic structure to contents, or by adding impossible worlds.

3

Hyperintensionality and Structure

A popular way to deal with hyperintensional concepts (such as knowledge, belief and information) is to add extra structure to an intensional account. In this chapter, I discuss and reject this structuralist approach.

3.1   Structured Content

A *structuralist* approach to hyperintensional phenomena proceeds by identifying contents with structured entities of some kind. ('Structuralism' here has nothing to do with 1960s French thought!) To get a handle on this idea of structure, let's contrast sentences, a paradigm case of structured entities, with sets of possible worlds, a paradigm case of unstructured entities. The latter are unstructured in the sense that a set of worlds contains no internal order. The set $\{w, u\}$ is identical to the set $\{u, w\}$. Sets, quite generally, are just unstructured collections of things. Contrast this with a *list* or *sequence*. The sequence (or ordered pair) of worlds $\langle w, u \rangle$ differs from the sequence $\langle u, w \rangle$. Hence neither sequence is identical to the set $\{w, u\}$. Sequences come with an order and can be thought of as sequences or lists of words. They are not merely collections of words, for obviously, the order of words in a sentence matters. 'Greg begged Meg' and 'Meg begged Greg' are different sentences. This is the sense in which sentences are structured entities.

A structuralist then takes content to be structured, much in the way that sentences are structured. In fact, many structuralists take the structure of content to be given by the syntactic structure of the corresponding sentences. Let's focus on a simple sentence (S),

(3.1) Greg begged Meg

which is composed of a noun (N) 'Greg' and a verb phrase (VP) 'begged Meg', itself composed of a verb (V) and a noun. We represent it using the syntax tree on the left in figure 3.1:

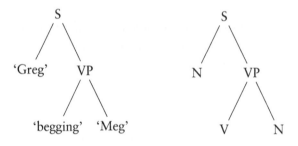

Figure 3.1: SYNTAX TREES

Here, we can think about the sentence's structure as the form of the tree, i.e. the way its branches link together its nodes, abstracted away from the lexical items 'Greg', 'begging' and 'Meg' that we find at the leaf nodes, as shown on the right in figure 3.1. In this sense, (3.1) has the same structure as

(3.2) Ed zapped Zed.

We get to structured contents for these sentences by taking their syntax trees and replacing the lexical items at their nodes with corresponding semantic items (King 1995, 1996; Salmon 2005). We might, for example, take these to be Greg (the person), the property *begging*, and Meg (the person). If so, we get the structured content shown on the left in figure 3.2. This is a *Russellian* notion of content, involving the very things the content is about. When talking about the content of sentences, as in this case, we have a Russellian proposition. (I'll talk of contents rather than propositions, but the arguments I run in this chapter could be phrased equivalently in terms of propositions.)

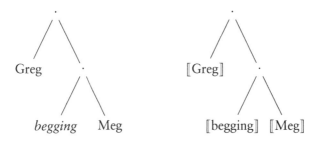

Figure 3.2: STRUCTURED CONTENTS

We can obtain other notions of structured content by placing other kinds of entities at the leaf nodes of the relevant tree. The general notion is that of the *semantic value* or *compositional value* of a lexical item '*l*', which I'll write '$[\![l]\!]$'. We might take the semantic value of a predicate, for example, to be a property, as on the Russellian view, but we might instead take it to be a possible-worlds intension (a function from possible worlds to extensions) or a Fregean sense. In general, structured contents are like syntax trees but with lexical items replaced by their semantic values, as shown on the right of figure 3.2. We can represent the same structure using nested sequences (in this case, nested ordered pairs), as:

$$\langle [\![\text{Greg}]\!], \langle [\![\text{begging}]\!], [\![\text{Meg}]\!] \rangle \rangle$$

In the next section, I'll begin to evaluate this structuralist account of content.

3.2   Hyperintensional Contents

In this section, I'll argue that the structuralist approach does some, but not all, of the work we would expect of a solution to the problems discussed in chapter 2. The approach can distinguish between necessarily equivalent contents. Consider these necessarily equivalent sentences:

(3.3) $1 + 1 = 2$

(3.4) $3 + 3 = 6$

(3.5) $e^{i\pi} = -1$

These express the structured propositions:

(3.3′) $\langle\langle[\![1]\!], [\![+]\!], [\![1]\!]\rangle, [\![=]\!], [\![2]\!]\rangle$

(3.4′) $\langle\langle[\![3]\!], [\![+]\!], [\![3]\!]\rangle, [\![=]\!], [\![6]\!]\rangle$

(3.5′) $\langle\langle[\![e]\!], [\![exp]\!], \langle[\![i]\!], [\![\times]\!], [\![\pi]\!]\rangle\rangle, [\![=]\!], [\![-1]\!]\rangle$

Each of these contents are distinct from the others. (3.3′) and (3.4′) have a common structure, but differ as to which entities instantiate that structure, whereas (3.5′) differs in structure from the others. We can thus differentiate between Anna's believing in (3.3) and her believing in (3.4), and distinguish both of these from her believing in (3.5). We can thus allow that she has any of these beliefs without having any of the others. The structuralist approach provides us with genuinely fine-grained hyperintensional contents.

So far so good. On the structuralist account, we are not limited to coarse-grained intensional contents. Nevertheless, the structuralist approach on its own does not make all of the fine-grained distinctions between contents that we require. We can see this easily by focusing on the following examples (borrowed from Dave Ripley (2012)):

(3.6) All woodchucks are woodchucks

(3.7) All woodchucks are whistle-pigs

Since whistle-pigs are woodchucks (and necessarily so), a structuralist view which takes semantic values of nouns to be extensions or intensions will hold that $[\![\text{woodchucks}]\!] = [\![\text{whistle-pigs}]\!]$. If so, both (3.6) and (3.7) express the proposition:

(3.6′) ⟨⟨[[All]], [[woodchucks]]⟩, ⟨[[are]], [[woodchucks]]⟩⟩

Yet one might believe (3.6) but not (3.7). Ripley (2012) makes the point vividly (for the case of *fearing*, rather than *believing*):

> Suppose Tama is familiar with both woodchucks and whistle-pigs, but isn't sure that they are the same kind of critter. He's noticed the similarities, though, and so he has his suspicions. Suppose further that Tama knows he is allergic to whistle-pigs, and knows that he has just been bitten by a woodchuck. In this scenario, ['Tama fears that all woodchucks are whistle-pigs'] is likely true, while ['Tama fears that all woodchucks are woodchucks'] is almost certainly false. (Ripley 2012, 106)

This is a variant of Frege's puzzle (§1.4), to which many responses have been given. The point is that structure alone does not avoid Frege's puzzle. It does not provide us with distinct fine-grained contents for pairs of cases in which we have no difference either in syntactic structure or in the corresponding semantic values.

A Fregean structuralist can avoid this conclusion by identifying the semantic contents of lexical items with senses, rather than extensions or intensions, and by insisting that the senses of 'woodchuck' and 'whistle-pig' differ. (Indeed, since Tama is unsure whether whistle-pigs are woodchucks, it seems reasonable for a Fregean to take 'woodchuck' and 'whistle-pig' to differ in sense in Tama's idiolect.) She will then treat propositions as structures with senses at their leaf nodes and will treat (3.6) and (3.7) as expressing distinct structured Fregean propositions.

Russellian structuralists cannot take this route out of the problem, for they identify the semantic values of names, indexicals and predicates with their referents. The Russellian view, as elaborated so far, incorrectly entails that anyone who believes that Richard Routley was an Australian logician thereby believes that Richard Sylvan was an Australian logician, given that Routley was Sylvan. (Soames (2002, 2005) comes closest to defending this consequence.)

Russellians may refine their view in a number of ways, in response to this problem. On Salmon's (1986) view, for example, believing that

A amounts to accepting some representational 'guise' corresponding to the proposition *that A*. (Salmon is non-committal about the nature of guises. What's important for present purposes is that an '*a*'-guise may be distinct from a '*b*'-guise, even when '*a*' and '*b*' co-refer.) Believing is thus a relation mediated by guises, much as it is a relation mediated by senses on the Fregean account. One may believe something of woodchucks under their 'whistle-pig' guise, but not under their 'woodchuck' guise.

Somewhat similarly, Richard (1990) takes the objects of belief to be enriched propositions: standard Russellian propositions with added representational elements. On Crimmins's (1992) view, belief reports contain contextually contributed *unarticulated constituents*, which refer to ideas (or idea-types) in the believer's mind (see also Crimmins and Perry 1989). On all these views, one may stand in the *belief* relation to, say, (3.6) without thereby believing (3.7).

Both Fregean and Russellian structuralists have at their disposal a means of capturing the fine-grained distinctions in content required for belief reports. However, these approaches deliver that fineness of grain specifically for the embedded *that*-clauses of attitude reports (and related cases). It would be problematic for these structuralist approaches, therefore, if similarly fine-grained contents were required elsewhere, outside the scope of any attitude verb. But there are such cases.

Consider again the situation from §1.4: we're going to see the 1972 Ziggy Stardust tour, but we're confused about who Ziggy is. You're pretty sure he's David Bowie. I'm unconvinced. Over the course of our discussion the following indicative conditionals are asserted:

(3.8) If Ziggy isn't Bowie, then Bowie isn't Bowie

(3.9) If Bowie isn't Bowie, then Bowie isn't Bowie

On most accounts of conditionals, (3.9) is true (although bizarre), since it has the form 'if *A* then *A*'. But (3.8) seems false. Just because Ziggy is Bowie, it doesn't follow that 'if Ziggy isn't Bowie, then *A*' is true for any *A* we like. The English indicative conditional is not the logician's material conditional, ' ⊃ '. Indeed, (3.8)'s falsity is one kind of case we should expect a good theory of English indicative conditionals to deliver. Or consider subjunctive versions of these conditionals:

(3.8^s) If Ziggy were not Bowie, then Bowie would not be Bowie

(3.9^s) If Bowie were not Bowie, then Bowie would not be Bowie

Since (3.9^s) is an instance of '$A \,\square\!\!\rightarrow A$' ('if A were the case then A would be the case'), it is true on any account. (3.8^s), by contrast, is *prima facie* false. Let's assume that it is indeed false.

Now here's the problem. In each pair (3.8)/(3.9) and (3.8^s)/(3.9^s), the conditionals have different truth-values and so must differ in content from one another. Within each pair, the contents of the two conditionals differ only if their antecedents differ in content from one another. But the antecedent of each conditional has the same structure and the same denotation, and there is no attitude verb to invoke guises, representational elements, unarticulated constituents or Fregean reference switches. Russellians and Fregeans alike appear committed to the view that, when not embedded within attitude verbs, 'Ziggy isn't Bowie' and 'Bowie isn't Bowie' express the same content, namely ($[\![\neg]\!]$, ($[\![$Bowie$]\!]$, $[\![=]\!]$, $[\![$Bowie$]\!]$)).

A Russellian or Fregean might respond to this worry by invoking theories which treat 'if' as an epistemic modal operator, along the lines of 'might' or 'may'. Such theories hold that the indicative conditional 'if A then B', as asserted by speaker s in context c, is true just in case all the A-worlds compatible with the evidence available to s in c (alternatively: compatible with what s knows in c) are also B-worlds (Kratzer 1986).

This account is similar to the Lewis-Stalnaker semantics for conditionals (Lewis 1973; Stalnaker 1968), but with the added restriction to worlds compatible with the speaker's current evidence or knowledge. If this kind of account is correct, then the claim that 'if' forces a Fregean reference switch, or invokes Russellian guises or unarticulated constituents, is perhaps plausible. (At least, it is as plausible as it is in the case of 'believes' and 'knows'.) After all, whether a situation is compatible with a speaker's evidence or knowledge may depend on how that situation is presented to the speaker. But if the epistemic account of 'if' is not acceptable, then there is no reason at all to suppose that 'if' forces a Fregean reference shift or invokes Russellian guises or unarticulated constituents.

Epistemic theories of 'if' fail because they trivialise conditionals where the antecedent is incompatible with the speaker's evidence or knowledge. As asserted by me,

(3.10) If Fermat's Last Theorem is false, then Andrew Wiles is a poached egg.

(3.10^s) If Fermat's Last Theorem were false, then Andrew Wiles would be a poached egg.

are both true, if interpreted in line with the epistemic account. I know that Fermat's Last Theorem is true and so no worlds representing it to be false are compatible with what I know. Yet both conditionals are false (at least, that is the judgement of many competent language users). Perhaps, given that I know Fermat's Last Theorem to be true, I shouldn't assert (3.10). But if I do, it would't be true. (3.10^s) is an even clearer case: I may have good reason to assert it, and it is certainly not true.

The epistemic reading of these conditionals gives the wrong results in each case. If we reject the epistemic reading in these cases, we should reject it for (3.8), (3.8^s), (3.9) and (3.9^s) too. But without the epistemic reading of these conditionals, both the Fregean's claim that 'if' forces a reference shift in the antecedent and the Russellian's claim that 'if' invokes guises or unarticulated constituents in the antecedent lose their motivation.

In this section, I've argued that structure on its own does not deliver enough fine-grained contents and that the extra machinery to which structuralists may appeal gives the wrong results in the case of certain conditionals. I have assumed that conditionals such as (3.8) and (3.10) are false and that conditionals with impossible antecedents can be nontrivially true. It is meaningful for rival logicians to debate. A logician can say, truly, 'if Dummett is right, then classical logic is wrong'; but if she says 'if Dummett is right, then I'm a fruitcake', she speaks falsely.

Theorising about conditionals is a difficult business, however. Perhaps conditionals in general are (strictly speaking) neither true nor false (Edgington 1986, 1995). Conditionals are not my central concern in this book and I do not want to rest my argument on their correct interpretation. In the remainder of this chapter, therefore, I'll develop an argument against the structuralist which makes no appeal to conditional constructions.

3.3   A Problem for Structuralists

In this section, I will argue that the structured account of content (whether Fregean or Russellian) is incompatible with platitudes about how definitions fix content and meaning. What's striking about the argument I'm going to run is that it does not trade on what, from a theoretical point of view, are the difficult aspects of content, such as how to handle indexicals (and other context sensitive terms), ambiguity, tense, descriptions, empty names and intensional constructions of any type. The argument can be run in a very simple extensional language.

So, to avoid unnecessary complications, I will focus on very simple artificial languages containing only names (all of which refer, none of which are ambiguous, indexical or descriptive), predicates and logical connectives. If structuralism about content fails in such amenable linguistic territory, then it clearly fails for any natural language in which we might be interested. I'll build such languages from a stock of constants $C = \{c_1, c_2, \ldots\}$ and predicates

$$P = \{F_1^1, F_2^1, \ldots, F_1^2, F_2^2, \ldots, \ldots\}$$

(where F_k^i is the kth predicate of arity i, i.e. taking i terms to form a sentence). I'll call a language *simple* when it is built from C, P and a stock of logical connectives only.

My argument will focus on the logical connectives of such languages, specifically, the familiar symbols '¬', '∧' and '∨', thought of as negation, conjunction and disjunction, respectively. A connective is a symbol whose syntactic type is a function from n sentences to a sentence. Unary connectives (such as '¬') are of syntactic type *sentences ⟶ sentences*, binary connectives (such as '∧' and '∨') are of syntactic type *sentences × sentences ⟶ sentences*, and so. On a (Fregean or Russellian) structuralist view of content, we have that

$$[\neg A] = \langle [\neg], [A] \rangle$$
$$[A \wedge B] = \langle [\wedge], [A], [B] \rangle$$
$$[A \vee B] = \langle [\vee], [A], [B] \rangle$$
$$[A \rightarrow B] = \langle [\rightarrow], [A], [B] \rangle$$

The argument goes as follows. It is highly plausible that anyone should accept:

(3.11) If we introduce a new term 't' to a simple language (as defined above) using an explicit definition, then for any sentences 'A' and 'B' of that language which differ only in the substitution of the definiendum 't' for its definiens, 'A' and 'B' have the same semantic value.

(Note that, since we are considering a simple language here, we can speak of a sentence's semantic value without relativising to context.)

In giving a definition of 't', one may intend to fix its meaning or merely fix its reference. Defining 'bachelor' as 'unmarried man' fixes the meaning of 'bachelor'. But in saying 'let 'Julius' name the inventor of the zip' (Evans 1982, 31), we merely fix the referent of 'Julius'. I am interested in meaning-giving definitions only here, of the form, 'by 't', we will mean …'. This stipulation fixes what 't' means (and hence fixes its semantic value) precisely by aligning it with the meaning (and hence the semantic value) of the provided definition. This is what (3.11) says.

It is also highly plausible that

(3.12) The semantic value of a connective governed by a truth-table is the truth-function determined by that truth-table.

In saying that a connective 'C' is governed by a truth-table, I mean that the truth-value of any sentence 'A' for which 'C' is the main connective (i.e., for which 'C' is the root node of its syntax tree) is determined exhaustively by a function on the truth-value(s) of the sentence(s) connected by 'C' (i.e., the child node(s) of 'C' in the syntax tree). Thus, '¬', '∧', '∨' and '→' in classical languages are governed by truth-tables, whereas '¬' and '→' in relevant and intuitionistic logics are not. When a connective is governed by a truth-table, (3.12) says that its semantic value is the truth-function (i.e., the function from truth-values or pairs of truth-values to truth-values) displayed by that truth-table. In familiar terminology, (3.12) says that when a connective is truth-functional, its semantic value is the relevant truth-function.

The problem for the structuralist is that (3.11), (3.12) and structuralism are mutually inconsistent. So if the motivations for (3.11) and (3.12) just sketched hold water, then structuralism must be false. For the remainder of this section, I'll give in detail the argument that (3.11), (3.12) and structuralism are mutually inconsistent. I will investigate possible structuralist responses to this problem in §3.4.

To begin with, let $\mathcal{L}_1$ be a simple language over C, P whose connectives are just '¬' and '∧', interpreted in the usual way as classical negation and classical conjunction. The well-formed sentences of $\mathcal{L}_1$ are just its atomic sentences closed under '¬' and '∧'. In saying that '¬' and '∧' are classical, I mean that they are both truth-functional connectives and so, by (3.12), have truth-functions as their semantic values. More precisely, $[\![¬]\!]$ is the function *neg* which takes *true* to *false* and vice versa, and $[\![∧]\!]$ is the function *conj* which takes *(true, true)* to *true* and all other pairs of truth-values to *false*.

Now let *disj* be that function from pairs of truth-values to truth-values which returns *true* just in case at least one of the input values is *true* and *false* otherwise. I'll stipulate that *disj* is not the semantic value of any name or predicate of $\mathcal{L}_1$. Then, I claim:

Theorem 3.1 *No sentence in $\mathcal{L}_1$ has any tuple containing disj as its semantic value.*

Proof: We prove this by induction on the complexity of sentences 'S' $\in \mathcal{L}_1$. If 'A' is atomic, i.e. of the form '$Rc_1 \cdots c_n$', then $disj \in [\![A]\!]$ only if $[\![R]\!] = disj$ or for some $i \leq n$, $[\![c_i]\!] = disj$, which we know to be not the case. Now suppose 'A' $\in \mathcal{L}_1$ is complex, and suppose that for all sentences 'B' of lower complexity than 'A', $disj \notin [\![B]\!]$. 'A' may be of the form '$\neg A_1$' or '$A_1 \wedge A_2$'. If the former, $[\![A]\!] = [\![\neg A_1]\!] = \langle neg, [\![A_1]\!] \rangle$. By hypothesis, $disj \notin [\![A_1]\!]$ and so $disj \notin [\![A]\!]$. If the latter, $[\![A]\!] = [\![A_1 \wedge A_2]\!] = \langle conj, [\![A_1]\!], [\![A_2]\!] \rangle$. By hypothesis, $disj \notin [\![A_1]\!]$ and $disj \notin [\![A_2]\!]$, and so $disj \notin [\![A]\!]$. Hence for every sentence 'A' $\in \mathcal{L}_1$, $disj \notin [\![A]\!]$. ∎

Next, suppose we expand $\mathcal{L}_1$ by introducing a new connective 'O' by definition, with '$A \circ B$' defined as '$\neg(\neg A \wedge \neg B)$'. Call the resulting language $\mathcal{L}_1^+$. Although $\mathcal{L}_1^+$ contains sentences which $\mathcal{L}_1$ does not, the following holds: for any sentence 'A' in $\mathcal{L}_1^+$ but not in $\mathcal{L}_1$, recursively replacing each instance of '$A_1 \circ A_2$' in 'A' with '$\neg(\neg A_1 \wedge \neg A_2)$' results in a sentence which is in $\mathcal{L}_1$. Given this fact, (3.11) entails that every tuple expressible by a sentence in $\mathcal{L}_1^+$ is also expressible by a sentence in $\mathcal{L}_1$. Given proposition 3.1, it follows that no sentence of $\mathcal{L}_1^+$ expresses a structuralist tuple containing *disj*. In particular, $[\![A \circ B]\!] \neq \langle disj, [\![A]\!], [\![B]\!] \rangle$.

But, as 'O' is a connective of $\mathcal{L}_1^+$ (its syntactic type is *sentences* × *sentences* ⟶ *sentences*), by (3.12) its semantic value is the truth-function fixed by its truth-table. By design, the truth-table for 'O' in $\mathcal{L}_1^+$ is the truth-table for *disjunction* and hence the semantic value of 'O' in $\mathcal{L}_1^+$ is the disjunction function *disj*, i.e. $[\![O]\!] = disj$. Then by definition, $[\![A \circ B]\!] = \langle disj, [\![A]\!], [\![B]\!] \rangle$. Contradiction.

We've shown that (3.11), (3.12) and structuralism are mutually inconsistent. Yet the structuralist is (plausibly) committed to each principle. If so, structuralism must be rejected.

3.4   Structuralist Responses

What responses to this problem are available to the structuralist? She has but three options: she may reject (3.11), reject (3.12), or modify structuralism. In the remainder of this chapter, I'll argue that none of these options are tenable.

Option 1: Reject (3.12)

The simplest way for the structuralist to avoid the problem above is to deny (3.12) and thus deny the final step of the argument. The claim would be that logical connectives in a purely truth-functional language need not have primitive truth-functions as their semantic values. Rather (as the reasoning above suggests), such connectives may have structured semantic values. For example, if '○' is introduced explicitly by setting '$A \circ B$' $=_{\text{df}}$ '$\neg(\neg A \wedge \neg B)$', as it was above, then the current move allows that:

$$\llbracket \circ \rrbracket = \lambda x \lambda y \langle \llbracket \neg \rrbracket, \langle \llbracket \wedge \rrbracket, \langle \llbracket \neg \rrbracket, x \rangle, \langle \llbracket \neg \rrbracket, y \rangle \rangle \rangle$$

This is the function which, when taking contents $\llbracket A \rrbracket$ and $\llbracket B \rrbracket$ as input, returns the structured tuple $\langle \llbracket \neg \rrbracket, \langle \llbracket \wedge \rrbracket, \langle \llbracket \neg \rrbracket, \llbracket A \rrbracket \rangle, \langle \llbracket \neg \rrbracket, \llbracket B \rrbracket \rangle \rangle \rangle$ as output. This function, $\lambda x \lambda y \langle \llbracket \neg \rrbracket, \langle \llbracket \wedge \rrbracket, \langle \llbracket \neg \rrbracket, x \rangle, \langle \llbracket \neg \rrbracket, y \rangle \rangle \rangle$, is not a truth-function. Its inputs are contents, not truth-values; and likewise its output is a content (a highly-structured tuple), not a truth-value.

Although this option denies (3.12), i.e. that logical connectives always have truth-functions as their semantic values, it nevertheless results in the correct truth-functional behaviour for contents. If $\lambda x \lambda y \langle \llbracket \neg \rrbracket, \langle \llbracket \wedge \rrbracket, \langle \llbracket \neg \rrbracket, x \rangle, \langle \llbracket \neg \rrbracket, y \rangle \rangle \rangle$ is fed with at least one true content, the resulting complex tuple will likewise be true; but when fed with two false contents, the resulting complex tuple will be false. So the correct truth-functional behaviour is obtained for '○', without identifying its semantic value with a primitive truth-function. This is a point in favour of the suggested approach.

A structuralist taking this approach might wish to modify rather than completely reject (3.12), as follows:

(3.12*) The semantic value of a connective governed by a truth-table
supervenes on (is determined by) the truth-function determined
by that truth-table.

Unlike (3.12), (3.12*) does not claim that the semantic value of a
logical constant is the truth-function determined by its truth-table,
but only that its truth-table determines what its semantic value is,
whatever it may be. This amounts to the claim that truth-functional
logical constants cannot differ in their meaning unless they differ in
their truth-table. Other features of a logical constant's use, such as its
written shape, or its pronunciation, or its frequency in a particular
paragraph, are irrelevant to what it means (i.e., to what it contributes
to the meaning of sentences in which it appears). This much seems
undeniable.

 Replacing (3.12) with (3.12*) will temporarily block the argument
from §3.3, but it is clear that it does nothing to avoid the problem.
We can run the first part of that argument as above, which did not
make use of (3.12), concluding that no sentence of $\mathcal{L}_1^+$ expresses
a tuple containing *disj*. But clearly, there are possible languages in
which a connective does have *disj* as its semantic value. Plausibly, in
any classical language in which '∨' is a primitive disjunction symbol,
'∨' has *disj* as its semantic value. For such cases, $[\![\vee]\!]$ is fixed as *disj* by
the truth-table assigned to '∨' in that language. But then, by (3.12*),
any connective in any other language which has been assigned that
same truth-table must thereby have the same semantic value as '∨'.
Since (by design) 'o' in $\mathcal{L}_1^+$ has the truth-table for disjunction, it too
must have *disj* as its semantic value, i.e. $[\![o]\!] = disj$ in $\mathcal{L}_1^+$. Then, just
as before, some sentences of $\mathcal{L}_1^+$ express tuples containing *disj* and
the contradiction remains. Thus (3.11), (3.12*) and structuralism
are jointly inconsistent, just as (3.11), (3.12) and structuralism are.

 A structuralist who wants to resolve the initial problem by rejecting
(3.12) cannot accept (3.12*) in its place. She must altogether give up
the idea that a connective's truth-table determines its semantic value
and hence its meaning. There is, however, a serious problem with
this approach. Consider a different simple language $\mathcal{L}_2$ over C, P in

which '¬', '∧' and '∨' are primitive truth-functional constants. We stipulate that the semantic values of these symbols in $\mathcal{L}_2$, $[\![¬]\!]$, $[\![∧]\!]$ and $[\![∨]\!]$, are primitive truth-functions, as fixed by their respective truth-tables. And let's associate both $\mathcal{L}_1^+$ and $\mathcal{L}_2$ with a proof system (e.g., a sequent calculus), with primitive rules for each of the connectives. There is then a straightforward translation from $\mathcal{L}_2$ to $\mathcal{L}_1^+$ (and back again), simply by replacing occurrences of '∨' with occurrences of '○' (and vice versa). This translation preserves the syntactic structure of all sentences. In fact, considered as formal languages, $\mathcal{L}_2$ and $\mathcal{L}_1^+$ differ only in as much as $\mathcal{L}_2$ differs from the corresponding language in which one writes '&' rather than '∧' for conjunction. In a formal sense, each of these languages are no more than notational variants.

The similarities between $\mathcal{L}_1^+$ and $\mathcal{L}_2$ do not, of course, stop at the syntactic level. The semantics for each language (in terms of truth-tables, say) is identical: in particular, the semantics (i.e., the truth-table) given for '∨' in $\mathcal{L}_2$ is precisely the semantics given for '○' in $\mathcal{L}_1^+$. Moreover, the proof-rules governing '∨' in $\mathcal{L}_2$ are precisely the proof-rules governing '○' in $\mathcal{L}_1^+$ (modulo the purely syntactic substitution of the one symbol for the other). Proof structure is isomorphic between the two languages. Yet, on the current view, '∨' in $\mathcal{L}_2$ does not mean what '○' means in $\mathcal{L}_1^+$: the symbols have different semantic values. Thus, neither their meanings nor their semantic values can be fixed either by their truth-table or by their proof-rules. In short, neither truth-conditions nor use (via proof) is sufficient to fix meaning, on this view. This is incompatible with most views of meaning, on which meaning supervenes either on truth-conditions or on use.

All that can give rise to this difference in meaning, on the current view, is the differing histories of '∨' and '○' in their respective languages. But in general, a difference in the histories of two words is not sufficient for a difference in their meaning. Factors such as when and how a word was introduced to a language are generally seen as irrelevant to what that word means. Indeed, our ability to find synonyms across natural languages does not require knowledge of when and how a particular word was introduced to its language. So a theory of meaning should entail that '∨' and '○' (as defined above) have the same meaning, and hence the same semantic value, regardless of their differing histories. As a consequence, (3.12*) cannot be rejected and the contradiction remains for the structuralist, even if she rejects (3.12).

Option 2: Amend Structuralism

A structuralist may try to avoid the initial problem by minimally amending her structuralist proposal. This move can be motivated as follows. (3.11) implies that, when we introduce a new term 't' by definition, $[\![t]\!]$ should be identical to the semantic value of the definiens. But semantic values are also supposed to inherit structure from the syntactic structure of the relevant term. These two requirements clash, since definiendum and definiens need not be syntactically structured in the same way (as in the argument in §3.3). If 't' is syntactically simple, then $[\![t]\!]$ should reflect this structural simplicity, even if 't' was introduced by definition involving a syntactically complex definiens.

On the face of it, a structuralist should abandon (3.11) and allow the substitution of definiens for definiendum to alter the content expressed. But this is a large cost for the account, for the very point of an explicit definition is to establish the meaning of a term, effectively by saying that *this* means what *this* means. Rejecting (3.11) entails rejecting this platitude. (I'll consider below whether the structuralist can bite the bullet here.)

A structuralist can, however, avoid the clash without rejecting (3.11). Instead, she may amend the structuralist proposal slightly, by identifying the contents of sentences not with individual structuralist tuples but instead with equivalence classes of structuralist tuples:

STRUCTURALISM* For a simple language (as defined above), the semantic value of a sentence is an equivalence class of structuralist tuples.

More precisely, given a structuralist tuple r, let Cr be the set of all structuralist tuples logically equivalent to r. (Structuralist tuples r_1

and r_2 are logically equivalent when there exist logically equivalent sentences 'A' and 'B' such that, on the structuralist account, $[\![A]\!] = r_1$ and $[\![B]\!] = r_2$.) On this theory, the semantic value of a sentence 'A' of a simple language is Cr, where $[\![A]\!] = r$ on the standard structuralist account.

This account remains a compositional account of the semantic values of sentences. Although semantic values are no longer composed of the referents of names, predicates and the like, they are still determined by those features. It is also very much in the spirit of standard structuralism, despite denying that the semantic values of sentences are structuralist tuples. I'll treat the present suggestion as a structuralist account. (The issue isn't whether this account should be called 'structuralist', but rather whether this small amendment to standard structuralism is viable.) On this usage, rejecting structuralism in the general sense requires one to reject STRUCTURALISM*.

In accepting STRUCTURALISM*, the problem from §3.3 is avoided. To see why, assume that '○' has been introduced by explicit definition just as above. Then $[\![A \circ B]\!] = Cr$ where

$$r = \langle [\![\neg]\!], \langle [\![\wedge]\!], \langle [\![\neg]\!], [\![A]\!] \rangle, \langle [\![\neg]\!], [\![B]\!] \rangle \rangle \rangle.$$

But by definition, r is logically equivalent to $\langle [\![\vee]\!], [\![A]\!], [\![B]\!] \rangle$ (since '$\neg(\neg A \wedge \neg B)$' is equivalent to '$A \vee B$') and so we have that $Cr = C\langle [\![\vee]\!], [\![A]\!], [\![B]\!] \rangle$. It follows that $[\![A \circ B]\!] = [\![A \vee B]\!]$ and so the problem from §3.3 does not arise.

Despite resolving the initial problem for the structuralist, this account cannot be the right story about content. On this account, if 'A' and 'B' are logically equivalent then $[\![A]\!] = [\![B]\!]$. In other words, this is an intensional but not a hyperintensional theory of content. It thereby reintroduces all the problems discussed in §§2.1–2.2. These are the very problems that motivated us to consider standard structuralism in the first place! Since our account of knowledge, belief and information requires hyperintensional contents, STRUCTURALISM* must be rejected.

Can this objection be sidestepped by using some non-classical notion of equivalence in STRUCTURALISM*? The idea would be to define

contents as equivalence classes of tuples, just as STRUCTURALISM*
says, but where that notion of equivalence is something other (and
weaker) than classical logical equivalence. This will allow there to
be classically equivalent sentences 'A' and 'B' which are nevertheless
assigned distinct contents qua equivalence classes of tuples.

Let's consider how this suggestion plays out in response to the
aboutness and truthmaking objections to the possible worlds account
of content from §2.2. (I'll discuss non-classical logics in relation
to knowledge and belief in §§6.2–6.4.) Both arguments focus on
instances of '$A \vee \neg A$'. 'Puss exists $\vee$ Puss doesn't exist' is about
Puss, not Rover and is (minimally) made true by Puss, not Rover. By
contrast, 'Rover exists $\vee$ Rover doesn't exist' is about Rover, not Puss
and is (minimally) made true by Rover, not Puss. So these sentences
must differ in their content.

If we are to defend STRUCTURALISM* by using a non-classical
notion of equivalence, therefore, this must be a notion on which not
all instances of '$A \vee \neg A$' are equivalent to one another. This rules out
the equivalence relation of paracomplete logics such as Strong Kleene
and paraconsistent logics such as LP (Priest 1979). We could run a
parallel argument for an intuitionistic notion of logical equivalence
by using instances of '$\neg\neg(A \vee \neg A)$' (all of which are intuitionistically
provably equivalent) in place of '$A \vee \neg A$'.

Indeed, the aboutness objection can be run for a logic L given a
pair of L-equivalent sentences 'A', 'B' where 'A' contains an atomic
sentence which 'B' does not. For example, in the relevant logic
R, 'A' is R-equivalent to '$A \wedge (B \vee A)$'. But 'Puss exists and (either
Rover or Puss exists)' is in part about Rover, whereas 'Puss exists' is
not. So STRUCTURALISM* comes out false even when 'equivalence' is
interpreted as equivalence in R.

What one would need to rescue STRUCTURALISM* from this
objection is a notion of equivalence on which 'A' and 'B' are
(provably) equivalent only if they share all their atomic sentences.
Humberstone and Meyer (2007) call this property of logics the
relevant equivalence property. But they show that no usable logic
which includes '$\wedge$' or '$\vee$' has this property: 'its prospects are

slim outside the sheltered environment provided by multiplicative fragments [i.e., languages without the extensional '∧' or '∨'] in which it flourishes' (Humberstone and Meyer 2007, 178). So whichever logic we use to understand 'equivalence', STRUCTURALISM* must be rejected.

Option 3: Reject (3.11)

The remaining option for the structuralist is to reject (3.11). As I noted above, this move is counterintuitive, since it allows that substituting definiens for definiendum can alter the meaning of a sentence, even in a simple language. In rejecting (3.11), one is saying that explicit definitions are not in the business of fixing the meaning of the definiendum as the meaning of the definiens.

If a structuralist takes this line, she still needs to specify just what the relation between the semantic values of definiens and definiendum is, if it is not identity. Clearly, an explicit definition establishes some close relation between the semantic values of the definiens and the definiendum, for the very point of a definition is to guarantee that (in extensional contexts at least) statements differing only in the substitution of definiendum for definiens cannot differ in their truth-value. In the case of syntactically primitive logical connectives (such as 'O'), the story might go as follows. With either (3.12) or the weaker (3.12*) in play, the semantic values of any connective given semantics via a truth-table will be a truth-function. Hence when we define '$A \circ B$' as '$\neg(\neg A \wedge \neg B)$', we specify that $[\![\circ]\!]$ is that truth-function whose behaviour on 'A' and 'B' is given by '$\neg(\neg A \vee \neg B)$'. This uniquely determines *disj* to be the semantic value of '$\circ$'.

This move blocks the argument from §3.3, in just the way that amending structuralism in favour of STRUCTURALISM* blocks the argument. Since $[\![A \circ B]\!] = \langle disj, [\![A]\!], [\![B]\!]\rangle$, we cannot arrive at the conclusion that no sentence of $\mathcal{L}_1^+$ expresses tuples containing *disj*, which we need to generate the contradiction. So the structuralist who rejects (3.11) in this way appears to be safe from the argument I ran in §3.3.

As I've already noted, rejecting (3.11) amounts to rejecting the identity of meaning between definiens and definiendum. That is counterintuitive. The structuralist can respond to this worry as follows. Syntactic structure is a constituent of semantic value and hence of a sentence's meaning. Semantics, on this view, is a many-layered beast. One of these layers concerns structure; notions such as *aboutness* are found at another layer. Indeed, pairs of sentences may differ in semantic value (and meaning) purely in virtue of syntactic differences and yet be about precisely the same things. Instances of '$A \wedge B$' and '$B \wedge A$' are cases in point. A structuralist can capture just how close '$A \wedge B$' and '$B \wedge A$' are in their semantic values (and meanings) by saying that their semantic values (and meanings) differ merely structurally (i.e., they differ merely in how they are syntactically structured).

If this structuralist account is correct, then we should expect that in those cases where explicit definitions do not establish identity of semantic value (or meaning) between definiens and definiendum, the resulting differences are merely structural (in the sense just described). As a consequence, substituting definiendum for definiens might alter the syntax of a sentence (and hence its meaning), but cannot affect what that sentence is about. More precisely:

(3.11*) If we introduce a new term 't' to a simple language using an explicit definition (as defined above), then for any sentences 'A' and 'B' of that language which differ only in the substitution of the definiendum 't' for its definiens, 'A' and 'B' are about precisely the same things.

The problem for this structuralist move is that, given structuralism and either (3.12) or (3.12*), we can generate counterexamples to (3.11*). Suppose we introduce a new connective '$\triangle$' into a simple language by definition as follows:

$$\text{`}A \triangle B\text{'} \quad =_{\text{df}} \quad \text{`}(A \wedge B) \wedge 1 = 1\text{'}$$

In other words, '$A \triangle B$' is true when 'A' is true, 'B' is true and $1 = 1$. This is a strange but perfectly legitimate definition. '$\triangle$' has the syntactic type *sentences × sentences ⟶ sentences*, and so is a connective of our language. If (3.12) holds, then $[\![\triangle]\!]$ must be a truth-function, whose truth-functional behaviour on '*A*' and '*B*' is given by its definition '$(A \wedge B) \wedge 1 = 1$'. In other words, $[\![\triangle]\!]$ must also be the conjunction function: $[\![\triangle]\!] = conj$.

Indeed, this result holds even in the absence of (3.12). For (as I argued above), the structuralist is committed at the least to (3.12*), which tells us that the semantic value of '△' must be shared by any connective with the same truth-table as '△'. But since (in some simple language) $[\![\wedge]\!] = conj$, it follows that (in the expanded language containing '△') $[\![\triangle]\!] = conj$ as well. Given the structuralist definition of content, it follows that

$$[\![\text{Puss exists} \; \triangle \; \text{Rover exists}]\!] = \langle conj, [\![\text{Puss exist}]\!], [\![\text{Rover exists}]\!] \rangle$$

whereas $[\![(\text{Puss exist} \; \wedge \; \text{Rover exists}) \wedge 1 = 1]\!] =$

$$\langle conj, \langle conj, [\![\text{Puss exists}]\!], [\![\text{Rover exists}]\!] \rangle, \langle [\![=]\!], 1, 1 \rangle \rangle.$$

These contents, and hence the sentences that express them, are about different things. The former is about just Puss and Rover, whereas the latter is about Puss, Rover and the number 1. Thus a △-sentence need not be about the number 1 whereas its definiendum always is, contradicting (3.11*).

A structuralist may respond to this objection as follows. Just because a content (qua structuralist tuple) contains some entity *x*, it doesn't follow that that content is about *x*. Logically complex contents are, perhaps, a case in point. It's strange to think that a sentence '*A* ∧ *B*' is (in part) about a truth-function, despite the fact that $conj \in [\![A \wedge B]\!]$. To paraphrase Wittgenstein (1922, §5.44), we shouldn't think that '¬*A*' is (in part) about negation, else '¬¬*A*' and '*A*' would be about different things. Hence we shouldn't think that a sentence '*A*' is about the number 1, just because 1 is an element of $[\![A]\!]$ (as in the example above).

What the structuralist says here may well be true, but it does nothing to help her position. The current objection to structuralism can be run by defining '$A \vartriangle B$' as '$(A \wedge B) \wedge T$', where 'T' is any logical truth whatsoever. This will guarantee that '$\vartriangle$' inherits the truth-table for '$\wedge$'. The objection can then be run by choosing a logical truth 'T' which is about something which neither 'A' nor 'B' is about. (If neither 'A' nor 'B' is about Puss, then 'Puss exists $\vee$ Puss doesn't exist' will do). So the response offered on behalf of the structuralist in the previous paragraph is ineffective.

I've argued that the structuralist must accept (3.11*), even if she rejects (3.11). But structuralism, (3.11*) and (3.12*) are mutually contradictory. So the structuralist cannot resolve the problem from §3.3 by rejecting (3.11). In short, the structuralist cannot avoid the problem by rejecting (3.11), by rejecting (3.12), or by amending structuralism to STRUCTURALISM*. Since these are her only options, structuralism should be rejected.

Chapter Summary

By augmenting (or replacing) the possible worlds account of content with syntactic structures, we obtain hyperintensional contents (§3.1, §3.2). The structuralist approach can draw distinctions between equivalent cases only when there is a structural difference. But not all of the cases for which we require a distinction are like this: there are equivalent, structurally identical cases which should be assigned distinct contents (§3.2). Structuralism cannot make sense of such contents. I then gave an independent argument against the structuralist approach (§3.3) and considered several responses on behalf of the structuralist (§3.4). As none of these are successful, I rejected structuralism. In the next chapter, I turn to the second option for developing the possible worlds approach into a hyperintensional account: adding impossible worlds to the picture.

4

Impossible Worlds

This chapter is a discussion of impossible worlds and their meta-physics. I argue against a number of accounts of possible and impossible worlds. I give a positive metaphysical theory of possible and impossible worlds in chapter 5.

4.1 Impossible Worlds

Impossible worlds are worlds according to which impossible things happen. If a world represents that such-and-such and it is impossible that such-and-such, then that is an impossible world. In this section, I'll introduce some clarifications and some arguments for believing in impossible worlds. Detailed discussion of what impossible worlds are will wait until §4.2.

Impossible worlds are not impossible entities, as round squares are. Round squares could not exist, but (on my view) impossible worlds do in fact exist. So whatever impossible worlds are, they are not entities like round squares. We call them 'impossible' because they represent impossibilities, such as a square's being round, as being the case. In this sense, an impossible world is like an Escher drawing. The drawing itself is perfectly possible, but what it represents is not. (Other philosophers who accept impossible worlds disagree with me here. Priest (2005) holds that there are impossible worlds, but denies that they exist. Yagisawa (2010) holds that there are impossible worlds and that they are genuinely impossible. I'll discuss these views in §4.2 and §4.3.)

Given our antecedent interest in thinking impossible thoughts, worlds which represent impossible states of affairs are an attractive option. As we will see below (§8.1), accepting impossible worlds gives us a way to form the fine-grained contents we need to analyse hyperintensional constructions. Those contents are just functions on worlds, as in the possible worlds account of content (§1.3), except the worlds in question will include impossible as well as possible worlds.

I said above that impossible worlds represent impossibilities. For some authors, this amounts to representing some logical contradiction as being true (Lycan 1994; Berto 2010). Such worlds are logically inconsistent. Or, more generally, one may hold that a world is impossible if it represents that A and it is impossible that A (Nolan 1997; Priest 2005). For others, impossible worlds are representations governed by some non-classical (e.g., intuitionistic) logic (Cresswell 1973). Any such world obeys the rule that, if it represents that A and 'A' entails 'B' in the logic in question, then that world also represents that B. I'll say that what such a world represents is *closed* under the logic in question. In general, such worlds are deemed impossible not because they represent contradictions or other impossible states of affairs, but because what they represent falls short of classical closure. Worlds governed by intuitionistic logic may fail to represent that $A \vee \neg A$, for example. From the perspective of classical logic, such worlds are logically incomplete.

I will take the view that a world can fail to be a possible world either by representing some impossible state of affairs, or by being incomplete. In the latter case, the worlds are impossible because of what they fail to represent, given what else they represent. (Such worlds have found a place in the semantics for relevant logic and epistemic logic. Berto (2012) and Rescher and Brandom (1980) give an overview of impossible worlds in logical semantics.) I will also adopt Nolan's (1997) plenitude principle: if it is impossible that A, then there exists an impossible world which represents that A. This ensures we have enough worlds to construct fine-grained epistemic contents (chapters 7 and 8).

Unlike Cresswell (1973), I will not insist that all worlds be governed by some non-trivial logic. If they were, then there would be non-trivial logical links of the form: if a world represents that *A*, then it also represents that *B*. Given that we want to use worlds to analyse notions such as knowledge, belief and information, it would follow that anyone who knows or believes that *A* must thereby know or believe that *B*. This view would then be hostage to counterexamples in which we imagine someone knowing or believing that *A* but not that *B*. I'll argue in chapter 6 that we should take this possibility seriously and so should adopt the view that worlds need not be closed under any non-trivial logic. If so, then we will arrive at a very liberal notion of a world, on which what a world represents need not, in general, obey any logical rules. Priest (2005) calls such worlds *open worlds*. I develop a position along these lines in chapter 5.

Some philosophers draw distinctions between various kinds of possibility (and impossibility), including nomic, metaphysical, logical and conceptual possibility (and impossibility). We might think of these notions in terms of compatibility or incompatibility with the laws of nature, with certain truths of metaphysics, with logical rules, and with certain conceptual truths, respectively. It is nomically impossible (but perhaps metaphysically possible) for the wave-function to evolve other than in accordance with the Schrödinger equation; and metaphysically impossible for Ziggy to be someone other than Bowie, for example. Yet both are logical and conceptual possibilities.

These distinctions will not play a large role in this book. I'll accept that there are nomically impossible worlds, metaphysically impossible worlds, logically impossible worlds and conceptually impossible worlds. As I'll argue in chapter 5, we can accept all of these worlds because worlds are mere representations, constructed set-theoretically from actually existing entities. Of all the worlds that exist, some agree with the laws of nature and some don't; some agree with the truths of metaphysics and some don't; some agree with classical logic and some don't; and some agree with conceptual truths and some don't. Those that agree are the possible worlds and those that disagree are the impossible worlds, relative to that notion of possibility. I'll hold that all of these worlds are of a kind, metaphysically. (I'll argue for that in §§4.3–4.5 below.)

Before digging deeper into the logic and metaphysics of impossible worlds (and of worlds in general), it is worth asking what reasons we have to believe in impossible worlds. Some adherents, including Naylor (1986) and Yagisawa (1988), argue as follows. Possible worlds are the ways the world could have been. Since there exist many ways the world could have been, there exist many possible worlds. But there are also ways the world couldn't have been. Taking quantification at face value, there exist such ways. They are the impossible worlds. (Sharlow (1988) argues that a modal realist, persuaded by the argument in favour of possible worlds, need not accept the argument in favour of impossible worlds.)

Arguing in this way, Yagisawa holds that 'if modal realism is to be accepted at all, we should not stop with the Lewisian modal realism', the thesis that there exist many worlds very much like our own (which I'll discuss in more detail in §4.2) 'but go all the way and accept the extended modal realism' (Yagisawa 1988, 203), the thesis that 'there are possible worlds in Lewis's sense and also impossible worlds in an equally realistic sense' (1988, 176). He makes the parallel with Lewis's argument for the existence of possible worlds explicit:

> There are other ways of the world than the way the world actually is. Call them 'possible worlds.' That, we recall, was Lewis' argument. There are other ways of the world than the ways the world could be. Call them 'impossible worlds.' That is the extended argument. (Yagisawa 1988, 183)

As it stands, this is rather unpersuasive (Berto 2012). Hardly anyone takes quantification at face value all the time. The definite description 'the average man', read in the Russellian way, is quantificational in form, but few believe in the existence of the average man. But Lewis's argument does not take as its premise that we assert truths using 'ways' talk about the world; rather, it takes as its premise that the best way to understand 'ways' talk about the world is by accepting the existence of those ways. As Lewis puts it, 'the price is right; the benefits in theoretical unity and economy are well worth the entities' (Lewis 1986, 4). So says Yagisawa, but allowing impossible worlds in addition to Lewis's ones.

Such cost-benefit analyses are notoriously difficult to evaluate and I would prefer not to be embroiled in such debates. In fact, as I'll argue in §4.5 below, Lewis's account cannot be the best way to understand 'ways' talk about worlds because his account is internally inconsistent. To anticipate chapter 5, my view is an *actualist* one, according to which every existing entity actually exists. I don't accept Lewis's or Yagisawa's 'ideology, paid for in the coin of ontology'. Nevertheless, I believe in possible and impossible worlds, albeit ones constructed from actually existing entities (chapter 5). The question for me is not why I believe in their existence: they are set-theoretic constructions from actual entities and so exist whether we like it or not. Rather, the question is why I think it philosophically worthwhile to discus their logical and metaphysical nature.

My answer is twofold. First, they provide the best account of epistemic notions of content, including knowledge and belief states, cognitive significance and information, and the content of informative deductions (chapter 8). Second, they provide the best successful account of conditionals of the kind we met in 3.2, such as the counter-possible conditionals

(3.8^s) If Ziggy were not Bowie, then Bowie would not be Bowie;

(3.9^s) If Bowie were not Bowie, then Bowie would not be Bowie.

Suppose that a counterfactual '$A \,\square\!\rightarrow B$' is true iff all closest A-worlds are also B-worlds (Lewis 1973; Stalnaker 1968). (3.8^s) comes out false on this approach, as it should, if we include worlds according to which Ziggy is not Bowie. Since it is metaphysically necessary that Ziggy is Bowie, such worlds are metaphysically impossible, although they remain logically possible. Presumably, all logically possible worlds are closer to ours (and perhaps to any other logically possible world) than any logically impossible world is. So all of the closest worlds to ours according to which Ziggy is not Bowie are logically possible, and hence do not represent that Bowie is not Bowie.

Conditionals are not my concern here and so I won't discuss counter-possibles any further. (Brogaard and Salerno (2013), Nolan (1997), Read (1995) and Routley (1989) discuss the application of impossible worlds to theories of conditionals. Just how we should think of similarity between impossible worlds is not at all clear, but then again, neither is it clear how we should think about similarity between possible worlds; see Nolan 1997.) For those attracted to the Stalnaker-Lewis possible worlds semantics for conditionals, it is very natural to extend the account to counter-possible conditionals via the addition of impossible worlds. This provides us with a strong, independent reason for theorising in terms of impossible (as well as possible) worlds.

4.2   The Metaphysics of Impossibility

The question of what worlds (possible or impossible) are is much debated amongst metaphysicians. In this section and for the remainder of the chapter, I will discuss what worlds (including impossible worlds) are and how they represent. But why discuss the metaphysics of worlds at all, given that my main interest is in semantic notions of content and information? As I said in the introduction, semantics rests on a basis of metaphysics. To use worlds which represent impossible states of affairs, I first need to say how they can do that. To understand the semantic story fully, we first need in place a metaphysical story of what worlds are and how they represent.

Some argue that we don't need a specific answer to this question in the case of impossible worlds. Graham Priest, for example, claims that 'any of the main theories concerning the nature of possible worlds can be applied equally to impossible worlds' (Priest 1997, 580). But, as we'll see in §4.3 and §5.2, this is far from the case. I'll argue that none of the theories of possible worlds in the literature can be extended to make good sense of impossible worlds. The metaphysics of impossible worlds is a pressing issue.

I'll begin by discussing the status of worlds in general, before discussing the specific case of impossible worlds. There are those who hold that worlds other than our own exist in much the same way that our own world, the universe in its entirety, exists. Just as our own world consists of spatiotemporally located entities which bear properties and which are related to one another in various spatiotemporal ways, so do other worlds, on this view. Let's call such worlds *genuine* worlds and the view which says there are genuine worlds other than our own *genuine modal realism*. Lewis (1973, 1986) is the main proponent of this view in the case of possible worlds; Yagisawa (1988, 2010) is its champion in the case of impossible (as well as possible) worlds.

(There is a huge literature on Lewis's proposals; Divers (2002) gives a good overview. One interesting debate is between Divers and Melia (2002, 2003, 2006) and Bremer (2003), on whether Lewis's proposal gives a reductive account of modality. I shan't consider that issue here.)

An opposing view holds that worlds other than our own exist but that they are not of a kind with the world around us. They are not genuine worlds, in the above sense; they are mere representations or models of ways things could or could not be. Following Lewis (1986), I'll call such worlds *ersatz worlds*. (Genuine worlds are also representations of ways things could or could not be, but they are not *mere* representations. A genuine world represents the existence of a unicorn by containing a real unicorn; an ersatz world represents the existence of a unicorn in some other, perhaps pictorial or linguistic, way.) There are many varieties of ersatz world on offer to the theorist, depending on how she wants to represent ways the world could or could not be; I'll discuss some of these below. I'll call the view which accepts ersatz worlds (but not genuine worlds) *ersatz modal realism*.

Both genuine and ersatz modal realism accept that worlds other than our own exist, or are real. An opposing view accepts that there are worlds other than our own, but denies that such worlds exist. This view takes its cue from Bolzano (1834), Meinong (1904) and Twardowski (1894), who held that some things have *being* but lack *existence*. (Schnieder (2007) compares Bolzano's and Meinong's views to one another.) The young Russell (1903) also held this view and, more recently, Linsky and Zalta (1994, 1996), Priest (2005) and Williamson (1998, 2000b) have supported some aspects of this approach. Priest holds that some things (things which it makes perfect sense to talk about and quantify over) do not exist (and do not have being either). Worlds other than ours, both possible and impossible, fall into this category on Priest's account.

These debates are sometimes phrased by contrasting *possibilist* with *actualist* views. The actualist holds that all of being is actual; the possibilist denies this. One can be a possibilist by holding that there are entities which do not exist, but could have existed (sometimes called 'classical possibilism'), or by holding that there exist entities which are non-actual (the Lewisian option). The former needn't say that there are round squares, as the Bolzano-Meinong-Twardowski view does, but only that there are possible entities which don't exist. Lewis has perhaps more in common with actualists than with classical possibilists, in that he does not accept a category of being beyond what exists (Lewis 1990). (van Inwagen (2008, 40–41) argues that Lewis isn't a possibilist at all.)

I shan't have much to say about classical possibilism, understood as the claim that merely possible entities have being but do not exist. I do not accept a notion of existence other than the all-inclusive one. We can (and often do) use restricted senses of 'existence'. On one such restricted use, 'exists' applies only to concrete spatiotemporal things. If Lewis is right and there are non-actual genuine worlds, then there is a further restricted use on which 'exists' applies only to actual things. But nothing metaphysical hangs on these uses. They are run-of-the-mill cases of restricted quantification, much as when one says 'there's no coffee left' (truly, but with the domain of quantification contextually restricted to one's house). We don't infer from this that things without one's house have a different mode of being from those within.

Neither do I accept the Bolzano-Meinong-Twardowski argument for entities which lack existence from the fact that we can think certain thoughts. Russell (in his idealist days) argued for the view as follows:

> *Being* is that which belongs to every conceivable term, to every possible object of thought. ... "*A* is not" must always be either false or meaningless. For if *A* were nothing, it could not be said not to be. ... Thus ... to mention anything is to show that it is. (Russell 1903, §427)

This argument trades on a bad semantic picture. What is to be explained is how we can talk meaningfully using names such as 'Superman' and descriptions such as 'a square circle'. Our semantics must associate these terms with semantic values of some kind. But to get to Russell's (and Bolzano's, Meinong's and Priest's conclusion), those semantic values must be non-existent beings, the purported denotations of those terms. This simply doesn't follow.

Quite generally, the semantic value of a term and the entity (if any) it denotes may come apart. We see this in the case of descriptions, for example, as Russell (1905) was soon to realise. Russell's contribution in 'On Denoting' (1905) isn't merely to semantics (in giving us the Russellian theory of definite descriptions). Perhaps more importantly, he gives us the metaphysical resources to see how the Bolzano-Meinong view can be avoided, whilst retaining the meaningfulness of terms such as 'the Golden mountain'. Russell warns us to not infer too much metaphysics from the way we use language. This book is very much written in that spirit: we meaningfully think, talk and reason about the impossible and yet there are no impossible things or states of affairs in reality.

Even saying that we think about Superman is misleading. We meaningfully think that Superman is Clark Kent; that he flies; and that he is loved by Lois Lane. These thoughts involve a Superman-concept. In this thin sense, they are thoughts about Superman, distinct from thoughts about Pegasus or Robin Hood. But in a more robust, world-involving sense, they are not about any thing, for there is no Superman for them to be about.

In what follows, therefore, I will assume that everything exists (*being* and *existence* are coextensive) and that worlds other than our own exist. The debate is then whether worlds other than our own are genuine worlds, or actually existing ersatz worlds.

To make best sense of the debate, it is helpful to be clear on what differentiates genuine worlds from ersatz worlds. The distinction is sometimes given as one between concrete and abstract entities. Indeed, Lewis's worlds are all wholly concrete, spatiotemporal entities. For Lewis, abstract entities such as sets, numbers and properties exist, but do not belong to this or that world (they are not parts of any world). This is no problem for Lewis, since those entities all exist necessarily and have all of their properties essentially. There is no gap between such entities having some property F and the possibility of such entities being F.

This picture of things has no room for abstract entities with impossible properties. Fermat's Last Theorem tells us that there are no three positive integers x, y, z such that $x^n + y^n = z^n$ for any integer $n > 2$. Yet, as someone might disbelieve the theorem, the impossible worlds approach to hyperintensional content requires worlds according to which there are such numbers. Clearly, we must not be allowed to infer from such a world that those numbers could or do exist and have those properties. Whatever we say about the metaphysics of worlds, we need worlds to differ amongst themselves with respect to abstract entities. As a consequence, we cannot characterise genuine worlds precisely as Lewis does, as maximal sums of spatiotemporally related objects. (A sum of objects $x_1, \ldots, x_n$ is the smallest object with $x_1, \ldots, x_n$ as parts.) Such worlds never differ amongst themselves with respect to abstract entities.

When considering whether a world counts as genuine, what's at stake is how that world represents. A Lewisian world represents the existence of a flying hippo by having a flying hippo as a part: a real flesh-and-blood flying animal, the kind you could bump into if you weren't careful. This way of representing is what is essential to being a genuine world. Such worlds represent *de dicto* the existence of an F by having an F as a part. These worlds walk it like they talk it.

This criterion concerns *de dicto* representation only. We should not insist that a genuine world which represents me as having a tail must contain me, entailed, as a part. According to Lewis (1986), there are good reasons for thinking that no entity is a part of more than one genuine world. If genuine world *w* had entailed-me as a part, then (giving that having a tail is an intrinsic property) I would have a tail, which I don't. This is Lewis's problem of *accidental intrinsics* (1986, 198–209), and it persuades him that each entity is a part of at most one world. Lewis holds that other worlds represent me by containing some representative, or *counterpart*, of me. (I'll discuss this point further in §4.5.) Even if Lewis's argument is ultimately rejected, we should still count Lewis's worlds as genuine worlds. So, as I'll use the term, a genuine world is a world which represents *de dicto* that *A* by being such that *A*.

Two features of genuine worlds, so defined, are worth noting. First, they obey the *exportation principle*: if world *w* represents something as being *F*, then something is *F*. For if *w* represents something as being *F*, then *w* contains an *F* as a part. As *w* is part of the totality of being, by the transitivity of parthood, that *F* too is part of the totality of being. (I'll consider ways for genuine worlds to avoid the exportation principle in §4.3.) Second, and as a consequence, genuine worlds commit us to non-actual entities. There are actually no flying hippos but there could have been. So some world represents that there are flying hippos. If that world is a genuine world, then it contains a flying hippo; and so there exists a flying hippo. This is strange, but consistent: there are flying hippos but no actual flying hippos (according to the genuine modal realist), just as there are penguins but no penguins here in Beeston.

4.3   Exportation and Impossible Worlds

The exportation principle is problematic for any account of impossible worlds, as Lewis (1986) notes. Exporting merely possible entities (or states of affairs) from genuine possible worlds lumbers us with a large and counterintuitive but still consistent ontology. Exporting impossible entities (or states of affairs) from genuine impossible worlds, by contrast, drags us into contradiction. There is an impossible world according to which there is a round square. If that world is genuine and we can export from genuine worlds, then there is a real entity which is both round and square. But it is a necessary truth that no square is round (that's why the round square was impossible to being with!), and so our exported round entity is also not round. Consequently, it both is and is not round: contradiction.

The problem seems to affect those taking the Bolzano-Meinong-Twardowski approach to impossible worlds, if they characterise those worlds as worlds which have impossible entities, or impossible states of affairs, as parts. Since such worlds are genuine parts of being, and have contradictory entities as parts, we infer (from the transitivity of parthood) that being itself has contradictory parts, described truly by some contradiction.

Yagisawa (1988, 203) appears to bite the bullet here for his extended modal realism (§4.1), the thesis that 'there are possible worlds in Lewis' sense and also impossible worlds in an equally realistic sense' (1988, 176). He accepts that one can tell the truth about impossible things by contradicting oneself. If so, some contradictions are true (simpliciter; not merely true-in-an-impossible-world). This is the *dialethist* position (Priest 1987), which Yagisawa (in his 1988 paper) is happy to entertain. But merely allowing for true contradictions, as the dialethist does, is not enough to alleviate the exportation worry. For even dialethists want to maintain that many sentences are not true. Dialethists make use of a paraconsistent logic, which does not support the inference *ex falso quodlibet*, $A, \neg A \vdash B$. The very point of rejecting this principle is that, without it, one cannot derive whatever one likes from a contradiction (as one can in classical and intuitionistic logic), thus permitting dialethists to hold that some sentences are not true.

If we can export contradictions from impossible worlds, however, every sentence will be true (simpliciter). Take any sentence *A* and any theorem of real analysis, stated as a universal quantification over real numbers. The latter is equivalent to some statement that there is no real number n such that Bn. Since that is a theorem, it is impossible for there to be a real number n such that Bn, and hence impossible for there to be a real number n such that $A \wedge Bn$. So there is an impossible world according to which there is a real number n such that $A \wedge Bn$. If that world is genuine then we can use the exportation principle: there is (simpliciter) an n such that $A \wedge Bn$. This contradicts our theorem (that there's no n such that Bn). But worse than that, from $A \wedge Bn$ we can (paraconsistently) infer that 'A', our arbitrarily chosen sentence, is true (simpliciter; not merely true by the lights of some impossible world).

Here is a further argument to the same conclusion. Paraconsistent logic usually defines a special atomic sentence, '$\perp$', the Church false constant, which (paraconsistently) entails 'A' for arbitrary 'A' (See, e.g. Restall 2004b). '$\perp$' cannot be true, so there is an impossible world according to which $\perp$. If that world is genuine, it follows that there is (simpliciter) an entity such that $\perp$, and hence (by exportation) that '$\perp$' is true (simpliciter). But then, since '$\perp$' entails 'A', it follows that 'A' is true, for arbitrary 'A': everything is true. This is just the conclusion the dialethist wanted to avoid by introducing her paraconsistent logic. So dialethists cannot accept genuine impossible worlds which support the exportation principle (as Lewisian genuine worlds do).

Yagisawa (2010) gives an alternative to the Lewisian account of worlds. His account is particularly interesting for our purposes, because he focuses explicitly on impossible worlds. Yagisawa treats modality much as *four-dimensionalists* treat temporal matters. On the latter view, entities exist and have properties at a time t by having *temporal stages* at time t which have those properties. Bertie is beagle-shaped this Monday in virtue of having a beagle-shaped this-Monday-stage; he was once a puppy in virtue of having a past puppy-stage; and he is always adorable in virtue of all his temporal states being adorable. Four-dimensionalism is thus a view about how objects persist through time. It is not in itself a view about what time is, or about whether non-present entities exist. But it does presuppose the eternalist ontology of time, on which past, present and future entities genuinely exist. Presentists deny this. (For an overview of these debates, see Sider 2003.) Actualism (the denial of the existence of any non-actual entities) is the modal analogue of presentism and the genuine modal realism we are currently discussing is the modal analogue of eternalism. The question then is, what is it for entities to exist and have properties according to a world?

Yagisawa's answer is that entities exist and have properties at a world w by having *modal stages* at world w which have those properties. Bertie is actually beagle-shaped in virtue of having a beagle-shaped actual-stage; he could have been portly in virtue of having a (merely) possible portly world-stage; and he is necessarily canine because all of his world-stages are canine.

This approach does not avoid the exportation worry. (What follows draws on Jago 2013a.) In the temporal case, some temporally extended entity such as Bertie has properties-at-time-t in virtue of having t-stages with those properties. This reduces Bertie's properties-at-a-time to properties had by his temporal stages. His Monday-stage is beagle-shaped, simpliciter; that stage is intrinsically beagle-shaped. Similarly, in the modal case, Bertie has properties-at-world-w in virtue of having w-stages with those properties. His w-stage is portly, simpliciter; that stage is intrinsically portly, even though Bertie (the collection of all his stages) is not. So the possibility of Bertie's being a portly beagle entails that there is a portly beagle stage, perhaps not actually, but out there somewhere in modal space. That stage is intrinsically portly and not merely portly-at-w (for some world w or other). But by the same token, the impossibility of Bertie's being a portly slim beagle entails that there is an intrinsically portly-and-slim beagle stage, certainly not actually, but out there somewhere in modal space. We can truly say that that stage of Bertie is both portly and not portly: we have not avoided contradiction.

Yagisawa might object that I confuse existence with reality here:

> It is important not to confuse reality with existence. When I say that possible worlds and mere *possibilia* are real, I do not mean that possible worlds and mere *possibilia* exist. Reality

and existence are not the same; the former is absolute, while the latter is relative. (Yagisawa 2010, 49)

According to Yagisawa, existence is always relative to some world or other. There is no existence simpliciter. Given this usage of 'exists', I would be wrong to infer from 'Bertie-stage b exists at world w' to 'Bertie-stage b exists simpliciter' and thus wrong to infer that there exists, simpliciter, a Bertie-stage that is both portly and not portly.

This response is besides the point, for two reasons. Firstly, it doesn't matter at all if Yagisawa calls 'reality' what others call 'existence'. For Yagisawa,

[Reality is] an absolutely basic notion in metaphysics. Reality is the comprehensive ultimate subject matter of metaphysics. ... reality is unique among ultimate subject matters of metaphysics in that any serious discussion of any ultimate subject matter of metaphysics is ultimately about reality, or some part or aspect of reality. (Yagisawa 2010, 40)

The word 'reality' is a label for the comprehensive ultimate topic of metaphysics. It is part of what I mean by 'ultimate' that reality is absolute and irreducible. (Yagisawa 2010, 49)

This is sufficient to establish that Yagisawa means by 'is real' and 'reality' what I (and many others) mean by 'exists' and 'existence'. So, phrased in my own idiolect (which, I think, is shared in these important respects by many), I was right to conclude that Yagisawa's account delivers the existence of a contradictory portly-and-not-portly Bertie-stage.

Secondly, even if the worry were substantial, the argument to absurdity can be run by deriving the reality (as opposed to the existence) of an entity with contradictory properties. Bertie's impossible portly-and-not-portly world-stage b exists relative to some impossible world w. So b is real and is portly-and-not-portly simpliciter. The reality of b is sufficient for the truth of a contradiction, and Yagisawa does not avoid absurdity.

To avoid this conclusion, the defender of genuine impossible worlds must not allow that Bertie is portly-at-w in virtue of having a portly modal part wholly at w. Rather, the story must be that Bertie's possible corpulence is irreducibly relational in form, holding between Bertie as a whole and w. On this view, Bertie is not beagle-shaped; he is beagle-shaped-at-@. (Yagisawa does hint at this, in saying that 'things being thus-and-so is generally relative to a metaphysical index' such as a world (2010, 49).) Crucially, on this view, *being beagle-shaped-at-@* does not reduce to having a beagle-shaped modal part at @, for the view is that *being beagle shaped* is irreducibly a relation to a world. So on this view, Bertie does not have modal parts at all. McDaniel (2004) defends a view along these lines, whereas Yagisawa (2010, 53) explicitly rejects it. (Transposed to the temporal case, the view says that objects do not have temporal parts, for each object is wholly present at each time. This is the three-dimensionalist view.)

This relational theory avoids the exportation worry because something's bearing the relational property *being-beagle-shaped* to world w does not entail that thing's possessing the monadic property *being beagle shaped*. In fact, on the view being described, there is no such monadic property. A feature of this account is that one and the same entity may exist in many worlds, for that entity may bear the *exists-at* relation to more than one world. If Bertie is portly-in-w_1 and slim-in-w_2, then Bertie is a common part of w_1 and w_2. Because of this feature, the view is sometimes called *genuine modal realism with overlap* (McDaniel 2004), the overlap in question being between worlds which have common parts.

There are worries with this approach to genuine worlds, even if we restrict ourselves to possible worlds. One worry is that it is not clear that the worlds in question are in any sense genuine worlds. They are not composed of concrete entities such as Bertie. Parthood, for the overlap theorist, is a triadic relation: my hand is a part of me at w_1, but not at w_2. So we cannot say that Bertie is a part (non-relationally) of world w, for this would require a dyadic parthood relation. Another worry with the view, as Lewis (1986, §4.2) notes, is that it treats aspects of an object that we usually think of as its intrinsic (non-relational) properties, such as shape, as extrinsic relational properties. Entities do not have intrinsic properties, on this view, for every property is possessed only relatively to some world or other. There is no question of how the object in question is, irrespective of how it is in this or that world. This is, to say the least, counterintuitive.

Yet another worry is that the account does not give a genuinely reductive theory of modality, because it cannot say what a possible world is without employing modal concepts. If this is so, then the account embraces a large ontology including non-actual entities, as Lewis's account does, but without Lewis's payoff of a reductive account of modality. (McDaniel (2004) discusses the problem and proposes a solution. Here isn't the place to evaluate it.)

Our topic here is not whether this is a plausible theory of possible worlds, but whether (assuming it works for possible worlds) it can be extended to give an account of impossible worlds. And the answer is it cannot. For suppose to the contrary that impossible worlds are of the realist-with-overlap variety and take the case of Richard Sylvan, the New Zealand logician, born Richard Routley. It is impossible for Routley to be other than Sylvan and hence impossible for Routley but not Sylvan to be a logician. So there is an impossible world w according to which Routley but not Sylvan is a logician.

On the overlap view, that is to say that Routley, but not Sylvan, bears the *being a logician* relation to world w. So, on this view, Routley bears a relation to w which Sylvan does not bear to w and hence, by Leibniz's law, Routley and Sylvan are not identical (simpliciter). But this is absurd: Routley is (or was) Sylvan! Consequently, overlapping genuine worlds are not a suitable treatment of impossible worlds. (One may worry about the use of Leibnitz's law here, on the grounds that it fails in hyperintensional contexts. But the context in which I applied it is extensional, given that the modal-realist-with-overlap analyses 'x is F in w' as a relation between x and w.)

In summary, neither Lewis's non-overlapping genuine worlds, nor Yagisawa's genuine worlds with modal stages, nor McDaniels's genuine overlapping worlds, are suitable candidates for being impossible worlds. Impossible worlds are not genuine worlds. Impossible worlds must be treated as ersatz worlds.

4.4   Hybrid Modal Realism

Berto (2010) and Rescher and Brandom (1980) discuss the *parity thesis*, which says that possible and impossible worlds are of a kind (either both genuine or both ersatz). As Berto notes, the thesis has had many supporters, including Rescher and Brandom, Priest (1997) and Yagisawa (1988, 2010). Since impossible worlds should be treated as ersatz worlds, we can either accept the parity thesis and take all worlds to be ersatz worlds, or deny the parity thesis and adopt a *hybrid* account, on which the possible worlds are genuine worlds but the impossible worlds are ersatz worlds.

Berto (2010) takes the latter option, accepting an ontology of genuine Lewisian possible worlds in addition to ersatz impossible worlds. He calls the resulting view *hybrid modal realism*, and develops it as follows. For Berto, atomic propositions are sets of genuine possible worlds. Ersatz worlds or 'world-stories' are then sets of atomic propositions (Berto 2010, 482), that is, sets of sets of genuine possible worlds. All the impossible worlds are ersatz worlds (2010, 481).

This way of developing the hybrid view faces two problems. First, Berto takes ersatz worlds to be sets of sets of genuine possible worlds, and this places logical constraints on the way in which those worlds represent. They cannot represent both that A and that B without thereby representing that $A \land B$, for example. (They may represent that A, that B, and that $\neg(A \land B)$, but this is not the same as failing to represent that $A \land B$.) Yet representing that A and that B, whilst failing to represent that $A \land B$, is precisely the kind of fine-grained content we require to make sense of certain epistemic states.

Second, Berto's approach conflates intuitively distinct contents. 'Hesperus is F' is true according to exactly the same set of genuine possible worlds as 'Phosphorus is F' and so any of Berto's ersatz worlds represents that Hesperus is F if and only if it represents that Phosphorus is F. As a consequence, Berto's account assigns the same content to 'Hesperus is F' as to 'Phosphorus is F', and so is no help with Frege-puzzle cases (§1.4).

These two worries are worries for Berto's development of hybrid modal realism, not for hybrid modal realism *per se*. They can be overcome by a hybrid modal realist if they can be overcome by a purely ersatz account of worlds, since a hybrid theorist can adopt all of those ersatz worlds (including ersatz impossible worlds) in addition to her genuine possible worlds. In chapter 5, I set out a theory of ersatz worlds for which these problems do not arise. There's nothing to stop a hybrid theorist adding those worlds to her account. (It's not as if actualists can take out a patent on certain set-theoretic constructions!)

In so doing, the hybrid modal realist will obtain a theory quite different from Berto's. Ersatz worlds will be constructed set-theoretically from genuine possibilia, but they will not be sets of possible worlds. They will be more fine-grained than any set of possible worlds. Propositions (and other notions of content) can then be defined in terms of sets of ersatz worlds. On this approach, the genuine worlds provide the genuine building blocks and tell us which ersatz worlds count as representing genuine possibilities. But unlike in Berto's account, the genuine worlds do not play a direct role in constituting contents. A hybrid theorist may adopt an account along these lines. I'll argue, however, that the actual world provides sufficient building blocks for all the ersatz worlds we need (chapter 5). If I'm right, then merely possible genuine worlds come into the picture only in determining which ersatz worlds represent genuine possibilities. This is already to minimise severely the role of genuine worlds in the theory.

Hybrid modal realism is viable only if genuine modal realism (with a plurality of genuine possible worlds of some kind) is viable. But the latter isn't viable. In the remainder of this chapter, I'll give an extended argument against genuine modal realism and consequently against hybrid modal realism. I'll return to impossible worlds in chapter 5, where (in line with the parity thesis) I give a construction of both possible and impossible ersatz worlds from actual entities.

4.5   A Problem for Genuine Worlds

In §4.3, I discussed several notions of genuine possible worlds. In this section, I will give an extended argument against the genuine modal realist, who takes possible worlds to be genuine worlds. I'll conclude that we should treat possible worlds, as well as impossible worlds, as ersatz worlds.

My argument will focus on the genuine modal realist's use of *counterpart theory* (§4.2), on which I'll say more below. I'll argue that the combination of genuine modal realism and counterpart theory leads to absurdity. But Lewis (and, plausibly, other defenders of genuine worlds: see §4.6) are committed to some version of counterpart theory. Hence genuine modal realism should be rejected. I'll focus at first on Lewis's account of genuine worlds, as it is the best worked-out and most plausible account of genuine worlds. But the argument also applies to the other notions of genuine worlds discussed in §4.3; I'll indicate why this is so in §4.6.

Counterpart theory (Lewis 1968, 1971, 1986) provides an answer to the question: how do other worlds represent me (or some other particular) as being a certain way? This is the question of *de re* modality. In §4.2, I briefly discussed the problem of accidental intrinsics. Suppose a genuine world represents me as having a tail by containing an entailed version of me. If that particular were numerically identical to me, then I would have a tail, which I don't. Having a tail isn't like having certain legal rights, which I might have in one country but lack in another. Having or lacking a tail is intrinsic to the particular in question. So, given that I don't have a tail, the entailed entity that's part of the other world can't be me. This is Lewis's problem of accidental intrinsics (1986, 198–209).

Lewis's response is that the entailed otherworldly entity is a representative, or *counterpart*, of me. A world represents me as having a tail by containing an entailed counterpart of mine. Something counts as one of my counterparts insofar as it resembles me in certain important ways. What those ways are is a highly context-sensitive matter.

This is the basis of counterpart theory. It contributes to a theory of *de re* modality as follows. I could have been at the beach right now, on Lewis's view, if and only if I have a counterpart in a possible world who is at the beach right now. I am necessarily (or essentially) a person if and only if all my possible-world counterparts are people. Lewis (1971, 1986) allows that there are worlds at which I have no counterpart (for I might not have existed) and worlds at which I have more than one counterpart. (This represents a departure from Lewis's original presentation of counterpart theory in Lewis 1968.)

Let's abbreviate 'y is a counterpart of x' as 'Cxy', 'x is a part of y' as 'Pxy' and 'w is a possible world' as 'Ww'. Then in general, the statement of possibility '$\Diamond A x_1 \cdots x_n$' (where '$x_1$' $\cdots$ 'x_n' are all the free variables in 'A') is analysed as

$$\exists w \exists y_1 \cdots \exists y_n (Ww \land Py_1 w \land Cx_1 y_1 \land \cdots$$
$$\land Py_n w \land Cx_n y_n \land A^w y_1 \cdots y_n)$$

where 'A^w' is just like 'A' except with its quantifiers restricted to world w (Lewis 1968). (In restricting quantifiers in 'A' to world w, we recursively replace each instance of '$\forall x B$' with '$\forall x (Pxw \to B)$' and each instance of '$\exists x B$' with '$\exists x (Pxw \land B)$'.) I will call this the *counterpart analysis* of '$\Diamond$'.

This analysis quickly runs into conflict with Lewis's metaphysics. Suppose that w is a world and e is a possible entity which isn't a part of w:

(4.1) $Ww \land \neg Pew$

By *possibility introduction*, the inference from 'A' to 'possibly, A', this entails

(4.2) $\Diamond(Ww \land \neg Pew)$

which, on the counterpart analysis, is equivalent to:

(4.3) $\exists v \exists x \exists y (Wv \land Pxv \land Cwx \land Pyv \land Cey \land Wx \land \neg Pyx)$

This, however, is inconsistent with Lewis's metaphysics, on which no world is a part of any other world:

(4.4) $\forall x \forall y ((Wx \wedge Wy \wedge Pxy) \to x = y)$

To see that (4.3) is inconsistent with (4.4), assume (from (4.3)) that there are entities v, x and y such that:

$$Wv \wedge Pxv \wedge Cwx \wedge Pyv \wedge Cey \wedge Wx \wedge \neg Pyx$$

Given (4.4), this entails that $x = v$ and hence (substituting 'x' for 'v') entails the explicit contradiction '$Pyx \wedge \neg Pyx$'. We have derived a contradiction (via *possibility introduction* and the counterpart analysis of possibility) from a premise which, given Lewis's metaphysics, is true.

(Divers (1999) calls problems such as this *advanced modalizing problems*. He presents two examples, 'it is possible that there are many possible worlds' and 'it is possible that there are natural properties', to which Lewis is committed via *possibility introduction* from his accepted metaphysics. Given the counterpart analysis, these are equivalent to '$\exists x (Wx \wedge \exists y \exists z (Pyx \wedge Pzx \wedge Wy \wedge Wz \wedge y \neq z))$' and '$\exists x (Wx \wedge \exists y (Pyx \wedge Ny))$', respectively, where '$N$' is the predicate 'is a natural property'. Lewis rejects both of these (Divers 1999, 221–3), for no Lewis-world contains another Lewis-world, and no world contains any natural property, for natural properties are transworld sets (Lewis 1986, 94).)

Before moving on to discuss how Lewis should respond, I want to head off two quick attempts to dismiss this as a non-problem. The first claims that I have illegitimately mixed a modal language containing '$\diamond$' with the language of counterpart theory. The second claims that the *possibility introduction* rule is not valid in the context of counterpart theory. Both moves can be dismissed quickly. The language we are interested in is neither a pure modal language (e.g., the language of quantified modal logic lacking the predicates of counterpart theory), nor a purely extensional first-order language quantifying over worlds. Rather, we are interested in the language in which Lewis states his analysis of possibility. This language, the language of *On the Plurality of Worlds* (Lewis 1986), contains both modal operators and the predicates of counterpart theory.

We are interested in Lewis's (1986) reductive account of modality, which makes use of a language (English, or some fragment of it) including both modal operators and the predicates of counterpart theory, and not merely in a translation from one language to another. It is thus no response to argue that counterpart-theory-talk and possibility-talk should be kept separate, precisely because this would preclude Lewis's reductive analysis of the latter in terms of the former.

What of the objection that the *possibility introduction* rule, which allows one to infer '$\Diamond A$' from 'A', is not valid in the current setting? Possibility introduction is equivalent to the factivity of necessity: *from '$\Box A$', infer 'A'*. This corresponds to axiom T: $\vdash \Box A \rightarrow A$. By factivity and *reductio*, 'A' entails '$\neg\Box\neg A$' which, by the duality of '$\Box$' and '$\Diamond$', is equivalent to '$\Diamond A$'. If one rejects the factivity of '$\Box$', then there is a strong case that one does not mean *it is necessary that* by '$\Box$'. So I will assume that rejecting *possibility introduction* is a weak option. (It's worth noting that Divers (1999), whose aim is to defend Lewis's approach, accepts *possibility introduction*.)

The Redundancy Account

A better response to the objection is set out by Divers (1999). I'll discuss this move, but argue that it does not genuinely avoid the problem. Divers's idea is to distinguish *extraordinary* from *ordinary* modal cases. In ordinary cases, '$\Diamond A$' is treated in accordance with the standard counterpart-analysis, as given above, whereas in advanced cases (such as the problem case above), Divers stipulates that:

(4.5) $A \leftrightarrow \Diamond A$ and $A \leftrightarrow \Box A$

In such cases, we simply ignore the modal operator in our analysis. Call this the *redundancy analysis* of '$\Diamond$' and '$\Box$'. Assuming that (4.2) is an advanced case (as it must be if the redundancy account is to help here), it is then analysed as (4.1), which is unproblematically true for Lewis.

When does a modal statement '$\Diamond A$' count as an advanced modalizing case? Divers says that ordinary modalizing is 'primarily about ordinary individuals' where 'an ordinary individual is a thing that is spatiotemporally located and has all of its spatiotemporally located parts spatiotemporally related to one another' (Divers 1999, 218), so that 'the ordinary individuals are *intra-world* individuals' (Divers 1999, 219). Such entities contrast with 'extraordinary or transworld entities—including the transworld sets whose members are individuals that are parts of different worlds and the transworld sums whose parts are parts of different worlds' (Divers 1999, 220). Advanced modalizing is then 'modalizing that is primarily about entities that are not ordinary individuals' (Divers 1999, 219).

To make best sense of Divers's proposal, we should not understand these remarks as giving a set of syntactic-and-semantic principles for classifying statements into the *ordinary* and *extraordinary* categories. (After all, worlds are not transworld entities. So if this were Divers's aim, he would be at risk of (incorrectly) treating his own example, 'it is possible that there are many possible worlds', as a case of ordinary modalizing.) Divers's aim is not to provide a translation scheme, on the model of Lewis's (1968) scheme. Divers's remarks are best taken as describing some of the typical indicators of extraordinary cases. His aim, instead, is to provide a non-ad hoc semantic story which avoids the advanced modalizing problem, given some prior understanding of whether a content counts as ordinary or extraordinary.

For the genuine modal realist, statements are in general ambiguous between (i) a world-restricted content, whose scope encompasses a single world only (usually, the world of utterance), and (ii) an unrestricted content, whose scope encompasses all the possible worlds. Using this distinction, a genuine modal realist can explain how we ordinarily say something true by uttering 'there are no unicorns', even though she insists that unicorns do exist. She does this by interpreting our ordinary utterance of 'there are no unicorns' as having the world-restricted content *that there are no unicorns in our world*. This is perfectly compatible with her insistence that there exist unicorns in other worlds.

In general, a world-restricted content has the form 'in world w, A'; its truth requires all entities referred to and quantified over by 'A' to be parts of w. (In particular, the world-restrictor 'in world w' restricts all quantifiers within its scope to world w, as set out at the start of this section.) According to Divers (1999, 228), prefixing '$\diamond$' to a sentence 'A' has the semantic effect of quantifying into the world-restrictor in 'A': if 'A' has the content *in w: B*, then '$\diamond A$' will have the content *for some world w, in w: B*. (See Divers's principle (Q), Divers 1999, 228 and Lewis 1986, 5–7.) In this way, world-restricted contents prefixed with '$\diamond$' behave in line with the standard counterpart analysis of '$\diamond$'. But contents containing no world-restrictor (the unrestricted contents) have nothing on which the semantic value of '$\diamond$' can operate. Thus prefixing a sentence 'A' expressing an unrestricted content with '$\diamond$' has no semantic effect. '$\diamond A$' then behaves in line with Divers's redundancy analysis.

Crucially for Divers and Lewis, there is no need to give a syntactic-or-semantic specification of when an utterance expresses a restricted or an unrestricted content. Context is important, but above all there is what Lewis calls 'the cardinal principle of semantics', namely 'interpret the message to make it make sense – to make it consistent, and sensible to say' (Lewis 1996, 566). Given this principle, we interpret the genuine modal realist to be asserting an unrestricted content when she utters (4.1), since this content (and not the corresponding restricted content) is true by her own lights.

Let's work through the idea in more detail. (4.1) is ambiguous between:

(4.1^r) In the actual world @: $Ww \wedge \neg Pew$

(4.1^u) (In all modal space:) $Ww \wedge \neg Pew$

The former is false, since if both w and e are parts of the actual world, then w must be the actual world, in which case $\neg Pew$ is false. But the latter is (by the general modal realist's lights) unproblematically true. The results of applying possibility-introduction to (4.1^r) and (4.1^u) are, respectively:

(4.2^r) For some world w', in w': $Ww \land \neg Pew$

(4.2^u) (In all modal space:) $Ww \land \neg Pew$

Since (4.1^u) is unproblematically true (for the genuine modal realist), (4.2^u) is too. Hence the argument via possibility-introduction is diffused, so long as one disambiguates (4.1) as (4.1^u). This is reasonable, since the other disambiguation of (4.1), (4.1^r), is false. So an appeal to charity in interpreting the genuine modal realist's utterance of (4.1) diffuses the problem.

This way of avoiding the problem, however, causes problems elsewhere in the theory of possibility. Consider Anna, who is taller than Bill. As Anna and Bill are perfectly normal humans, it seems clear that it is a contingent matter that Anna is taller than Bill. Any theory which flatly denies this does a bad job of capturing our concept of possibility. Now suppose further that Anna and Bill are not worldmates of one another. Then any world-restricted disambiguation of

(4.6) Anna is taller than Bill

is false. The world-restricted reading (for some world w) of (4.6) is 'in w, Anna is taller than Bill'. Since the 'in w' restriction requires the particulars in its scope to be parts of w, this reading of (4.6) is false for any w. So, appealing to Lewis's 'cardinal principle of semantics', we should disambiguate to the unrestricted reading of (4.6), which (according to Lewis) is true. Then prefixing this content by either '$\Diamond$' or '$\Box$' is redundant, on Divers's account. We can thus infer from the unrestricted content of (4.6) to

(4.7) It is necessary that Anna is taller than Bill.

This seems reason enough to reject this account of how modal operators work. For intuitively, (4.7) is false as (4.6) is contingent, even if Anna and Bill are not worldmates.

The genuine modal realist is likely to claim that (4.7) is harmless, since (on the redundancy account) it says no more than (4.6). Objecting to (4.7) with the embedded (4.6) understood as having unrestricted content begs the question against Lewis, she will say. However, it is not enough for the genuine modal realist to find an acceptable reading of (4.7). The data to be explained is the deep intuition that (4.6) is contingent. On the current proposal, the genuine modal realist cannot say that (4.6) is contingent in any sense. She can accept

(4.8) Anna is taller than Bill $\wedge$ $\Diamond\neg$Anna is taller than Bill

but only if there is a shift in linguistic context between the first and the second conjuncts. Each occurrence of 'Anna is taller than Bill' in (4.8) must have a different content (the former unrestricted, the latter world-restricted) in order for (4.8) to come out true. But this is not the same as saying that a particular utterance of (4.6) is a contingent truth.

To be a contingent truth, an utterance must have a content (i.e., express a proposition) which is true but which could have been false. It is clearly no good if some other proposition could have been false! And this is precisely what the genuine modal realist cannot accept in the case of (4.6). To claim that the unrestricted content of (4.6) could have been false amounts to the claim that it is false, on the current view (since it contains no world-restrictor). But then, to assert that that very content is contingent is to assert that it is both true and false: a contradiction. So as a matter of logic, the current proposal is debarred from asserting the contingency of (4.6).

We cannot avoid the problem by reading (4.6) as saying, 'Anna has height n; Bill has height m; and $n > m$' (which is contingent). The approach is a non-starter. It will treat 'Anna is younger than her father' as 'Anna's age is n, her father's age is m, and $n < m$', and hence (incorrectly) as a contingent truth. So we must reject this suggestion.

The genuine modal realist might try to explain away our intuition that (4.6) is contingent as a mistake. Perhaps, she might say, we (mistakenly) infer from (4.8) that (4.6) is contingent. But the judgement that (4.6) is contingent is far more robust that this. It is a central part of my concept of contingency that such facts about the heights of humans are contingent matters. Given my concepts of a human body and of height, I can be sure that, if Anna and Bob exist and have human bodies, then which of them is tallest is a contingent matter. The current proposal conflicts with this. At best, it captures some other concept of contingency, and hence captures concepts of possibility and necessity other than our everyday ones.

(The genuine modal realist is not adverse to questioning common sense. She says there are flying pigs, whereas common sense denies this. But the whole point of developing such an account is surely to give an account of our modal concepts. My claim here is that the approach fails in this respect.)

Lewis's notion of genuine worlds is in deep trouble. That notion requires counterpart theory, but the combination of counterpart theory, Lewis-worlds and regular modal reasoning generates contradictions. In the next section, I show how to generalise the argument.

4.6   Generalising the Argument

I've argued that Lewis's account of genuine worlds is untenable. In this section, I generalise the argument to Yagisawa's (2010) and McDaniel's (2004) accounts of genuine worlds, as well as Rosen's modal fictionalism (1990).

Yagisawa

On the face of it, the argument against Lewis's combination of general modal realism and counterpart theory does not affect Yagisawa's (2010) account of modality (§4.3), precisely because he does not adopt counterpart theory. According to Yagisawa, Bertie could have been portly in virtue of Bertie having a portly world-stage. For some world-index w, Bertie has a portly w-stage, hence Bertie could have been portly: and with no mention of counterparts. But Yagisawa faces a nasty dilemma, as follows.

Necessarily, any entity whatsoever that's F is either necessarily F or contingently F. Take Bertie's portly w-stage (call it b_w). Is b_w necessarily or contingently portly? Suppose the former. According to Yagisawa, any ordinary entity x (such as Bertie) is possibly F iff, for some world-index u, x has a u-stage that's F. As Bertie has a necessarily portly w-stage b_w, it follows that Bertie is possibly necessarily portly: it is possible that it is necessary that Bertie is portly. But '$\Diamond \Box A \to \Box A$' is a theorem of the most plausible alethic modal logic, $\mathbf{KT5}$ (or $\mathbf{S5}$). Hence (assuming $\mathbf{KT5}$), it follows that Bertie is necessarily portly. But this is false, since Bertie is in fact lithe, and not at all portly. To avoid that conclusion (given the assumption that Bertie's w-stage is necessarily portly), Yagisawa must reject $\mathbf{KT5}$ as the correct logic of metaphysical modality, which is a highly questionable move.

(Yagisawa does suggest that metaphysical accessibility is not an equivalence relation (Yagisawa 2010, 156). Accessibility seems to be reflexive, transitive but non-euclidian, on Yagisawa's approach; hence Yagisawa must accept $\mathbf{KT4}$ but not $\mathbf{KT5}$ as the correct logic of metaphysical modality. Thus, whatever is necessary is necessarily necessary, but something can be possibly necessary without being necessary, on Yagisawa's view. Yagisawa says that u is metaphysically accessible from w iff all metaphysical laws of w are also metaphysical laws of u (Yagisawa 2010, 153, 156). As a consequence, such-and-such could have been the laws of metaphysics even though they are in fact not. That seems dubious, especially if you want to delineate the realm of genuinely metaphysically possible worlds as those that conform to all the laws of metaphysics: see §5.6.)

We can run the argument without assuming $\mathbf{KT5}$, however. Bertie is actually lithe in virtue of his lithe actual Bertie-stage, $b_@$. If that stage is necessarily lithe, then Bertie is actually necessarily lithe. On anyone's view, if actually A then A, and hence Bertie is necessarily lithe. But this is false, since Bertie could have been non-lithe (as Bertie's portly w-stage attests).

So Yagisawa must assume that world-stages do not have all their properties of necessity: Bertie's actual-stage $b_@$ is contingently lithe (and so could have been portly), and his w-stage b_w is contingently portly (and so could have been lithe). These possibilities cannot be analysed as possibilities for ordinary objects (such as Bertie) are analysed: b_w itself does not have modal stages (other than itself), and so does not have a lithe world-stage. But b_w is related, in an important way, to a lithe world-stage, namely $b_@$ (Bertie's actual-stage). The relation between the world-stages b_w and $b_@$ is that they are both world-stages of Bertie. This relationship between world-stages behaves like a counterpart relation (for stages): we can say that such-and-such world-stages are Bertie-counterparts of one another when they are amongst Bertie's world-stages. Stage s could have been F iff there is a world w and a w-stage s_w which is both F and a counterpart of s.

In this way, an analogue of the argument against Lewis can be run. Say that world-stages s and s' are *worldmates* ($W s s'$) when they both exist at the same world-index (i.e., iff they are both w-stages). Now consider any two world-stages s_1 and s_2 which are not worldmates: $\neg W s_1 s_2$. By *possibility introduction*, it's possible that they are not worldmates: $\Diamond \neg W s_1 s_2$. By the analysis of possibility for stages just given, there is a world u and there are u-stages s_1^u and s_2^u such that s_1^u is a counterpart of s_1, s_2^u is a counterpart of s_2 and $\neg W s_1^u s_2^u$. But since s_1^u and s_2^u are both u-stages, by definition they are worldmates: $W s_1^u s_2^u$. Contradiction. Hence Yagisawa's theory is in the same predicament as Lewis's. It cannot live without counterpart theory, but the combination of counterpart theory, Yagisawa's metaphysics and regular modal reasoning is inconsistent.

McDaniel

McDaniel (2004) avoids the argument just run against Yagisawa, for he does not treat ordinary objects as having modal stages. Rather, properties of objects become relations between objects and worlds (§4.3). This is the sense in which there is identity across worlds: one and the same entity exists relative to more than one world but (unlike in Yagisawa's account) not in virtue of having stages in those worlds. So counterpart theory is not required for ordinary objects, on McDaniel's view.

Nevertheless, McDaniel still makes use of counterpart theory for the *de re* modal properties of spacetime regions (McDaniel 2004, 149). A spacetime region is a region of a world; it doesn't make sense to say that a region exists relative to a world, or that a given region exists ('is wholly present') in more than one world. So according to McDaniel, modal properties of regions are given in terms of their counterparts, just as in Lewis's account. We can then run the argument just used against Yagisawa's account, with spacetime regions in place of world-stages. Regions r and r' are worldmates (Wrr') when they are spatiotemporally related to each other. Now suppose regions r_1 and r_2 are not worldmates. Then possibly, they are not worldmates: $\Diamond \neg W r_1 r_2$. By the counterpart-theoretic analysis of *de re* modality for spacetime regions, there is a world w containing counterparts r_1' and r_2' of r_1 and r_2, respectively, such that $\neg W r_1' r_2'$. But r_1' and r_2' are both regions of w, hence are spatiotemporally related, hence are worldmates: $W r_1' r_2'$. Contradiction.

McDaniel's account is in the same predicament as Lewis's. It requires counterpart theory (for spacetime regions), but the combination of counterpart theory, McDaniel's metaphysics and regular modal reasoning is inconsistent. Lewis's, Yagisawa's and McDaniel's accounts are the best worked-out theories of genuine worlds. They all suffer from internal inconsistency. So we should reject the idea that possible worlds are genuine worlds.

Modal Fictionalism

I've argued against the view that possible worlds are genuine worlds. We can run a similar argument against *fictionalism* about possible worlds (Rosen 1990). This view is an attempt to reap the theoretical benefits of Lewis's (or some other) account of genuine worlds, but without the ontological costs. It does this by analysing modal language using a fiction of possible worlds (which might be Lewis's *On the Plurality of Worlds*, plus an encyclopaedia of all actual, non-modal truths). The modal fictionalist (unlike the genuine modal realist) will not assert that there literally are flying hippos at other worlds. Instead, she will assert that *according to the fiction* there are flying hippos at other worlds and hence (literally) that there could have been flying hippos. In general, modal fictionalism treats '*A*' as being literally true iff '$A^@$', the counterpart-analysis of '*A*' relativised to the actual world, is true according to the fiction.

Modal fictionalism fails because the argument given in §4.5 against Lewis's account of worlds shows that the fiction is inconsistent. By running that argument, we can derive a contradiction within the fiction. Moreover, since the fiction is governed by classical logic, any classical consequence of something true in the fiction is itself true in the fiction. So, given that the fiction is inconsistent, every sentence whatsoever is true in the fiction. We can then derive the literal truth of an arbitrary sentence '*A*' as follows. First, translate '*A*' into its counterpart-analysis, '$A^@$'. This is true according to the fiction (since every sentence is) and so, by the modal fictionalist analysis, '*A*' is (literally) true. We have derived the literal truth of an arbitrary sentence '*A*', which is absurd. Consequently, modal fictionalism is not a tenable position.

Chapter Summary

We have good reason to accept impossible worlds into our ontology, for they provide the best way to make sense of conditionals with impossible antecedents (§4.1). We can think of impossible worlds (and worlds in general) either as genuine worlds or as ersatz worlds, and as really existing or as beings that lack existence (§4.2). And we might treat impossible worlds in the same way as possible worlds, or adopt a hybrid account (§4.4).

The main conclusion of the chapter is that neither impossible worlds (§4.3) nor possible worlds (§4.5, §4.6) should be treated as genuine worlds. Both possible and impossible worlds are ersatz worlds, in line with the parity thesis. The task in the next chapter is to set out an account of ersatz possible and impossible worlds in more detail.

5

Constructing Worlds

In this chapter, I present a metaphysical account of possible and impossible worlds. These worlds provide the basis for the accounts of content in chapters 7–8. I consider a problem faced by accounts of ersatz worlds: the problem of aliens. I argue that existing solutions are not tenable and develop a new account, based on a metaphysics of facts.

5.1 Ersatz Worlds

In the previous chapter, I argued that both possible and impossible worlds should be treated as ersatz worlds. There is thus no relevant ontological distinction between possible and impossible worlds. (I'll briefly address the question of when a world counts as a possible world in §5.6.)

Ersatz worlds are worlds constructed from actual entities but which represent non-actual entities and states of affairs, much as a novel represents a merely possible situation using actual sentences of English and an Escher drawing represents an impossible situation using actual paper and ink. Indeed, speaking broadly, we may adopt ersatz worlds which represent either in a linguistic way, as a novel does, or in a pictorial way, as a realistic painting or architect's scale model does (Lewis 1986, chapter 3).

Lewis also considers worlds which represent in some other, unspecified, 'magical' way. Such a world represents such-and-such, and there's no further explaining how or why it does so. This is fine when we're doing formal semantics (e.g., building possible worlds models for a modal logic, as in §1.2). We take a function which assigns sentences of the object language to worlds, and we're not interested in why sentence '*A*' is or isn't assigned to world *w*. But my interest here isn't merely in formal semantics. To give a genuinely philosophical account of content in terms of worlds, I need to explain how those worlds represent what they represent. So I'll set 'magical' ersatz worlds to one side.

Linguistic and pictorial ersatz worlds each have their advantages in constructing possible worlds. (Chapter 3 of Lewis 1986 is the classic discussion of these issues.) But when we turn to impossible worlds, the linguistic approach has a clear advantage over the pictorial approach. Escher was ingenious in finding ways to depict many impossible situations pictorially, but the applicability of these or any other pictorial techniques is fairly limited.

Just consider the hugely varied kinds of impossibility which we can represent. There are explicitly contradictory situations: a winter scene in which it is both snowing throughout and not snowing at all. There are mathematical impossibilities: Fermat's Last Theorem turning out false. And there are incomplete situations: Bertie being adorable (but being neither small nor large; neither thin nor fat; neither old nor young; and having no particular appearance whatsoever). These are all situations we want our worlds to represent, yet it is hard to see how they could be represented pictorially. Accordingly, I will focus on the linguistic approach to constructing ersatz worlds. This approach has been defended, in different ways and for different purposes, by Carnap (1947); Hintikka (1962, 1969); Jeffrey (1983) and, more recently, by Melia (2001) and Sider (2002).

On the linguistic approach, ersatz worlds are sets of sentences in some 'worldmaking' language. This can be any language we like, as long as some important constraints are met. First, we need a method of interpreting sentences of the language, so that we can say what a given sentence represents. Second, the language should be disambiguated and precise, so that it is always a determinate matter what a given sentence represents. Third, the language must be expressible enough to represent all the possible and impossible situations we want to represent and to represent distinct (possible or impossible) situations as distinct situations.

The first two desiderata can be met in a number of ways. Lewis (1986, 145–6), following Carnap (1947), suggests the *Lagadonian* approach, according to which we take actual particulars to be our names and actual properties and relations to be our predicates. Each name and predicate is interpreted as denoting itself. Thus flesh-and-blood Bertie counts as a name in the language, referring to himself.

This isn't a language like English, but that doesn't matter in the slightest. All that matters is that we have a precisely specifiable, compositional system of representation: a language in the formal sense. Atomic sentences are sequences of an n-place predicate (that is, a property or relation) and n names (or other referring terms). We can set aside special set-theoretic constructions to serve as our connectives, quantifiers and variables. We thus have uncountably many names in our language (each real number is a name for itself, for example) and hence uncountably many sentences. We can also allow infinitely long sentences. We can allow for infinitely long quantifier-prefixes and we can allow our conjunction and disjunction symbols to operate on (possibly infinite) sets of sentences, resulting in infinitely long conjunctions and disjunctions.

In this way, the Lagadonian approach can avoid the cardinality objection from Lewis (1973, 90) and Bricker (1987, 340–3). The objection, in short, is that there are more possibilities than there are sets of sentences and hence that sets of sentences are no good at representing all the possibilities without conflation. How do we know how many possibilities there are? A common thought (see Lewis 1986, 143 and Bricker 1987, 340–1) is that a continuum of points, with each point either occupied or unoccupied by matter, is possible; and each such configuration of matter-at-points is a distinct possibility. There are $\beth_2$ such configurations (where $\beth_2$ is the cardinality of the power set of the continuum), hence at least $\beth_2$ many distinct possibilities. But there are only $\beth_1$ sets of sentences in a countable language; hence some possibilities must be ignored or conflated, on the linguistic approach. As this objection works only against ersatz approaches with a countable worldmaking language, it does not affect the above proposal. The cardinality objection was one way to argue that linguistic ersatzism does not represent all the possibilities without conflation. It did not work (at least, not against the version of linguistic ersatzism I am considering). But there is another, more worrying, argument to the very same conclusion. It is to that argument I now turn.

5.2   The Problem of Aliens

In this section (which draws on Jago 2013d), I consider 'an apparently devastating problem' for linguistic ersatzism, 'the problem of descriptive power' (Sider 2002, 281) or, as it is often called, the *problem of aliens*. The problem, as it affects ersatz accounts of possible worlds, concerns entities which do not exist, but which could have. (I'll come to ersatz impossible worlds below.) I don't have a sister, but I could have had one. So some possible world represents me as having a sister and represents her as being various ways. She could have been older and taller than me, better at chess and with a penchant for a glass of port. Moreover, a possible world which represents someone as being all these things should represent her as having these properties contingently. That is, in the possible situation we are imagining, my possible sister likes port, but could have hated the stuff. Call my merely possible sister an *alien particular*. The actualist says there are no alien particulars, yet needs the resources to represent them. How can she do this? Clearly not in the Lagadonian way, given that there are in fact no alien particulars.

There is another, more worrying, version of the problem of aliens, which focuses on alien properties rather than alien particulars. Lewis describes a case:

> Think of an ersatz philosopher who lives in a simpler world than ours. The protons and neutrons (if we may call them that)

of his world are indivisible particles. There are no quarks; and so the distinctive properties of quarks, their so-called flavours and colours, are not instantiated by anything at all in his simpler worlds. ... They are alien to that world. (Lewis 1986, 159)

This otherworldly philosopher could not construct a Lagadonian language which names all the properties we have at our world and so he could not construct an ersatz world which represents our world. He misses out on real possibilities.

But then, Lewis asks, why suppose that we are not in a situation much like the otherworldly philosopher? Is it not possible that the properties which are fundamental to our world (whatever they turn out to be, if anything at all) could have been present in some other world, a world at which some other properties are fundamental? In the situation we are imagining, our fundamental properties are constituted by more fundamental properties, properties which are not present at our world (just as our quark-properties of charm and strangeness are not present in the world which 'bottoms out' with protons and neutrons). If so, we cannot give a Lagadonian name to those possible properties alien to our world and so cannot unambiguously represent the world we are imagining.

Perhaps an actualist ersatzer should not accept that there are such possibilities. After all, Lewis's description of the relevant possibilities is couched in his genuine modal realist language, talking of those other worlds much as we would talk about other times or places. (Lewis concedes this (1986, 160) but nevertheless hopes that the ersatzer 'would find it compelling to say, simply, that there might have been other natural properties (or universals) than there are'; otherwise 'he gets the facts of modality wrong' (1986, 160). I agree with Lewis here.)

Even if this way of responding to Lewis has some weight, it will not help our current project of constructing ersatz worlds. Lewis's argument with the ersatzer concerns just the possible worlds, whereas we are interested in the impossible as well as the possible worlds. If it is not possible for there to be universals other than those that actually exist, then it is impossible for there to be such universals, and so some impossible world must represent those universals as existing! So if linguistic ersatzism does not have the resources to represent such eventualities, we are in trouble, regardless of whether such eventualities are possible or impossible. Following this line of reasoning, the task of responding to the objection may seem insurmountable for the Lagadonian approach (and for linguistic ersatzism in general).

This is the problem of alien particulars and alien properties, as it affects the Lagadonian ersatz approach. I'll now sketch some possible replies. An ersatzer may reply by claiming that the particulars and properties in question do in fact exist and hence that they may be named. Or she may claim that the possibilities and impossibilities in question can be represented, absent the relevant names and predicates. The foremost problem with the former approach is that actualists should deny that Pegasus, Superman and my (merely possible) sister exist in any sense, so this response looks to be a non-starter in the case of alien particulars. In the case of alien properties, there is perhaps a little more elbow room, since it is a controversial matter which properties actually exist. An ersatzer taking this route would have to claim that there actually exist properties which are not actually instantiated; that is, properties which nothing actually has. This line of thought is unpopular, to say the least.

In the case of possible (but not impossible) situations, Melia (2001), Sider (2002) and Skyrms (1981) adopt the latter strategy, holding that the possibilities in question can be represented even though the relevant names and predicates do not exist. Skyrms, agreeing that 'there might be other things that play the role of our objects; other things that play the role of our relations' (1981, 201), holds that we should allow 'new' properties and relations to be represented. But 'the only significance of these new blocks [i.e., non-actual particulars and properties] lies in their arrangement vis-à-vis each other and vis-à-vis the elements of the real world' (1981, 201). We can implement this suggestion using *Ramsey sentences*: existentially quantified second-order sentences specifying the existence of certain properties, relations and particulars, together satisfying some holistic description (Lewis

1970). If P is the class of all actual particulars and U the class of all actual properties and relations, then the worldmaking sentence

$$\exists x (\bigwedge_{y \in P} \{x \neq y\} \wedge Ax)$$

says that there is a non-actual individual which satisfies the open sentence Ax, and

$$\exists X (\bigwedge_{Y \in U} \{X \neq Y\} \wedge AX)$$

says that there is a non-actual property or relation which satisfies the open sentence AX.

(I am doubtful that these formulae in fact abbreviate any well-formed sentences of the worldmaking language. P must be a proper class, since it is supposed to contain all actual particulars (and hence all sets). Thus the worldmaking language cannot be formulated in ZF set theory, in which the notion of a class is present only informally. Whether or not ZF should be assumed as the background for the formal definition of the ersatz language is moot. Alternatives: von Neumann-Bernays-Gödel set theory permits talk of proper classes but not quantification over them, as the ersatzer requires. Morse-Kelley set theory does allow quantification over proper classes, but is not finitely axiomatizable (Morse 1965). Again, the extent to which this affects the ersatzist programme is moot.)

This approach builds in the identity of indiscernibles for non-actual particulars and universals. We introduce distinct possibilia through such existential sentences only if we use distinct (indeed, non-equivalent) open sentences Ax in each. Some philosophers, *haecceitists* (e.g. Kaplan 1975), object at this point. I could have had two sisters and, in that possible situation, the properties had by the first sister (in that situation) could have been had by the second.

There are distinct possibilities here, says the haecceitist. In one, sister$_1$ has properties $F_1, \ldots, F_n$, whereas sister$_2$ has properties $G_1, \ldots, G_m$; in the other, sister$_2$ has properties $F_1, \ldots, F_n$, whereas sister$_1$ has properties $G_1, \ldots, G_m$. The two situations are qualitatively identical with respect to the two sisters, but are nevertheless distinct possibilities. So says that haecceitist. If she is right, then the erstazer's move above fails, for it discerns just the one possible situation, described as a situation in which there are two non-actual individuals, both sisters of mine, one of whom has properties $F_1, \ldots, F_n$, the other of whom has properties $G_1, \ldots, G_m$.

An ersatzer might refuse to take the example seriously, holding instead that qualitatively identical possible situations are numerically identical. But pressure can be put on this stance by considering a similar example, this time focusing on properties instead of particulars. Suppose there is a situation in which things are just as they actually are, except all the negative charges have switched places with all the positive charges. In this situation (so the story goes), everything behaves as things actually do; yet this situation is distinct from ours, since properties have switched roles. As Lewis says, 'the two possibilities are isomorphic, yet different', for 'there are more ways than one to make [some] Ramsey sentences, or [some] Ramsified ersatz worlds, come true' (Lewis 1986, 162). If so, then the descriptive ersatz approach conflates possibilities which should be kept distinct.

This argument assumes property haecceities (Robinson 1993, 19) or *quiddities* (Black 2000), the idea that 'nothing *constitutes* the fact that a certain quality playing a certain nomological role in that world is identical with a certain quality playing a different role in ours; they just are the same quality, and that's all that can be said' (Black 2000, 92). Quidditism is by no means universally accepted. Dispositional essentialists such as Bird (2007), Ellis and Lierse (1994), Mumford (2003), Shoemaker (1980) and Swoyer (1982) deny quidditism, for they tie the nature and identity of a property to its dispositional or nomological role. Alternatively, one may treat properties much as Lewis treats particulars: as worldbound entities, standing in counterpart relations to other properties (Heller 1998). If so, then quidditism will be false.

Denying quidditism will help the ersatzer only if her concern is limited to the genuine possibilities, however. The dispositional essentialist (or other anti-quidditist) says: it is not possible for a property P and its nomological role R to come apart. She thereby describes an impossibility in which property P and role R are distinct. So, given our concern for representing the impossibilities, we need the means to represent such impossible situations. In short, it may be correct to deny both haecceitism and quidditism, but it won't help us in our quest for ersatz impossible worlds.

Melia (2001) and Sider (2002) both take a different approach to constructing ersatz possible worlds. They accept (at least, for the sake of argument) that we want to represent mere haecceitistic and quidditistic differences. Melia presents the following analogy. Suppose there is a catalogue for an abstract painting collection, accidentally printed in black and white. Fortunately, no two colours in the catalogue have come out the same shade of grey and so the catalogue never conflates two paintings. However, it does not tell us to which colour a particular shade of grey corresponds. By analogy, Melia says, we can allow that it is indeterminate which possibility a particular ersatz world represents and yet not conflate any possibility with any other. I'll discuss the details of Melia's proposal below. Before that, I will consider Sider's approach.

Sider concedes (as Melia does) that it is often indeterminate which possibility a given ersatz world represents. Hence, says Sider, a plurality of ersatz worlds will conflate possibilities. Sider's proposal is to replace the plurality of ersatz worlds with a single *ersatz pluriverse*, so that 'quantification over possibles is interpreted, not as quantification over surrogates [i.e., ersatz worlds], but rather as truth of a quantified sentence according to a single surrogate' (Sider 2002, 288). That single surrogate is a *pluriverse sentence* (in the Lagadonian language), which has the form:

> There are worlds $w_1, w_2, \ldots$, non-actual particulars $x_1, x_2, \ldots$ and non-actual properties $X_1, X_2, \ldots$ such that $\ldots w_1 \ldots$ and $\ldots w_2 \ldots$ and $\ldots$

where each world-conjunct '$\ldots w_i \ldots$' has the form 'x_1 exists in w_i, has property X_2, and $\ldots$'.

Crucially, the quantifiers in a pluriverse sentence occur outside the world-conjuncts. Because of this, it is easy to say, for example, that there are distinct properties F and G and that everything that is F in w_1 is G in w_2 and vice versa. Sider has given us a description of all of modal space, rather than a separate description for each ersatz world.

Of course, a pluriverse sentence like this is (by actualist lights) false (and necessarily so), since is asserts the existence of particulars and properties which do not exist. Nevertheless, it represents all the possibilities in one fell swoop. A pluriverse sentence represents the possibility of flying pigs by entailing the existence of a world w where there exist flying pigs. Indeed, what pluriverse sentences represent is none other than a plurality of genuine possible worlds. (In this respect, Sider's approach bears some similarities to Rosen's modal fictionalism (1990), discussed in §4.5.) If successful, Sider has shown how to reap the benefits of Lewis's pluriverse without accepting Lewis's ontology of non-actual entities.

I have already argued that Lewis's metaphysics of worlds both requires and is incompatible with his counterpart theory (§4.5). That argument shows that, to the extent that Sider's pluriverse sentences describe Lewis-style modal spaces, they are incompatible with counterpart theory. But Sider accepts counterpart theory (2002, 281) and so his official account at least is untenable. (There may be ways to develop a version of Sider's approach which does not use counterpart theory. But insofar as pluriverse sentences represent modal spaces comprising genuine possible worlds, any such account would face the worries for genuine worlds discussed in §4.3.)

Let us suppose that this objection can be overcome somehow. We can then ask: can Sider's approach be extended to include impossible as well as possible worlds? To represent impossibilities, we need to consider *extended pluriverse sentences*. These have the same form as Sider's pluriverse sentences, but assert the existence of impossible as well as possible worlds. Such sentences will include world-conjuncts such as 'x_i exists in w_j and x_i is round and x_i is square' (where both x_i and w_j are existentially quantified variables).

This approach faces a painful dilemma: either the extended pluriverse sentence represents *implicitly* by entailment, as on Sider's original account (2002, 288), or it represents *explicitly* by containing an appropriate sentence as a conjunct. Inconsistent world-conjuncts trivialise the former approach. An inconsistent world-conjunct entails every '*A*', for Sider's entailment is classical (2002, 294). An extended pluriverse sentence *S* will implicitly represent that *A* for any '*A*' whatsoever. This grossly misrepresents both the possibilities and the impossibilities. In particular, an extended pluriverse sentence cannot implicitly represent a structured space of impossible worlds and hence cannot be used in a theory of epistemic content or counter-possible conditionals. So, if we are to extend Sider's approach to represent impossibilities, the extended pluriverse sentence cannot represent by entailment.

(Note that it would not help if the extended pluriverse sentence were to represent implicitly by some non-classical notion of entailment. If '*A*' entails '*B*' under that notion of entailment, then any world that represents that *A* will also represent that *B*. But it might be impossible that *A* and not *B*, in which case, there should be a world which represents that *A* but does not represent that *B*. This point is crucial if we are to capture epistemic contents using impossible worlds. I'll discuss the issue further in §§6.2–6.4.)

Suppose instead that the extended pluriverse sentence *S* represents explicitly. Then *S* represents that there's a world such that *A* if '*A*' (expressed in the worldmaking language) is a conjunct of some world-conjunct of *S*. This move avoids the trivialisation worry just discussed. But now, if any '*A*' is to be a necessary truth, it must be a conjunct of every possible world-conjunct. This raises cardinality worries. For any set *X*, *X* necessarily exists and so the worldmaking sentence '*X* exists' must be a conjunct of *W*. But worldmaking sentences themselves are set-theoretic constructions. Thus, the worldmaking sentence corresponding to '*W* exists' must be a member of *W*.

If *W* is used as a name for itself, as Sider supposes, then *W* is part of a non-well-founded membership chain $W \in \cdots \in W$, contradicting the axiom of regularity. (There do exist non-well-founded set theories (Aczel 1988), but these are non-standard. It is pure hubris to think that the correct theory of content should dictate what set theory should look like!) Moreover, for every set X, there will be a membership chain $X \in \cdots \in W$. But there can be no such set W, since no set contains all sets. World-conjuncts are 'too big' to be sets. They must be proper classes. But by definition, no proper class is a member of another class and so cannot be conjoined into a quantifier-prefixed pluriverse sentence. So there can be no extended pluriverse sentence that represents explicitly.

Could we escape the dilemma by taking the possible-world-conjuncts to represent implicitly and the impossible-world-conjuncts to represent explicitly? No, we cannot. Consider a situation just like the actual state of affairs (mathematical universe included) which, in addition, contains a round square. That is impossible and so there should be an impossible world representing it fully. But the situation contains all sets, so cannot be represented explicitly by a worldmaking sentence qua set-theoretic construction. As in the previous case, that world-conjunct is too big to be a set, but cannot be a proper class either. However we define representation, there can be no extended pluriverse sentence that incorporates impossible-world conjuncts.

Does Melia's account ameliorate the problem? I do not think so, for as far as I can see, his account is (modulo unimportant details) very similar to Sider's account. To avoid conflating possibilities, Melia introduces new worldmaking constants, which he calls *pixels*, governed by 'the convention that sentences containing these extra pixels are interpreted as existentially quantified sentences' (Melia 2001, 26). Melia then says

> since one and the same pixel can appear in *different* stories, ... simply let the pixels represent the same non-actual entity across different stories, and different pixels represent different non-actual entities across different stories. (Melia 2001, 27)

This allows 'the linguistic ersatzer [to] write down stories which differ only over which entities play which roles' (2001, 27). To implement this notion of representation, it is clearly not sufficient to think in terms of what each story (world) represents individually, for this will not guarantee that distinct pixels represent distinct non-actual entities across stories (worlds). To implement the suggestion, we need to represent the possibilities holistically, with all stories within the scope of a block of pixel-quantifiers. But this is just Sider's proposal. What we obtain, in spelling out Melia's proposal explicitly, is one of Sider's pluriverse sentences. So Melia's account will fall to the same objections as Sider's.

The problem of aliens is a deep and perplexing problem for ersatz constructions of worlds and it is made harder by our need to construct impossible as well as possible worlds. It is not the case that 'any of the main theories concerning the nature of possible worlds can be applied equally to impossible worlds' (Priest 1997, 580). Far from it: none of the theories of possible worlds (genuine or ersatz) discussed so far can be extended to impossible worlds. In the remainder of this chapter, I attempt to remedy this situation.

5.3   Dealing with Aliens

In this section (which draws on Jago 2012 and Jago 2013d), I set out my strategy for dealing with the problem of aliens. Recall that the ersatzer has two kinds of strategy available to her. She may accept that she cannot name all the possible particulars, properties and relations but nevertheless try to describe the possibilities and impossibilities without conflation; or she may claim that, somehow, she can name all the possible particulars, properties and relations. The latter approach is incompatible with the Lagadonian way of naming entities, but the former approach seems incapable of representing the possibilities without conflation, let alone representing the impossibilities.

I will, for the time being, focus on the problem of alien properties for this is, I think, the real crux of the matter. Let us remind ourselves of the problem, as we encountered it at the start of §5.2. It could be that something is an F, even though nothing is in fact an F. As we have seen, it seems that we cannot represent *Fness* by saying 'there is some non-actual property, such that …', without thereby conflating *Fness* with some other non-actual property, in a way that will simultaneously allow us to represent impossible situations. An option briefly mentioned above, but not yet discussed, is to allow that the properties in question do in fact exist. Since they are not possessed by anything, someone making this move would have to argue that properties can exist even if uninstantiated.

What could such a philosopher possibly mean by 'property'? Those who argue against uninstantiated properties take the following strategy. First, list out all the things philosophers have meant by 'property'; second, run through each notion, showing how it does not support uninstantiated properties (or at least, does not support enough uninstantiated properties for the actualist's purposes). Thus Lewis:

> What does the ersatzer mean by 'property'? … there are many different conceptions of properties; and not all of these are available to an ersatzer. He cannot mean what I mean: the set of all instances, at this world or any other. … Is a property, for him, some sort of abstraction from a predicate? … Are his properties universals? Or sets of duplicate tropes? … Is it that, although the uninstantiated ones among his properties do not technically qualify as universals or tropes, at any rate they are *of a kind* with the instantiated universals or tropes that really are present in things? But what does 'of a kind' mean here? (Lewis 1986, 160–1)

and Sider:

> The properties required for the reply could not be sets of their instances … Nor could they be immanent universals (in the sense of D. M. Armstrong) which are supposed to be "wholly present in their instances" and incapable of existing uninstantiated. Even Michael Tooley, whose "transcendent" universals can exist uninstantiated in certain cases, would not accept [all] uninstantiated universals [required by the actualist] … For Tooley, uninstantiated universals are accepted only when they play a role in the laws of nature …. (Sider 2002, 285)

Both Lewis and Sider seem to be correct that these notions will not allow uninstantiated properties. I think we could make sense of uninstantiated properties, but I will not pursue this line of thought, since I do not need them. For there is a way of representing each possible property without conflation, even having accepted that there are no properties but those that actually exist, all of which are instantiated. To motivate the idea, we should return to the basic thought that properties are ways things can be. As I look around me, I see that the room is many ways. Over here is a mess of musical instruments; over there is clear of mess. There's a hole in one wall, and gaps in the window-frame, making the room cold. Now there's music playing; now I hear the silence between songs. Containing particular presences, absences, holes, gaps, noises and silences are all ways the room is.

Most philosophers ban the absences, holes, gaps and silences from the realm of existence, or else allow them to exist but only by reducing them to 'positive' presence. Absence is viewed as a kind of metaphysical baseline, populated here and there with presence. The possible ways of the world correspond to the possible distributions of presence; and for each way, the story about the distribution of presence is the whole story. I disagree with this way of viewing the world. As I see things, the ways the world is not can be as vital, primitive and fundamental as the ways the world is. If so, we should allow negative ways things can be, or negative properties, into our ontology (Barker and Jago 2012).

This move is rejected by most philosophers and so it requires a good deal of clarification and defence. I will attempt to do so below. But first, let's see what we gain by allowing negative properties into our ontology. Let us focus on some alien property, F. This might be the property *having ¼ charge*, or *having spin 3*. Since F is an alien property, nothing is F. And let us suppose furthermore that it is a fundamental feature of our world that things are not F. Then, on my view, it is a fundamental feature of the world that things lack *Fness*. Fundamental features of reality are captured in our ontology. In particular, properties capture the ways things fundamentally are. So I capture this fundamental feature in terms of the negative property, *lacking Fness* or *non-Fness*, which everything possesses. All fundamental entities, as well as you and I, Bertie and the Sydney Harbour bridge, possess *non-Fness*.

Our task, recall, is to represent the alien property *Fness*. Now, just as we can take two properties G, H and set-theoretically represent the conjunctive property *being G and H*, or the disjunctive property *being G or H*, we can take a positive property G and set-theoretically represent the negative property *non-Gness*. To do so, we just need set-theoretic entities to act as predicate conjunction, disjunction and negation. Similarly, combining predicate negation with the negative property *non-Fness*, we represent *Fness* (Jago 2012). So we have unambiguously represented the alien property F, without conflation, and without supposing that F must actually exist.

(A quibble: won't this negated negative property represent *non-non-Fness*, rather than *Fness*? Given our interest in fine-grained hyperintensional representations, it is good to attend to such worries. But in this case, it is up to us how our predicate negation works, so long as we can precisely specify how it represents. If $(\neg, F)$ is our set-theoretic negation of property F, then let's specify that $(\neg, F)$ represents *non-Fness*, $(\neg, non\text{-}Fness)$ represents *Fness*, and $(\neg, (\neg, X))$ represents whatever (X) represents (Jago 2011). In this way, predicate negation toggles between positive and negative properties and double-negations 'cancel out' in the rules for interpreting negated predicates. If we wanted, we could introduce another predicate negation symbol, which does not cancel out in this way.)

It is crucial to this account that negative properties are not themselves negated properties, or otherwise constructed from positive properties. To do so would make negative properties ontologically dependent on positive properties, which will not achieve our aims. We want *non-Fness* to exist independently of whether *Fness* exists (and in the case just described, precisely because *Fness* does not exist). It is crucial to this account that (at least some) negative properties are ontologically independent of any positive property.

On this story, we avoid worries about uninstantiated properties, but only at the cost of allowing negative properties into the ontology. Yet isn't this just as bad? Why think that there are such properties? Are they even so much as coherent? I will defend the move to incorporate negative properties into our ontology in the next section.

Before that, there is one loose end to tie up: what of Lewis's and Sider's challenge to say just what I mean by 'property'? As they point out, it is not clear that the common notions of a property support uninstantiated properties; is it any clearer that they support negative properties? Yes, it is. Whether we think of properties as immanent universals, tropes or (for genuine modal realists such as Lewis) sets of instances, there is no compelling reason not to accept negative versions of such properties.

Nevertheless, I will not treat properties as primitive universals or tropes. Instead, I will treat them as abstractions from worldly facts. My reason for doing so is that we need to explain both how a particular possesses a property and, relatedly, what in the world makes a particular truth true. Take the first problem. Suppose both particular *a* and property *Fness* exist; it is still open whether *a* possesses that property. So what else is required for *a* to possess *Fness*? Perhaps a further relation of *instantiation*. But already, *a*, *Fness* and *instantiation* exist; what further is required for *a* and *Fness* to feature in the *instantiation* relation? This problem is often called 'Bradley's regress' (Armstrong 1997, 30, 114–5).

We cannot account for the phenomenon of property possession simply by adding more entities to the mix. Unless, that is, we begin with entities which are neither particulars nor properties, but rather particulars-possessing-properties, such as *Bertie's being adorable*. These entities are worldly facts (Armstrong (1997, 2004) speaks instead of 'states of affairs'). These facts are substantial non-linguistic entities. The world as a whole is the totality of all the facts (as Wittgenstein (1922, §1.1) had it). The question of whether *a* possesses the property *Fness* is then reduced to the question, does the fact *that a is F* exist?

Facts also answer the second question, what makes '*a* is *F*' true? That sentence is true if and only if *a* possesses *Fness*, which amounts to the existence of the fact *that a is F*. That fact suffices for that truth; it necessitates it; it is the thing in the world in virtue of which the sentence is true, rather than false. In short, that fact is the truth's *truthmaker* (Armstrong 1997, 2004; Mulligan et al. 1984).

I think of facts as primitive entities, some of which are metaphysically fundamental. They are not, as Wittgenstein (1922, §2.0272) would have it, 'configuration[s] of objects' in which 'objects fit into one another like the links of a chain' (§2.03). Nor are they Armstrong's (1997) non-mereological compositions of universals and 'thin particulars' (that is, particulars 'abstracted in thought' from their properties' (Armstrong 1997, 109)). Metaphysically, facts are not made up of non-fact-like constituents. They are metaphysically primitive and unstructured. (If there are logically complex facts, then the claim is that the logically atomic facts are primitive and unstructured.)

Nevertheless, we conceptualise and classify facts in terms of particulars and properties, as when we say that the fact *that Bertie is adorable* is about Bertie and involves *being adorable*. I am in agreement with Skyrms:

> Facts are primitive entities. Nevertheless we can say something about their nature in terms of the way in which we classify them. An atomic fact can be completely characterized by a relational-classification (e.g. is-a-loves-fact) and its coordinate object-classifications (e.g. with John standing in the first place of the loving relation and Mary in the second). We may then, in the vulgar way, think of an atomic fact as associated with a representation consisting of a $n + 1$-tuple: an n-ary relation followed by n objects. (Skyrms 1981, 200)

Facts are not n-tuples, but we can represent or model facts as n-tuples (as van Fraassen (1969) does).

What then of properties? They are *abstractions* from facts. This notion of abstraction is a primitive of the theory, just as naturalness is for Lewis's sets-of-possibilia (Lewis 1983), as resemblance is for resemblance nominalists (Rodriguez-Pereyra 2002), and as exact similarity is for trope theorists (Williams 1953). We can, nevertheless, model property-abstraction as an operation which, given a fact, returns a function from particulars to facts. Given the fact *that Bertie is adorable*, property-abstraction 'abstracts Bertie away' and leaves us with the property — *is adorable.*

We can model this property as a function from particulars to facts which, given *a* as input, returns the fact *that a is adorable* as output. On this model, properties are 'unsaturated' entities. This does not deny them existence; they are entities in their own right, albeit dependant ones. For a property — *is F* to exist, it must be an abstraction from some fact *that a is F*. This requires something to be *F*. So, on this view, properties cannot exist unless they are possessed by some particular. Hence (in line with Lewis's and Sider's arguments), there are no uninstantiated properties.

Much more could be said about the nature of facts and of property abstraction, but here is not the place. (I say much more about a formal theory of property-abstraction in Jago 2011.) In the next section, I turn to the pressing task of defending negative properties. I do so by defending negative facts. If there are negative facts, such as *that Bertie is not portly*, then property abstraction delivers negative properties. So the weight of justification falls on negative facts. I should point out, however, that the arguments I give below in favour of negative facts could be applied directly in favour of negative properties. So suppose you disagree with me over the metaphysical priority of facts over properties. Suppose you think that properties are primitive and somehow get together with particulars to produce facts. Then no worries: simply read the arguments below as arguments directly in favour of negative properties.

5.4 Negative Facts

It is common to paint a vampiric image of negative facts (and, by association, negative properties) and this undoubtedly contributes to their unpopularity. But this bad press is unjustified. My aim in this section (which draws on joint work with Stephen Barker in

Barker and Jago 2012) is to extricate negative facts (and negative properties) from the realm of the metaphysically undead. I'll first look at objections which claim it is not even coherent to talk of negative facts or negative properties. To dispel these worries will require me to say a little more about how I think of such facts. I will then look at worries that negative facts are ontologically excessive, for (it is claimed) they add to our ontology but do nothing.

Mumford (2007) runs an objection of the first kind; he doubts that negative facts are even coherent. He says that

> A fact … is taken to be some kind of existent in the world.
> … But … can it really be a fact in the world that there is no
> hippopotamus in the room? This sounds like an absence of a
> fact, and an absence is nothing at all. (2007, 46)

I take Mumford's point to be that a negative existential fact would be an absence of something, but an absence is nothing at all, i.e., a non-existent object. But of course, we want our negative facts to exist just as much as our positive facts. So, to meet Mumford's worry, one must show how negative facts qua absences can have any existence at all.

There is a tendency, in using absence-talk, to confuse what is absent with the absence itself. There are no hippos in the university lake. Hippos (amongst other things) are what is absent from the lake; but the absence of hippos in the lake is perfectly real. That absence is not itself a hippo. Talk of absences (and of lacks and the ways things aren't) picks out negative facts, just as talk of the ways things are picks out positive facts. When one says 'the absence of a hippo in the lake', one denotes the negative fact *that there is no hippo in the lake*. Thus, when there is an absence of hippos in the lake, the fact *that there is no hippo in the lake* exists. That fact is not a lake-dwelling hippo. Indeed, the fact exists precisely when there's no hippo in the lake.

A related worry, pushed by Molnar (2000, 84–5) and others, is that everything that exists is positive. But negative facts are not positive, says Molnar, and so are debarred from the realm of being. I'm not sure exactly what Molnar might mean by 'positive' in this context. I see what it would be for a representation (such as a sentence) to be positive or negative, but facts are not representational entities. (Parsons (2006, 591–2) expresses doubts about the coherence of describing entities as 'positive' or 'negative'.) Still, I take Molnar's point that there is but one notion of existence. I agree and so I must not treat negative facts as existing in some special sense of 'existence'.

I claim that both negative and positive facts exist. Facts of both kinds may be fundamental entities, irreducible to any other entities. But to say that there is more than one fundamental kind of entity is not to say that entities in each category come with their own 'special' kind of existence, distinct from the way in which the entities in other categories exist. The standard model of particle physics posits sixteen kinds of fundamental particle. Each kind of particle is characterised by a unique combination of mass, charge and spin. But the standard model does not tell us (and is not interpreted as telling us) that there are sixteen kinds of existence. Rather (if the standard model is correct), there are sixteen fundamental kinds of thing, all of which exist in precisely the same sense as each other. Similarly, I say that there are two fundamental kinds of fact (positive and negative) and both positive and negative facts exist in exactly the same way.

Facts, including negative facts, are often spatiotemporally located entities. Their spatiotemporal location is given by the spatiotemporal location of their concrete constituents. The fact that Fred is happy at time t is spatially located where Fred is at t and temporally located at t. A positive relational fact is located where and when its relata are located insofar as the relation is instantiated by them. The location of the fact that Uluru is 25 kilometres from Kata Tjuta is a discontinuous region, comprising the regions occupied by Uluru and Kata Tjuta. Likewise for negative facts: the fact that the Eiffel Tower is not next to the Sydney Opera House is located at the discontinuous region occupied by the Eiffel Tower and the Sydney Opera house.

Positing negative facts, as I do, is distinct from positing negated facts, as others do (e.g., Fine (1982), Zalta (1993) and Restall (2004a)). (Zalta, like Armstrong, speaks of states of affairs, rather then facts.) On these views, negated facts have a complex structure similar to that of negated sentences. The identity of a negated fact thus depends on the fact thereby negated. As mentioned above, this is not the picture I have in mind. I hold that at least some negative facts are absolutely fundamental entities, which do not have their identity fixed by any other thing. Facts in general are substantial, worldly entities. They are not (in general) abstract or theoretical entities and, in particular, they do not have a structure which can be interpreted as the negation of some other entity.

I turn now to the second kind of objection, that negative facts contribute nothing to the workings of the world (Molnar 2000). Along these lines, Armstrong holds that 'whatever truthmakers are postulated should make some sort of causal/nomic contribution to the working of the actual world' (2004, 39). (Presumably, Armstrong means that concrete truthmakers should contribute to the causal/nomic workings of the world. We should not object to sets or numbers merely on the basis that they are non-causal.) One might dispute Armstrong's and Molnar's premise here. But a stronger response is to grant it, and show that negative facts meet the challenge. This is the route I take. Negative facts contribute to the workings of the world in the following ways.

Causation

Ordinary intuition does not shrink from using negative-talk in relation to causal claims. We are happy to assert that Bob's not watering the plants caused them to die. The enemies of causation by absence frequently contend that such claims are not cases of real causation. Dowe (2001) argues that the truth-conditions of such claims are captured in terms of counterfactuals: had Bob watered the plants, his doing so would have caused the plants to live. But two concerns arise here. First, it is not clear that such counterfactual paraphrasing works. We can imagine cases of preemption involving negative causation. Suppose that, had Bob watered the plants, an evil scientist would have sprayed poison on them, so that they would have died anyway. Still, we want to say that Bob's not watering the plants caused them to die. Second, even if the counterfactual paraphrase strategy worked, it would not provide a compelling argument that real causation takes only the positive form. It would show only that there are interesting counterfactual conditions mirroring causation by absence.

Dowe (2009) offers a further argument against causation by absence, based on Hall 2004. He argues that if you let negatives cause, then you are going to violate the principle from Special Relativity (STR) that no signals can travel faster than the speed of light. Dowe interprets that principle as entailing that all effects occur within the forward lightcone of the cause. Dowe's argument depends on the premise that negative facts are located, which I accept: a negative fact is located at the (possibly discontinuous) spatiotemporal region where its concrete constituents are located.

Now suppose that Bob's not watering his plants in Glebe, Sydney, caused their death at t^*. Bob did not water the plants because he was kidnapped by Tralfamadorians, aliens who whisked Bob away, sequestering him in a zoo 2 million light years from earth. The four dimensional region that is the location of the fact *that Bob did not water his plants* is a discontinuous region, part of which is in Glebe and part of which is located 2 million light years away. It is true that the effect in Glebe, the plant's dying, is not in the forward light cone of Bob in Tralfamadore. But what's relevant to the STR principle is not just Bob's location at t^*, but rather the location of the fact *that Bob did not water his plants* at t^*. As this fact's location includes parts of Glebe, its (discontinuous) forward light cone includes the effect. There is no violation of STR, as understood by Dowe.

Constitution

Donuts are material objects. The thing about donuts is that they have holes. If you get rid of the donut hole by filling it up with more donut-dough, then there is no longer a donut. The hole, just like the donut as a whole, is a part of reality. We can understand holes in terms of negative facts. On this view, the negative fact which constitutes the hole is a part of reality.

One might resist this view by treating holes either as non-entities (i.e., there really are no holes), or as immaterial entities (and hence not constituted by material negative facts), or by treating them as entities which do not require negative facts to exist. The first view has trouble explaining the seemingly obvious fact that there is a hole in the donut, without which, the donut would not exist. Casati and Varzi (1994) take the second option, treating holes as immaterial entities. Yet we can perceive holes, gaps, dents and the like; this strongly speaks against their being immaterial. Lewis and Lewis (1970) take the final option, identifying holes with hole-linings, i.e., the inner surfaces of the surrounding things. But this view does not accord with the fact that holes can be filled up.

A better view is that holes are negative facts. If there is a donut hole then there is a spatial region r involving the instantiation of donut-dough which is intimately connected with an absence thereof (in the related region r'). That absence is a negative fact, the fact *that there is no donut-dough in region r'*. That fact is itself a material entity, located at region r'. That negative fact is a donut hole insofar as it is surrounded, spatially, by an appropriate positive fact or facts (those that constitute the presence of donut-dough in region r). A negative fact thus constitutes a hole only contingently. Destroy the donut-dough in r and the negative fact remains, but is no longer a hole.

On this view, holes are very much material objects. One can fill a hole without destroying it. Indeed, the donut-hole is not an empty region; it is filled with air, or perhaps cream. This theory can be extended to analyse gaps, dents and the like, by fine-tuning the account of regions in which negative facts are located and their relation to the surrounding positive facts.

The existence of holes (and gaps, dents and so on) provides reason to believe in negative facts. But should we really believe in holes? We should. Holes are explanatory. The basic concepts of topology depend on holes: solids without holes and solids with one or more holes represent a basic distinction in topology. Many physical processes involve holes. Osmosis, for example, is a process partly explained by holes in molecule-thick surfaces; the physical process is inextricably bound up with holes. Holes enter into physical processes and, to that extent, so do negative facts.

Perception

I can see Bertie, and this reassures me that he exists. I can hear that he's barking and see that he's restless. This reassures me that those facts, *that Bertie is barking* and *that Bertie is restless*, exist. I am not merely seeing Bertie, I am seeing that he is certain ways, and his being those ways amounts to the existence of the corresponding facts. But I can also see that Bertie isn't portly; I can see he isn't a leopard; and I can see that he's not sharing a room with a hippo. I see that Bertie, or the room, or the world, isn't a certain way, and that things aren't that way amounts to the existence of negative facts. On this view, I literally see the negative facts that Bertie isn't a leopard and that there is no hippo in the room. Since negative facts can be causally efficacious (as pointed out above), it is not so surprising that we can (and frequently do) perceive negative facts. And that we can perceive negative facts provides reason to believe in negative facts.

In this section, I have argued that the vampiric image of negative facts as amongst the metaphysically undead, or of non-existence masquerading as existence, is not part of any serious conception of negative facts. The idea of negative facts is coherent and there are many good reasons to want them around.

The world is such that either it is a given way or it isn't. If a positive fact *that A* does not exist, then the negative fact *that not A* exists. The world is closed with respect to the facts there are: there are no gaps between the positive and the negative facts. The representational strategy for properties is then simple. From facts, we abstract properties. In particular, abstraction from positive facts gives us positive properties and abstraction from negative facts gives us negative properties. Actually existing properties represent themselves; alien properties are represented by negations of their actually existing compliments. If *Fness* does not exist, then the fact *that a is not*

F exists (§5.3). Property abstraction from this fact gives us the negative property of *non-Fness* and property-negation gives us the worldmaking predicate (¬, *non-Fness*), which represents *Fness*.

On this account, we have distinct representations of distinct alien properties. Suppose it is a fundamental fact that nothing is *F* and a distinct fundamental fact that nothing is *G*. (This might be because something could have been *F* without being *G*.) Since these facts are distinct, the abstracted properties *non-Fness* and *non-Gness* are likewise distinct and hence our worldmaking representations of *Fness* and *Gness* are distinct as well.

The vexed question of the identity conditions for these properties (and the corresponding representations) must be framed in terms of the identities of facts. *Non-Fness* and *non-Gness* are distinct just in case they are abstracted from distinct classes of facts. When a fact is a fundamental entity, as many negative facts are, we cannot further demand an explanation of its identity. It is what it is, primitively.

In sum, this approach allows us to represent alien as well as actual properties without conflation. I now turn to the problem of representing alien as well as actual particulars.

5.5   Representing Particulars

How are non-actual particulars represented in the worldmaking language? There are three cases to consider. The first case concerns merely possible particulars. The second concerns impossible particulars. The third concerns fictional characters.

Merely possible particulars

In this section (which draws on Jago 2013d), I'll revisit the idea, from §5.2, of representing non-actual particulars using property-bundles. Since we have named all the possible properties, we can help ourselves to any bundle of possible properties. But, as we saw in §5.2, using property-bundles qua definite descriptions to represent possibilia forces us to conflate what should be distinct possibilities.

These are possibilities which are qualitatively indistinguishable but with different particulars playing the relevant roles.

I propose that we represent mere possibilia using property-bundles, interpreted in line with proper names and demonstratives rather than definite descriptions. The function of names and demonstratives is to refer to a particular, whereas the function of descriptions is to describe. Names and demonstratives (when non-empty) pick out some particular, but do not attribute any properties to it. According to some, descriptions can be used in a referential, non-attributive way too. Suppose it's a common belief between us that Anna won the bake-off. Donnellan (1966) maintains that I can then use 'the winner's biscuits are amazing' to mean *that Anna's biscuits are amazing*. He claims that, in this context, I can use 'the winner' merely to single out Anna, rather than to attribute the property of *winning the bake-off* to her. Indeed, Donnellan says, my use of 'the winner' in this context may succeed in picking out Anna even if (unbeknownst to us) someone else won the bake-off.

It is controversial whether this use of English descriptions is a genuine semantic feature, as Donnellan claims, or merely a pragmatic phenomenon (Kripke 1977). But even if English descriptions cannot be used non-attributively in the way Donnellan says they can, we can imagine artificial devices that do. Kaplan (1978) introduces just such a device, the DTHAT operator. It takes a definite description 'the F' and picks out the unique F, but does not attribute *Fness* to that particular. 'DTHAT(the F)' is semantically rigid, in the sense that it picks out the same particular in each possible world. (By contrast, 'the F' may differ in what it picks out across possible worlds.) The descriptive condition 'F' in 'DTHAT(the F)' tells us what is picked out, but not how it is said to be.

Property-bundles in our worldmaking language are to be interpreted in a similar way. The bundle $b = \{F_1, \ldots, F_n\}$ will behave like 'DTHAT(the $F_1 \wedge \cdots \wedge F_n$)', as a non-attributive and semantically rigid way of representing a possible particular. I'll call property-bundles like b *bundle-names*. As with 'DTHAT' terms, they tell us what is being represented, but not how it is being represented.

Given our actualist assumptions, there are no such things as merely possible particulars and so bundle-names for mere possibilia are empty. Nevertheless, they have representational content, for they combine with worldmaking predicates to represent that such-and-such is the case. Consider a bundle-name b_{sister} = $\{\dots, being\ MJ's\ elder\ sister, \dots\}$. Using b_{sister}, we can write world-making sentences which represent situations in which I have an elder sister. For simplicity, I'll say that b_{sister} represents a merely possible elder sister of mine, although this has to be understood as meaning only that b_{sister} contributes to sentences representing *that some elder sister of mine is such-and-such*.

This approach solves the worry from §5.2 about conflating distinct possibilities. I could have had an elder sister. But she, like anyone, could have been an only child. We can't describe this possibility by saying that I could have had an elder sister who's an only child. What we can do is describe a fiction in which I have an elder sister, perhaps by giving her the name 'Molly'. According to that fiction, Molly is my sister, but could have been an only child. The worldmaking bundle-name b_{sister} works very much like 'Molly' does in this example. Both are empty, yet contribute to meaningful representations in which I have an elder sister. And crucially, both contribute to logically consistent representations in which I don't exist, for neither name attributes *being MJ's elder sister*.

Impossible particulars

How should we represent impossible particulars? A logically impossible particular would be one ruled out by the rules of logic alone. (I will assume that the logic in question here is classical logic.) But, strictly speaking, logic does not rule out any particulars. What logic rules out is particulars being a certain way: it rules out things being both F and *non-F* and (suitably extended to include mathematical axioms) rules out things being both square and round. So our question here should be: how are we to represent logically impossible situations, those situations ruled out by the rules of logic alone? (Not all the impossibilities discussed so far are of this nature. It is impossible for something to be both red all over and blue all over, and impossible for a bachelor to be married; but not impossible because of logic. 'x is red' does not logically entail 'x is not blue' and 'Bill is a bachelor' does not logically entail 'Bill is not married'.)

Logical impossibility requires logical structure. So, if we can represent logically primitive situations and we have a means to combine those representations in a way which mirrors the construction of complex sentences of a logical language, then we can represent the logically complex situations too. But we have such a way of combining representations, for our worldmaking language contains logical vocabulary (connectives, variables and quantifiers). If we can represent a's being F, for example, then we can represent a situation in which a is both F and not-F.

The case is similar for logically possible but metaphysically impossible situations when such impossibilities are logically complex. One such situation is a situation in which Bill is a married bachelor. This is not ruled out by the laws of logic, but it is impossible. (It is *a priori* or conceptually impossible, hence metaphysically impossible.) The impossibility derives from the conjunction of 'Bill is married' and 'Bill is a bachelor'. But since we can easily represent each of these possible situations individually and we have a way of conjoining them in our Lagadonian language, it is easy to represent Bill's impossible situation.

Things get tricky only when we try to represent logically primitive impossible particulars. To get a handle on the issue, suppose it is impossible for some entity to exist, but not in virtue of any combination of properties we are supposing it to possess. A round circle and the largest natural number are impossible entities, but are easy to represent linguistically by description in our worldmaking language. If there is a problematic case, it concerns a particular which could not exist purely because of the very thing it is, irrespective of what properties it has.

Kripke (1980) argues that we have such examples. He argues that, although there are possible situations in which a man does all the things Sherlock Holmes does in the Conan Doyle stories, nevertheless there are no possible situations in which someone is Sherlock Holmes (1980, 157–8). Indeed, it will turn out that fictional characters pose a problem for the theory being developed, regardless of whether we agree with Kripke that nothing could be Holmes. Accordingly, I now turn to the issue of representing fictional entities.

Fictional Entities

How are we to represent situations involving Holmes in our worldmaking language? Suppose we take the name 'Holmes' to be associated with a description, outlining some or all of the things attributed to Holmes in the Conan Doyle stories. Then whether or not someone could have been Holmes, it will turn out that it is trivially impossible that Holmes exists and is not a detective. For, on this view, any representation that Holmes exists represents him as being a detective; hence any representation that Holmes exists and is not a detective represents him as being both a detective and not a detective. But it is not trivial that Holmes, if he exists, is a detective. Somebody might wonder whether the Holmes of the Conan Doyle stories is a detective or a magician.

Perhaps we could paraphrase away such wonderings as wonderings about whether Conan Doyle wrote stories about a detective or a magician (and we have absolutely no problem representing either eventuality). But there is a good sense in which, in our imaginations at least, fictional characters take on a life of their own, untethered to their authors. So we should not take our worldmaking language to represent Homes only by description. It should contain a proper name to perform this representational duty, just as English contains 'Holmes'.

Some argue that authors of fictional works play a creative role: they literally create new fictional entities, *ficta*, when writing their fiction (Salmon 1998; Thomasson 1999; Voltolini 2006). Ficta are thought of as abstract objects, although ones created at a particular time and by a particular author (on whom these ficta are dependent for their existence). On this view, it is literally true that Holmes exists and that he is an abstract entity and hence not a detective. The intuitive data, by contrast, is that Holmes doesn't exist. (Perhaps this worry can be overcome: one might claim that what's intuitive is that there is no concrete entity Holmes. Yagisawa (2001) argues against this move; Goodman (2004) defends the view.)

Even if we set this worry to one side, the view is problematic. In the sense in which Holmes is a detective ('in the fiction'), he is inessentially so: he could have been a chemist, or a violinist. He might have done all the things Watson did and vice versa. But it is hard to see how abstract entities, as ficta are taken to be, can have any of their intrinsic properties non-essentially. Suppose we treat ficta as bundles of properties, with those properties specifying how that entity is in the fiction. Holmes will then be some bundle of properties {*is a detective, lives at 221b Baker Street, is a cocaine addict,* ...}. That bundle is the very bundle it is because it contains those very properties. So it is hard to see how we can treat Holmes, qua that bundle, as having those properties non-essentially. This is, in essence, the problem we encountered in §5.2 for the view that treats mere possibilia as property-bundles.

Note that a defender of ficta cannot escape the problem by reading 'Holmes could have been F' as 'Conan Doyle could have represented Holmes as being F'. For then, 'according to the Sherlock Holmes stories, Holmes could have been F' would come out as 'according to the Sherlock Holmes stories, Conan Doyle could have represented Holmes as being F'. The former is true for some F, whereas the latter is false (for any F), since Conan Doyle isn't represented anywhere in his stories.

A better approach is as follows. (The following draws on Jago 2013d.) There are no ficta (just as there are no merely possible particulars). Nevertheless, there are contentful worldmaking names which contribute to representations such as *that Sherlock Holmes solved the case.* Those fictional names are property-bundles, interpreted in the non-attributive, semantically rigid way. The worldmaking name h representing Holmes is a property-bundle {*is a detective, lives at 221b Baker Street, is a cocaine addict,* ...}.

As Conan Doyle wrote the novels, he associated the English name

'Sherlock Holmes' with h, by virtue of ascribing the properties $F \in h$ to Holmes. He did not create an abstract entity (how could he?); neither did he describe someone of whom it is *a priori* that he is a detective living in 221b Baker Street. It is coherent to think that Holmes lived elsewhere, or that he was a chemist, or that he did all Watson was said to have done and vice versa. The view I'm suggesting makes sense of these facts.

There is a worry with this approach, however. One might want to say that, in some sense, the English names 'Superman' and 'Clark Kent' represent the same thing (in a way that 'Superman' and 'Darth Vader' do not). If so, we should say likewise for the corresponding worldmaking names. But the approach I've described so far does not allow us to say this. We can say that, according to some world w, Superman is Clark Kent; but we cannot say that the worldmaking names corresponding to 'Superman' and 'Clark Kent' represent the same person, simpliciter, for there is no such person for them both to represent.

The best response to the worry is to deny that those worldmaking names literally co-represent. Co-representation is possible only in the case of names for existent entities, on this view: worldmaking names b_1 and b_2 co-represent just in case some particular uniquely satisfies both property bundles. As a consequence, distinct worldmaking names for fictional entities will never co-represent. Nevertheless, it remains true that, according to the Superman stories, Superman is Clark Kent. These stories represent that Superman is Clark Kent; another story may (consistently) represent otherwise.

On the view I am suggesting, we can say something positive and true using (English or worldmaking) names such as 'Superman' only by using *that*-clauses, or by using constructions such as 'according to the fiction, ...'. (We can say plenty of negative true things, of course: 'Superman does not exist'; 'Superman is not my dad' and so on.) It is true that Alice hopes that Santa will come, that Bob wishes that Superman exists, and that the stories represent that Superman is Clark Kent. But it is false that 'Superman' and 'Clark Kent' represent something and hence false that they represent the same thing.

One might object: surely each Superman story represents the same superhero! This I must deny, for there is no such superhero. Instead, we should say that the word 'Superman' has the same content and meaning in each story. Moreover, we can treat all the Superman stories as a combined fiction, in which 'Superman' has a consistent meaning (and according to which Superman exists and does such-and-such).

5.6   Constructing Worlds

I have so far (§§5.3–5.5) described a worldmaking language which is capable of representing actual, possible and impossible situations. In this section (which draws on Jago 2013d), I clear up a few loose ends surrounding the construction of ersatz worlds in terms of this language.

In the worldmaking language described so far, actual entities name themselves. There is thus a 1-1 correspondence between actual entities and their names. However, one of our aims is to use ersatz worlds to model an agent's beliefs (and other attitudes). Our agent may have beliefs about a given object thought of in different ways, as in Frege-puzzle cases (§1.4).

In §3.2, we encountered agents who are unsure whether Ziggy Stardust is David Bowie. But Ziggy Stardust is David Bowie and so, as things stand, we have just one Lagadonian name corresponding to both 'Ziggy Stardust' and 'David Bowie'. Consequently, the only way we have to represent a situation in which Ziggy is not Bowie is via the trivially impossible representation, *that Bowie is not Bowie*. But that was not what our agents were wondering! To account for the content of their wonderings, we need to represent *a posteriori*, non-trivially impossible situations in which Ziggy is not Bowie.

The most promising response to this worry is to replace all Lagadonian names in the worldmaking language with non-attributive property-bundles, all of which uniquely pick out the particular in question. There will in general be multiple such names-qua-bundles for each actual particular. When distinct names qua property-bundles are uniquely satisfied by the same particular, those names co-refer and thus give us distinct ways of representing (by name) one and the same individual. On this approach, all worldmaking names are property-bundles, irrespective of whether the supposed referent exists.

We originally adopted the Lagadonian approach to naming actual particulars because of its simplicity: we could state the interpretation rule for names simply by using the identity predicate. Replacing Lagadonian names with bundle-names does complicate the worldmaking language's interpretation, but not in a significant way. We still interpret all predicates in the Lagadonian way. We then add the general rule that bundle-names are interpreted as described above, in line with DTHAT. There is thus no need to provide a separate interpretation rule for each property-bundle.

I've set out how we should treat predicates and names (including fictional names) in the worldmaking language; now I turn to the construction of worlds from these sentences. Ersatz worlds are sets of worldmaking sentences. These worlds represent by inclusion (and not by entailment): for a worldmaking sentence 'A', a world w represents that A if and only if 'A' $\in w$. For an English sentence 'A' which translates to the worldmaking sentence 'A^*', world w represents that A if and only if 'A^*' $\in w$. (Not every worldmaking sentence translates to an English sentence, since the worldmaking language, unlike English, contains denumerably many names and predicates. But every English sentence (suitably regimented) can be translated into a worldmaking sentence.) To allow the maximum of flexibility, I am going to count every non-empty set of worldmaking sentences as a world. Consequently, many worlds are incomplete, in the sense that (for some 'A') they represent neither that A nor that $\neg A$.

We can classify worlds via a number of syntactic tests. A world is *prime* iff it contains a disjunct of each disjunction it contains. A world is *maximal* iff it contains either 'A' or its negation, for each sentence 'A' of the worldmaking language. A world is *logically possible* (with respect to some logic L) iff it is closed under L-consequence but does not contain every sentence of the worldmaking language.

Just when a world represents a genuine metaphysical possibility is a thorny issue and one I do not propose to say anything about here. Ersatzers typically resort to primitive modal facts, of the form: world *w* is possible. An alternative is to accept what Cameron (2009) calls the *deflationary* account of necessity. On this story, there are many sets of worlds which are candidates to be the set picked out by 'the possible worlds'. But there's nothing metaphysically special about the set which does get picked out in a given context (and different sets will be picked out in different contexts).

On Cameron's view, if *X* is picked out in some context as the set of possible worlds, 'there is nothing more to be said about why they are the possible worlds than that they are in the group I singled out to be called that' (2009, 15):

> We draw the distinction [between possible and impossible worlds] where we do not because it is more eligible than any of the other distinctions but because of our interests. There seems, then, to be nothing more required in accounting for why these worlds are the possible worlds than to account for why they occur on one side of the division we draw rather than the other, and that is easy to account for. (Cameron 2009, 15)

This is an attractive view for those, like me, who think there is no relevant ontological difference between the possible and the impossible worlds.

A third alternative is to think of the metaphysically possible worlds as those that conform to the laws of metaphysics, in roughly the way that the logically possible worlds conform to the laws of logic. We might take the laws of metaphysics to be a complete and correct metaphysical theory, settling questions about the nature of material objects, abstract entities, properties and the like, plus an inventory of identities of the form 'water is H_2O', 'Ziggy Stardust is David Bowie' and the like. (We might treat this third option as an instance of Cameron's deflationary strategy. The view would be that there are many sets of worlds eligible to be selected by 'metaphysically possible world', and which set is selected depends on which principles of metaphysics are operative in that context.)

I mention these three options in passing only; my aim is not to settle on one of them here. My concern in this chapter has been to represent all the possible and impossible situations, not to give an account of modal talk.

The worlds just described represent (by inclusion) such-and-such as being the case. In the case of logically possible worlds, saying what is the case thereby fixes what is not the case. But since worlds may be incomplete and inconsistent, what is the case and what fails to be the case (according to such worlds) need not be exhaustive or mutually exclusive. Consequently, it is sometimes useful to represent both what is the case and what is not the case as separate categories.

We can do this using *double worlds*, familiar from the semantics of relevant logic (Dunn 1966, 1976, 1986). A double world w is a pair of sets of worldmaking sentences, $\langle w^+, w^- \rangle$. Such a pair $\langle w^+, w^- \rangle$ represents that it is the case that A iff 'A^*' $\in W^+$ and that it is not the case that A iff 'A^*' $\in W^-$, where 'A^*' is the worldmaking translation of 'A'. Thus, w^+ captures what is the case according to w, and w^- captures what fails to be the case according to w. Double-worlds will come into play in §7.4.

With an account of ersatz worlds on the table, it might now seem an easy task to give an account of content and of epistemic states. We simply adopt the possible worlds approaches from chapter 1, substituting ersatz worlds for possible worlds. Contents are treated as sets of ersatz worlds and epistemic states are analysed in terms of the space of ersatz worlds structured with epistemic accessibility relations. But things are not nearly so simple. The approach faces a serious problem, which threatens to destroy our entire project. Epistemic notions must respect the meanings of the logical connectives 'and', 'or', 'not' and 'if ... then', whilst avoiding logical idealisation. This is the *problem of bounded rationality*, which I will clarify and discuss in the next chapter.

Chapter Summary

I adopted the linguistic approach to ersatz worlds, with worlds constructed from a worldmaking language (§5.1). This approach can overcome cardinality objections (§5.1) but, like any approach to ersatz worlds, it faces the problem of aliens (§5.2). I argued that neither Sider's nor Melia's response to the problem is ultimately tenable, either as an account of worlds in general or as an account of possible worlds (§5.3).

I took a different approach: alien properties can be represented, without conflation, using only what actually exists (§5.3). This approach relies on an independently-motivated ontology of positive and negative facts (§5.4). Particulars (actual, merely possible and impossible) are represented using non-attributive bundle-names (§5.5). Ersatz worlds are then sets of (or, in the case of double worlds, pairs of sets of) worldmaking sentences (§5.6).

6

The Problem of Bounded Rationality

My aim in this chapter is to clarify and discuss the problem of bounded rationality. This is the problem of accounting for the normative connections between logically-related contents whilst avoiding logical idealisation. This is a very serious problem, close to a paradox, which deserves serious consideration. In this chapter, I set out the problem in more detail and argue that a number of proposed solutions do not work. I develop a solution to the problem in chapters 7 and 8.

6.1   The Problem of Bounded Rationality

In this section, I set up the problem of bounded rationality, which confronts our attempts to give an account of epistemic content. We will see that the problem is more complex than previous accounts of content would have us believe. My starting point is the observation that there is something very counterintuitive in the claim that some agent knows that $A \wedge B$ but does not know that A; or that some agent knows that A but not that $A \vee B$; or knows both that $A \rightarrow B$ and that A but not that B.

These are platitudes, but ones which we will do well to remember. Notice that I don't say that anyone who knows that $A \wedge B$ must also know that A, or that anyone who knows that A must also know that $A \vee B$, or that anyone who knows both that $A \rightarrow B$ and that A must also know that B. I am pointing out how strange and counterintuitive it is to assert that so-and-so knows that $A \wedge B$ but not that A (and similarly for the $\vee$ and $\rightarrow$ examples). The same goes for belief ascriptions: it is highly counterintuitive to assert that so-and-so believes that $A \wedge B$ but not that A (and similarly for the $\vee$ and $\rightarrow$ examples).

Why is this? To say that an agent believes that A is not the claim that the agent currently has some 'A'-like token in her head. Rather, as Davidson (1985), Dennett (1987) and Stalnaker (1984) emphasise, a belief attribution is part of a holistic attempt to make best sense of the agent's behaviour (§2.4). Similarly for knowledge ascriptions. But it seems that making best sense of an agent who exhibits $A \wedge B$-type behaviour (the kind of behaviour that leads us to attribute the belief that $A \wedge B$ to that agent) will also involve ascribing to her the belief that A and the belief that B (and similarly for ascribing beliefs involving other logical connectives). Embedded within our practice of ascribing attitudes to agents are strong normative connections between an inference rule's input and output propositions.

Of course, someone might claim to believe that $A \wedge B$ but not that A, or claim to believe that A and that $A \rightarrow B$ but not that B. But it is then very tempting to say that she is confused about what '$\wedge$' or '$\rightarrow$' means, or at least that she disagrees with us on the logical properties of '$\wedge$' or '$\rightarrow$'. So we do not have to take an explicit self-ascription 'I believe that $A \wedge B$, but not that A' at face value. In fact, I hold that we should not take such self-ascriptions at face value.

I want to allow that competent language users make mistakes, even in deploying such basic words as 'and' and 'or'. Being competent with a word (or the corresponding concept) does not imply that one never misapplies it. I might well say 'and' when I really should have said 'or'; or during the course of a proof, I might try to use rules for conjunction when I should have used the rules for disjunction. Such cases might be daily occurrences and I certainly do not want to rule them out. The point is that we do best not to treat such cases as direct evidence for the agent in question having such-and-such beliefs.

Take a parallel case: you buy fifteen penny-sweets, paying with a £1 coin; the cashier counts the sweets and gives you 65p in change.

As Dennett (1987) says, we do not think the cashier has really weird beliefs about basic arithmetic. It's not that he believes that, say, fourteen sweets plus one sweet is thirty-five sweets, or that 100p less 15p is 65p. Rather, we assume he has made a mistake in counting, or in working out the change; or perhaps he wasn't concentrating on the task at all. Trying to make sense of his action in terms of specific beliefs and desires (those that would predict 65p change from £1, after spending 15p) is likely to be a theoretical dead end. Besides, if we point out his mistake and he subsequently corrects the change, it's strange to think of this as a change in his beliefs (other than in the trivial sense that he then gains new perceptual beliefs).

In short, because a belief ascription is part of a holistic attempt to make sense of the agent's behaviour, there will be cases (such as the cashier's miscalculation) that defy a belief-and-desire-type explanation. On Dennett's view, we need to idealise from an agent's actual behaviour in order to make a holistic ascription of beliefs and desires to her: 'one starts with the idea of perfect rationality and revises downwards as circumstances dictate' (Dennett 1987, 21). Part of that idealisation involves, at the least, acknowledgement of the strong normative link between '$A \wedge B$' and 'A', and between '$A \rightarrow B$', 'A' and 'B'. This is part of what drives us from an ascription of a belief that $A \wedge B$ to an ascription of a belief that A and from ascriptions of a belief that $A \rightarrow B$ and a belief that A to an ascription of a belief that B.

Set against these remarks are the empirical facts that we do not know all consequences of what we know and do not believe all consequences of what we believe. If we assumed that anyone who believes the premises of an inference rule also believes the conclusion, for all the standard inference rules, then we would be guilty of treating ordinary agents as ideal agents, which they are not.

This is the *problem of bounded rationality*. It is the conflict between normative principles of rationality and the fact that the agents with which we are concerned have limited cognitive resources. It is a problem specifically for assigning contents to attitudes of rational but cognitively bounded agents, such as ourselves.

If our aim was to assign a system of representations to a digital thermometer, we would not face the problem. We could say that the thermometer represents that A iff 'A' has the form 'the local temperature is currently $n°C$' and the thermometer currently reads $n°C$; or we could say that the thermometer represents that A iff the thermometer currently reads $n°C$ and its being $n°C$ entails that A. On the first approach, the thermometer is never assigned logically complex representations; on the second, it is treated as representing that A whenever A is a logical truth. But given how each notion of representation is defined, both cases are utterly unproblematic (for we can say, 'by 'represents', we mean only that ...'.) Similarly, if we were interested in the belief states of a hypothetical mathematically ideal agent, then we would not encounter the problem.

The problem is not simply that, if we use standard modal logic in our analysis of belief or knowledge, or if we treat propositions as sets of possible worlds, then we end up treating agents as being logically omniscient. These are artefacts of theories and we can take or leave those theories (see §2.4). The deep problem is that both the normative principles of rationality and the fact of non-omniscience seem non-negotiable. But together, they take us into the realm of philosophical paradox (on which, more in §6.4).

The problem of bounded rationality is not limited to accounts of epistemic states. A further instance concerns the cognitive significance of an utterance. One of the features of cognitively significant utterances such as 'whistle-pigs are woodchucks' is that they have the potential to be surprising, and learning of their truth can affect one's behaviour. Tama might be surprised to learn that woodchucks are whistle-pigs and, on learning so, he might seek medical attention (§3.2). But he wouldn't at all be surprised to hear that woodchucks are woodchucks, and telling him so makes him no more likely to seek a doctor.

Some hold that all logical truths are like 'all woodchucks are wood-chucks' in this respect: they are supposedly cognitively insignificant and trivial. As we saw in §2.2, Wittgenstein holds that 'there can *never* be surprises in logic' (1922, §6.1251). But, as I pointed out there, logic contains innumerable surprises. First-year logic students are surprised to learn that either $A \to B$ or $B \to A$, and Löwenheim's theorem has perplexed many professional logicians.

A natural way to explain the surprise value of such results is to appeal to their informativeness. If logical results could not possibly be informative, then how can they be so surprising? One would most naturally characterise the import of Russell's famous letter to Frege of June 16, 1902 as informing Frege of the paradox of Basic Law V, via a logical deduction. And we naturally say that a model checker will inform us whether a particular design meets a certain requirement (§2.1).

At least some results in logic are informative. But how can a logical theorem be informative, when it is true regardless of how the world happens to be? We can put the question in terms of the reasoning required to establish the theorem in question. It seems clear that deductive reasoning can be informative, in the sense that we can gain new information purely by engaging in deductive reasoning. If any theorem is itself informative, then it must be informative to deduce that theorem from zero premises. Since the information contained in the theorem cannot come from the premises of the deduction (since there are none!), engaging in the deduction itself must be an informative process.

Yet a feature of formal deductive reasoning is that it proceeds in tiny steps, each of which are guaranteed to preserve truth. Each of those tiny steps, taken in isolation, looks as trivial and uninformative as 'all woodchucks are woodchucks'. It is often said that each valid step of a deduction is trivial and tells us nothing new: it merely restructures information already contained in the premises (if there are any). Indeed, this seems to be a prime reason for thinking that logical truths are uninformative (since they can be derived from zero premises). There is, to be sure, something very counterintuitive in the claim that the deductive move from '$A \land B$' to 'A', or from 'A' to '$A \lor B$', or from '$A \to B$' and 'A' to 'B', is informative.

So we have another instance of the problem of bounded rationality, in which normative principles conflict with empirical facts. In this case, the normative principles linking (for example) '$A \wedge B$' to 'A', or '$A \rightarrow B$' and 'A' to 'B', seem to dictate that such inferences are trivial and uninformative. Failing to grasp those inferences is (at least, in non-theoretical contexts) the best possible evidence we could have that the agent in question does not grasp the relevant logical concepts. The empirical fact is that, for agents such as us, some logical truths and some valid deductions are informative.

Michael Dummett considers a similar problem to this in 'The Justification of Deduction' (1978a). He notes that

> When we contemplate the simplest basic forms of inference, the gap between recognising the truth of the premises and recognising that of the conclusion seems infinitesimal; but, when we contemplate the wealth and complexity of number-theoretic theorems which, by chains of such inferences, can be proved … we are struck by the difficulty of establishing them and the surprises they yield. (1978a, 297)

This observation leads Dummett to wonder how a deduction can be both justified and useful. If it is justified, it must be guaranteed to preserve truth from premises to conclusion. But to be useful, it must inform us of something, so that 'a recognition of its truth need not actually have been accorded to the conclusion when it was accorded to the premisses' (1978a, 297).

Yet how (wonders Dummett) can the move from premises to conclusion be informative, if the former already guarantee the latter? As he notes, 'no definite contradiction stands in the way of satisfying these two requirements' (i.e., being both justified and informative) and yet 'it is a delicate matter so to describe the connection between premises and conclusion as to display clearly the way in which both requirements are fulfilled' (1978a, 297).

Although Dummett's problem is not the same as the one I am concerned with here, his description of the problem is apt in our case. The problem is to describe the nature of the connection between premises and conclusion, so as to ensure that the meanings of (e.g.) '$\wedge$' and '$\rightarrow$' guarantee that '$A \wedge B$' entails 'A' and that '$A \rightarrow B$' and 'A' together entail 'B' (and that this fact is grasped by anyone who understands '∧' and '→'), whilst allowing room for some inferences to be informative and cognitively significant.

I'll now consider some responses to the problem. In seeing why they don't work, we will get more of a grip on the problem and on what a solution would look like.

6.2   Selected Worlds

A solution to the problem of bounded rationality must respect the meanings of the logical constants, but must simultaneously avoid treating agents as being logically omniscient. A popular thought in response to this kind of problem runs as follows. To respect the meanings of the logical constants, their truth-conditions must not be meddled with too much, for too much meddling with their truth-conditions amounts to changing their meaning. Nevertheless, there is a minimal way to alter the truth-conditional semantics of classical logic so as to avoid logical omniscience in an epistemic setting.

The proposal is to allow for incomplete and inconsistent situations which nevertheless respect the meanings of the logical constants. The former are situations which, for some 'A', represent neither that A nor that ¬A; the latter are situations which, for some 'A', represent both that A and that ¬A. Given that any set of worldmaking sentences counts as a world (§5.6), we already have such representations at our disposal. The question is, do they help us solve the problem of bounded rationality?

We can view the proposal as follows (drawing on Jago 2007). From the worlds constructed in §5.6, we select only those which are logically constrained in an appropriate way. One way in which worlds must be constrained, for example, is that a world which represent that A ∧ B must also represent that A and that B and vice versa. Call the worlds which meet all the logical constraints (set out below) the *selected worlds*. The thought then is that the selected worlds maintain enough logical structure to count as respecting the meaning of the logical constants. And yet, we can show that epistemic agents modelled using the selected worlds are not logically omniscient.

Now for the details. World w is a selected world if and only if:

$$'\neg\neg A' \in w \quad \text{iff} \quad 'A' \in w$$
$$'A \wedge B' \in w \quad \text{iff} \quad 'A' \in w \ \& \ 'B' \in w$$
$$'\neg(A \wedge B)' \in w \quad \text{iff} \quad '\neg A' \in w \text{ or } '\neg B' \in w$$
$$'A \vee B' \in w \quad \text{iff} \quad 'A' \in w \text{ or } 'B' \in w$$
$$'\neg(A \vee B)' \in w \quad \text{iff} \quad '\neg A' \in w \ \& \ '\neg B' \in w$$
$$'A \rightarrow B' \in w \quad \text{iff} \quad '\neg A' \in w \text{ or } 'B' \in w$$
$$'\neg(A \rightarrow B)' \in w \quad \text{iff} \quad 'A' \in w \ \& \ '\neg B' \in w$$

These conditions look very much like the conditions we give for logically possible ersatz worlds. The difference is that for selected worlds, unlike logically possible worlds, we do not require consistency or completeness: a selected world w may contain both 'A' and '$\neg A$' (so that it is inconsistent), or it may contain neither (so that it is incomplete). In the case of logically possible worlds, what a world represents as failing to be the case is fixed by what that world represents as being the case. So, if w were a logically possible world, the clauses above for negated sentences ('$\neg\neg A$', '$\neg(A \wedge B)$', '$\neg(A \vee B)$' and '$\neg(A \rightarrow B)$') would be redundant. But not so for selected worlds.

The restrictions above are restrictions on what a selected world represents, that is, on what it represents as being the case. A different, but equivalent, way of setting things up is to consider both what a world represents as being the case and what it represents as failing to be the case. The former gives us a notion of *truth-at-a-world* (that is, what the truths are, according to the world in question); the latter a notion of *falsity-at-a-world* (that is, what the falsehoods are, according to the world in question). The connection between the two is that a selected world w represents that it is not the case that A if and only if it represents that it is the case that $\neg A$: '$\neg A$' is true according to w if and only if 'A' is false according to w. The interaction between truth-at-a-world and falsity-at-a-world can be captured by selecting double worlds (§5.6), pairs $w = \langle w^+, w^- \rangle$. We think of w^+ as the set of truths according to w, and w^- as the set of falsehoods according to w.

We can then reformulate our conditions as follows. A pair $w = \langle w^+, w^- \rangle$ is a selected double world if and only if:

$$
\begin{array}{lll}
\text{'}\neg A\text{'} \in w^+ & \text{iff} & \text{'}A\text{'} \in w^- \\
\text{'}\neg A\text{'} \in w^- & \text{iff} & \text{'}A\text{'} \in w^+ \\
\text{'}A \wedge B\text{'} \in w^+ & \text{iff} & \text{'}A\text{'} \in w^+ \ \& \ \text{'}B\text{'} \in w^+ \\
\text{'}A \wedge B\text{'} \in w^- & \text{iff} & \text{'}\neg A\text{'} \in w^- \ \text{or} \ \text{'}\neg B\text{'} \in w^- \\
\text{'}A \vee B\text{'} \in w^+ & \text{iff} & \text{'}A\text{'} \in w^+ \ \text{or} \ \text{'}B\text{'} \in w^+ \\
\text{'}A \vee B\text{'} \in w^- & \text{iff} & \text{'}\neg A\text{'} \in w^- \ \& \ \text{'}\neg B\text{'} \in w^- \\
\text{'}A \rightarrow B\text{'} \in w^+ & \text{iff} & \text{'}\neg A\text{'} \in w^+ \ \text{or} \ \text{'}B\text{'} \in w^+ \\
\text{'}A \rightarrow B\text{'} \in w^- & \text{iff} & \text{'}A\text{'} \in w^- \ \& \ \text{'}\neg B\text{'} \in w^-
\end{array}
$$

These worlds correspond to models of paraconsistent and paracomplete logics. A paraconsistent logic is one which is contradiction-tolerant: in paraconsistent logics, unlike in classical logic, a contradiction does not entail everything. The inference *ex falso quodlibet*, or 'from a contradiction, everything follows', $A \wedge \neg A \vdash B$, is not valid in paraconsistent logics. The inference is sometimes called the *explosion principle*, since in logics where it holds, contradictions cause the derivability relation $\vdash$ to 'explode', allowing any sentence whatsoever to be derived. Paracomplete logics are those in which arbitrary inferences to excluded middle are not valid: $A \nvdash B \vee \neg B$. A logic is paraconsistent and paracomplete when both types of inference fail. Priest (1987, 2008) gives the background to these logics.

(Note that I am not suggesting we replace classical logic with a paraconsistent or paracomplete logic as an account of what follows from what. The question of which inferences are in fact valid is (let us suppose) settled exclusively by classical logic. The question here is not whether we should accept such-and-such inferences, but rather, which worlds should be used to model epistemic states and information contents.)

The inference $A \wedge \neg A \vdash B$ fails when 'A' may be both true and false and the inference $A \vdash B \vee \neg B$ fails when 'B' may be neither true nor false. Models of paraconsistent and paracomplete logics allow a sentence 'A' to be true, false, both or neither, just as selected worlds do. We can define such models in several ways. One option is to replace the standard valuation function a relation, which relates a given atomic sentence 'p' to either, both or neither of the classical truth values (Dunn 1976). Alternatively, we can retain a valuation function V but allow Vp to be any subset of $\{true, false\}$, with $Vp = \{\}$ corresponding to *neither true nor false* and $Vp = \{true, false\}$ corresponding to *both true and false* (Belnap 1977). We can then define a single 'true-in-a-model-M' relation $\vDash$ by setting $M \vDash p$ iff $true \in Vp$ and $M \vDash \neg p$ iff $false \in Vp$ (and similarly for the relational version). We then give clauses for '$\neg\neg A$', '$A \wedge B$', '$\neg(A \wedge B)$' etc. in parallel to the clauses for single selected worlds above.

Alternatively, we can define an additional 'false-in-a-model-M' relation $\dashv$, setting $M \dashv p$ iff $false \in Vp$. We then give '$\vDash$' and '$\dashv$' clauses for each of '$\neg A$', '$A \wedge B$', etc. in parallel to the clauses for double selected worlds above. Models of these kinds have a long history in the epistemic logic literature, going back to Lakemeyer (1986, 1987, 1990), Levesque (1984) and Wansing (1990), particularly in connection with worries about logical omniscience.

A case can be made that selected worlds (and selected double worlds) respect the (classical) meanings of the logical constants. After all, the claim might go, the clauses given above are just like the classical clauses. (One might, with justification, feel the claim is rather dubious. But let's allow it, for argument's sake.) So let's turn to the other part of the problem of bounded rationality: avoiding logical omniscience and capturing the information content of logical truths and valid deductions.

Let's briefly remind ourselves of how we model epistemic states (§1.2). We take our cue from the epistemic logic approach of Hintikka (1962). Epistemic (and doxastic) states are captured via relational structures on a space of worlds (which represents only what is epistemically possible). Knowledge amounts to what is true according to all accessible worlds. My gaining new information is modelled in terms of my ruling out certain worlds. What I have learnt in gaining that information is a matter of the difference between what I knew before and what I know now. Some of the worlds which I considered to be possible before (worlds which were epistemically accessible to me) I now no longer consider to be possible. As a result of learning something new, fewer worlds are epistemically accessible to me. I have gone one step closer to discovering which out of a set of worlds is the actual world.

We can avoid modelling agents as being logically omniscient, therefore, if there is a classically valid inference from premises $\Gamma = \{`A_1`, \ldots, `A_n`\}$ to conclusion 'C' and there are selected worlds according to which each of 'A_1', \ldots, 'A_n' is true but 'C' is not true. We could then build a model according to which an agent knows each of 'A_1', \ldots, 'A_n' but does not know that 'C'. And indeed there are such selected worlds. In fact, very simple classical inferences, including *modus ponens*, can fail to be preserved by the selected worlds. How can this be? Recall that selected worlds are constrained so that '$A \rightarrow B$' is true according to w if and only if either 'A' is false or 'B' is true according to w. The twist is that 'A' may be both true and false according to selected world w. If so, then both 'A' and '$A \rightarrow B$' are true (the latter in virtue of 'A' being false), even if 'B' is false.

Thus, there are selected worlds according to which both 'A' and '$A \rightarrow B$' are true, but 'B' is not true. We can then model agents who know that A and that $A \rightarrow B$, but not that B. In just the same way, we can account for agents who believe that A and that $A \rightarrow B$ but not that B. We can also model agents who do not know (and do not believe) all logical truths, for not all logical truths are true according to all selected worlds. If 'A' is neither true nor false, according to w (i.e., 'A' $\notin w^+ \cup w^-$), then neither '$A \vee \neg A$' nor '$A \rightarrow A$' is true according to w. We can then model agents who do not know (and do not believe) these basic logical truths.

This approach can also make an attempt to capture the information content of logical truths and valid deductions, in terms of the worlds they rule out. An instance of '$A \vee \neg A$' fails to be true at worlds according to which '*A*' is neither true nor false. Its information content is the set of all remaining selected worlds, and this content counts as informative since it does not include all selected worlds. Moreover, different instances of '$A \vee \neg A$' are assigned different sets of selected worlds as their contents: '$p \vee \neg p$' forces '*p*' (but not '*q*') to take at least one truth-value, whereas '$q \vee \neg q$' forces '*q*' (but not '*p*') to take at least one truth-value. So '$p \vee \neg p$' and '$q \vee \neg q$' are assigned different contents, as they should be.

Finally, let's consider the information content of the *modus ponens* deduction from '*A*' and '$A \rightarrow B$' to '*B*'. We can think of this as the difference between the content of the premises and the content of the premises plus the conclusion. There should be a change between these contents just in case the deduction is informative. In our present case, the combined content of '*A*' and '$A \rightarrow B$' consists of those selected worlds according to which both '*A*' and '$A \rightarrow B$' are true. Given the '$\wedge$'-restrictions on selected worlds above, this is just the content of '$A \wedge (A \rightarrow B)$'. This content contains worlds according to which both '*A*' and '*B*' are true, plus worlds according to which '*A*' is both true and false (irrespective of '*B*'). Adding the content of the conclusion '*B*' (giving us the content of '$(A \wedge (A \rightarrow B)) \wedge B$') further rules out those selected worlds according to which '*B*' is not true. Because the content narrows from premises to premises-plus-conclusion, the inference counts as being informative.

The selected worlds approach certainly accounts for epistemic states and information content better than the possible worlds approach. Nevertheless, it is not the correct approach. I'll now discuss several serious problems facing the account. First, note how the selected worlds approach classifies some very simple inferences, including *modus ponens* and *disjunctive syllogism*, $A \vee B, \neg A \vdash B$, as being informative. *Disjunctive syllogism* is classed as informative, on the selected worlds approach, for the same reason *modus ponens* is. If '*A*' is both true and false and '*B*' is not true according to *w*, then the premises but not the conclusion are true, according to *w*. A *disjunctive syllogism* inference excludes such worlds and so counts as informative.

By contrast, *conjunction elimination*, $A \wedge B \vdash A$ and *disjunction introduction*, $A \vdash A \vee B$, are classed as being uninformative. In the former category we find those classical inferences which are paraconsistently invalid, whereas those in the latter category are classical inferences which remain paraconsistently valid.

The first objection to the selected worlds approach is that it is incorrect to categorise basic inferences in this way. Why think that *modus ponens* is informative, if *conjunction elimination* is not? After all, *modus ponens* is just as integral to the meaning of '→' as *conjunction elimination* is to the meaning of '∧' and so there is just no reason for declaring the former but not the latter to be informative. Note that the proponent of the selected worlds approach cannot respond by claiming that the meaning of '→' is such that *modus ponens* is invalid. That would certainly provide a reason for not treating *modus ponens* and *conjunction elimination* on an informational par, but it would just as clearly hinder the task of explaining how valid inferences can be informative.

Indeed, it is vital to the present approach that the logic generated by selected worlds (a paraconsistent and paracomplete logic) treats some inferences which are in fact valid as being invalid. As a consequence, those such as Beall (2006) and Priest (1979, 1987) who think that a paraconsistent logic gives the correct account of validity of arguments must accept either that we know all logical consequences of what we know in that logic (which they take to be all the logical consequences, simpliciter), or else that selected worlds do not help with the problems of logical omniscience and bounded rationality.

(Priest (2005) opts for the latter disjunct. His account of epistemic content uses worlds with a much finer grain than the selected worlds discussed here. He calls these very fine-grained worlds *open worlds*, because what they represent is not closed under any rule of inference (except *identity*, $A \vdash A$). Open worlds correspond to the (single) ersatz worlds constructed in §5.6.)

A proponent of the selected worlds approach may respond to the worry by offering a different account of the information content of a valid deduction. Instead of treating the information contained in a deduction from premises 'A_1',...,'A_n' to conclusion 'C' as the difference between the information content of '$A_1 \wedge \cdots \wedge A_n$' and that of '$A_1 \wedge \cdots \wedge A_n \wedge C$', we could treat it as the combined information content of the premises and the negated conclusion, i.e. of '$A_1 \wedge \cdots \wedge A_n \wedge \neg C$'. Call this notion *information**.

This approach does not draw an unprincipled and ad hoc distinction between informative* and uninformative* inferences. Consider *conjunction elimination* once more (which was previously deemed uninformative). Since '$A \wedge B \wedge \neg A$' has a non-trivial information content, containing worlds according to which 'A' is both true and false and 'B' is true, *conjunction elimination* is deemed informative*. Indeed, on the present suggestion, every inference whatsoever is deemed informative*! Consider the simplest inference of all, $A \vdash A$. It is assigned a non-empty information* content, the set of all selected worlds according to which 'A' is both true and false.

This consequence is, if anything, worse than treating some but not all basic inferences (such as *modus ponens*) as being informative. There is simply no reason for taking $A \vdash A$ (for example) to be informative. So the response in terms of information* gets us nowhere; it merely trivialises the notion of deductive information. What we want of an account of deductive information is for it to treat all the basic inferences (including those captured by standard introduction and elimination rules) as being uninformative, whilst allowing that other, more complex deductions (including Gödel's incompleteness proofs, Andrew Wiles's proof of Fermat's last theorem and the like) are highly informative.

There is another, deeper problem with the selected worlds approach: it fails to explain why the worlds it provides are suitable tools for analysing epistemic notions. Recall that the selected worlds approach tries to avoid the logical omniscience problem by providing epistemically accessible worlds which are not closed under classical consequence. But by definition, world w can be epistemically accessible from world w' for agent i only if i considers w to be possible (for all she knows at w'). The worlds epistemically accessible from w' for i capture what is epistemically possible for i (at w').

Thus, to be eligible for being epistemically accessible (from any world), world w must represent the kind of situation which an agent could reasonably take as an epistemic possibility. There must be some possible state of information an agent could be in, wherein she considers matters and declares what world w represents to be a possibility (perhaps by saying, 'things might be so', or 'could be, for all I know').

We can abstract from the cognitive situations of particular agents and think in terms of a prior notion of an epistemically possible world. This notion captures a deep sense of epistemic possibility (Chalmers 2010, 62–3), in that it is not tethered to a particular agent's epistemic situation. It is this notion of a world which is primary when discussing knowledge, belief and epistemic concepts of content and information. It is *deeply epistemically possible* that A iff some epistemically possible world represents that A.

We can also say that it is *deeply epistemically necessary* that A iff every epistemically possible world represents that A. This notion of epistemic necessity captures what is epistemically unavoidable. If it is epistemically necessary that A then all agents, regardless of their epistemic situation or competence, know that A. It is thus a substantive question whether anything is epistemically necessary in this sense. (I'll return to the issue in §8.4.) We cannot assume that it is epistemically necessary that A when it is not epistemically possible that $\neg A$, for we must be open to the possibility of incomplete epistemically possible worlds which represent neither that $\neg A$ nor that A. Such worlds destroy the duality between 'it is epistemically possible that' and 'it is epistemically necessary that'.

We capture epistemic states by imposing a relational accessibility structure on the deep epistemic possibilities. Changes in information then correspond to changes in this relational structure. All of this takes place relative to a fixed class of deeply epistemically possible worlds. Worlds which are not deeply epistemically possible can have no effect whatsoever on epistemic notions.

The selected worlds approach proposes to identify the class of deeply epistemically possible worlds with the class of selected worlds. But this cannot be correct, for some selected worlds are explicitly contradictory, whereas no epistemic possibility is explicitly contradictory. It is not deeply epistemically possible that $A \wedge \neg A$ and so it is never epistemically possible that $A \wedge \neg A$ for any agent. The situation is not that, when an agent considers the matter, she realises that it is not the case that $A \wedge \neg A$ and thereby comes to reject worlds according to which 'A' is both true and false. Rather, such worlds were never on the table to be considered as possibilities in the first place, precisely because they are not deeply epistemically possible. (I return to this issue in §7.5.)

So it cannot be that all of the selected worlds are deeply epistemically possible worlds. None of the 'glutty' worlds, according to which some 'A' is both true and false, are deeply epistemically possible. The objection is not that the selected worlds approach is incompatible with a rational agent's belief in each instance of '$\neg(A \wedge \neg A)$'. For this is paraconsistently equivalent to '$A \vee \neg A$', which is true according to any selected world which assigns some truth-value to 'A'. The objection is not that the approach conflicts with what rational agents do in fact believe. Rather, the objection is that the very notion of an epistemically possible world excludes such obviously glutty worlds.

If we exclude such worlds from our analysis of epistemic concepts, however, we re-introduce many of the problems faced by the standard possible worlds account. To see why this is so, we can return to our model of an agent who knows that p and that $p \rightarrow q$ but not that q, which we can represent visually as follows:

The nodes (circles) represent worlds; the '$+p$' and '$-p$' labels represent what's true and what's false according to those worlds, respectively; and the arrows represent the agent's accessibility relation. At each world, '$p \rightarrow q$' is true, so both 'p' and '$p \rightarrow q$' are true according to each world accessible from w_1, but 'q' is not, since it is not true according to w_2. Hence w_1 represents the agent as knowing that p

and that $p \to q$ but not that q. Similarly, w_2 represents the agent as knowing that p and $p \to q$, but not that q.

But if we now remove w_2-type worlds from these models, on the grounds that they are not deeply epistemic possible, then all we are left with is:

which represents the agent as knowing that q as well as that p and that $p \to q$. To avoid modelling her as knowing that q, we will need to introduce accessible worlds at which 'q' is not true:

But then '$p \to q$' is not true according to w_3, and so the agent is no longer represented (by either w_1 or w_3) as knowing that p and that $p \to q$. In short, without explicitly contradictory worlds in play, the selected worlds approach can no longer model an agent whose knowledge is not closed under *modus ponens*.

Exactly the same reasoning applies to the account of informative inference. Previously, *modus ponens* was treated as an informative inference because there are worlds which represent that A and that $A \to B$ but not that B. But all such worlds are glutty worlds, representing both that A and that $\neg A$. If we exclude such worlds from the analysis, then *modus ponens* inferences are deemed uninformative, since any of the remaining worlds which represent that A and that $A \to B$ must also represent that B.

The basic notion of a deeply epistemically possible world is highly puzzling. This is the very feature which makes the problem of bounded rationality so difficult. If we are to model epistemic states and epistemic contents using sets of worlds and relational structures on them, then we have to admit logically impossible worlds into the account. But trivially impossible worlds cannot feature in any account of rational (but non-ideal) attitudes and all glutty selected worlds are trivially impossible.

Our problem is difficult because it requires us to find worlds which are logically impossible, but not trivially so. Lewis captures this idea nicely in stating his dissatisfaction with paraconsistent logic:

> I'm increasingly convinced that I can and do reason about impossible situations. [...] But I don't really understand how that works. Paraconsistent logic [...] allows (a limited amount of) reasoning about *blatantly* impossible situations. Whereas what I find myself doing is *reasoning about subtly impossible situations, and rejecting suppositions that lead fairly to blatant impossibilities.* (Lewis 2004, 176, my emphasis)

It is this seemingly ineffable notion of a *subtle* inconsistency that holds the key to the problem of bounded rationality. In the next section, I consider an attempt to make sense of logical models which are impossible, but subtly so.

6.3   Urn Worlds

In this section (which draws on Jago 2007), I discuss an attempt by Hintikka (1975a) and Rantala (1975) to provide formal models which 'look possible but which contain hidden contradictions' (Hintikka 1975a, 476). They aim to characterise models 'so subtly inconsistent that the inconsistency could not be known (perceived) by an everyday logician, however competent' (Hintikka 1975a, 478). As we saw in the previous section, selected worlds are not appropriate in an account of epistemic content, precisely because whenever they represent the impossible, they represent the trivially impossible. If Hintikka and Rantala are successful in their aim, then we have good candidates to play the role of epistemically possible worlds in our account of content.

The models Hintikka and Rantala describe are based on Hintikka's (1973a; 1973b) game-theoretic models of classical first-order logic, which themselves develop the ideas of Henkin (1961) and Peirce

(1992). The world is viewed as an urn from which individuals are drawn by two players, called '∀' and '∃'. In a game $G(\forall x A)$, player ∀ must pick an individual from the urn satisfying 'A'; if she picks individual a, the game continues as $G(A[x/a])$. Similarly, the game $G(\exists x A)$ requires ∃ to pick an individual a satisfying 'A' and continues as $G(A[x/a])$. Analogously, ∀ decides whether $G(A \wedge B)$ proceeds as $G(A)$ or as $G(B)$ whereas ∃ decides how $G(A \vee B)$ should proceed. The game $G(\neg A)$ proceeds as the inverse game $G^{-1}(A)$, in which the players swap roles.

In this way, nested quantifiers represent constraints on sequences of draws from the urn. Just as in probability theory, individuals can but need not be replaced after being drawn from the urn. Models in which individuals are always replaced immediately after being drawn are the *invariant* models; all others are *changing* models. Invariant models provide a classical first-order semantics, whereas changing models are non-classical (and correspond to what Hintikka (1975a) terms the *exclusive* interpretation of the quantifiers).

Hintikka's idea is that, given a sentence of certain game-theoretic complexity, there is a set of changing models 'which vary so subtly as to be indistinguishable from invariant [i.e., classical] ones at a certain level of logical analysis' (Hintikka 1975a, 483). Hintikka (somewhat unfortunately) calls such models 'impossible possible worlds'. For the formal details, Hintikka draws on Rantala's (1975) notion of an *urn model*:

Definition 6.1 (Urn sequence) An urn sequence Δ over a domain $\mathcal{D}$ is a countable sequence $\langle D_i \mid i \in \mathbb{N} \rangle$ where $D_1 = \mathcal{D}$ and, for $i \geq 1$, $D_i \subseteq \mathcal{D}^i$ (the ith Cartesian power of the domain $\mathcal{D}$) such that, for some $a' \in \mathcal{D}$:

$$\langle a_1 \cdots a_i \rangle \in D_i \text{ only if } \langle a_1 \cdots a_i a' \rangle \in D_{i+1}$$

and, for all $a' \in \mathcal{D}$:

$$\langle a_1 \cdots a_i \rangle \in D_i \text{ if } \langle a_1 \cdots a_i a' \rangle \in D_{i+1}.$$

Definition 6.2 (Urn model) An urn model $\mathfrak{M}$ is a pair $\langle \mathcal{M}, \Delta \rangle$, where $\mathcal{M}$ is a classical first-order model with domain $\mathcal{D}$ and Δ is an urn sequence over $\mathcal{D}$. An urn model $\mathfrak{M}$ satisfies a sentence 'A', $\mathfrak{M} \vDash_u A$, when $\exists$ has a winning strategy in the game $G(A)$ played in $\mathfrak{M}$.

Definition 6.3 (*d*-invariant models) Let $\delta_i =$

$$\{a_i \mid \exists a_1 \cdots \exists a_{i-1} \langle a_1 \cdots a_{i-1} a_i \rangle \in D_i\}$$

For any $d \in \mathbb{N}$, an urn-model $\mathfrak{M} = \langle \mathcal{M}, \langle D_1 D_2 \cdots \rangle \rangle$ is *d*-invariant iff $D_1 = \delta_1 = \delta_2 = \cdots = \delta_d$.

Here, δ_i is the set of individuals available at draw i. The *d*-invariant models behave as classical models for all sentences 'A' with quantifier depth no greater than d. (The quantifier depth of 'A' is the greatest n such that there is a quantifier in 'A' embedded within $n - 1$ other quantifiers (or 0 if 'A' is quantifier-free).) For such 'A', if $\mathfrak{M} = \langle \mathcal{M}, \Delta \rangle$ is *d*-invariant, then $\mathfrak{M} \vDash_u A$ iff $\mathcal{M}$ classically satisfies 'A'. Yet a valid sentence with quantifier depth d need not be satisfied by a d'-invariant model, for any $d' < d$.

Unlike selected worlds (§6.2), changing urn models do not verify classically unsatisfiable sentences only at the cost of making some sentences both true and false (the non-subtle way!). The approach also comes with a well-defined, non-trivial notion of consequence and an accompanying proof-theory (Hintikka 1970, 1973b). (Sequoiah-Grayson (2008) discusses Hintikka's proof theory in detail and comes to conclusions similar to those offered below.) As I'll argue in §6.4, however, the assumption that epistemic contents are closed under logical rules (other than identity) is rather dubious.

Urn models seem to be both logically respectable and good candidates for playing the role of the deeply epistemically possible worlds. Or rather, we would adopt Hintikka's and Rantala's ideas by treating only those single ersatz worlds w which correspond to some urn model $\mathfrak{M}$ (such that w represents that A iff $\mathfrak{M} \vDash_u A$) as deeply epistemically possible worlds.

There are several serious problems with using urn models in this way. The first problem is this. In using these models, Hintikka works with a notion of an agent's logical competence, measured in terms of quantifier depth d. The rough idea is that greater competence correlates with the ability to reason correctly with sentences involving higher numbers of embedded quantifiers. (In an epistemic logic setting, the epistemic accessibility relation of an agent with competency d is constrained so that all accessible urn-model-worlds are d'-invariant, for all $d' \leq d$ (Hintikka 1975a). That agent is then modelled as an ideal agent up to the limits of her competency, but no further.)

We could, if we want, replace Hintikka's individualistic notion of competency with a communal one, reflecting standards of linguistic understanding, or our communal expectations on rational (but non-ideal) agents. The idea, very roughly, would be that persistent logical mistakes falling below the standard would reflect the failure to grasp the relevant concept fully, whereas mistakes persistently over the threshold would instead reflect errors in calculation, lack of cognitive resources and the like.

Quantifier depth is not a good measure either of logical competence or of communal standards of (non-ideal) rationality, however. Suppose Anna completes a (correct) proof, in which no sentence has a quantifier depth greater than d, of a mathematical statement 'A'. If she completed the proof through skill and not random luck, her achievement reflects her competence and so we must assign her a competence of at least d. Then, no d'-invariant model was ever an epistemic possibility for Anna, for any $d' \leq d$. But since 'A' appears in the proof, it must have a quantifier depth no greater than d and so is true in all d-invariant models. Consequently, in a Hintikka-style model of knowledge, Anna is modelled as having known that A all along; and in a model of content, her proof is modelled as being contentless and uninformative. This is just what we want to avoid.

This objection shows only that we shouldn't link the d parameter directly to an agent's competence (or communal standards of competence). Let's grant, for the sake of argument, that d can be fixed meaningfully in some other way, so as to avoid the objection. Even then, a further problem remains. Given that $\delta_1 = \mathcal{D}$ in any urn model with domain $\mathcal{D}$, we can show that, for any 'A' which contains no embedded quantifiers and any urn model $\mathfrak{M} = \langle \mathcal{M}, \Delta \rangle$, $\mathfrak{M} \vDash_u A$

iff M classically satisfies 'A' (Rantala 1975, 466, theorem 1). As a consequence, agents are modelled as being logically omniscient with respect to all such sentences and all inferences involving only such sentences are deemed contentless. This gets things wrong: if valid deductions can be informative at all, then surely at least some purely truth-functional (quantifier-free) inferences are informative. It's not as if the first-year logic class struggles only with those inferences involving embedded quantification!

Hintikka's use of urn models represents an improvement (in certain respects) on using selected worlds to capture the epistemically possible worlds, but it renders too many inferences uninformative. The root of problem is that using urn models in this way establishes an absolute cut-off point between potentially informative and necessarily uninformative inferences (depending on whether they involve embedded quantifiers). But, as I argue in the next section, in reality there is no clear cut-off. This is because content, and hence whether an inference is informative or not, is an inherently vague matter.

6.4   Vague Epistemic Possibilities

I have discussed and rejected two approaches to the problem of bounded rationality (§6.2 and §6.3). I will set out my response to the problem in chapters 7 and 8. Before that, I want to discuss the problem in a slightly different form (drawing on Jago 2013e), to understand why the selected worlds and urn models approaches (and other similar approaches) make so little progress.

The following principles all seem reasonable. If w is an epistemically possible world (i.e., everything w represents is epistemically possible) and w represents that A and that B, then a world w' just like w but which in addition represents that $A \land B$ must also be epistemically possible. Similarly, if an epistemically possible world w represents both that A and that $A \rightarrow B$, then a world w' just like w but which also represents that B must be epistemically possible too. And so on, for other cases connected in this immediate way by an inference rule. These principles have the same rational force which leads us to say that the inference from '$A \to B$' and 'A' to 'B' is uninformative and that anyone who believes both that A and that B thereby also believes that $A \wedge B$.

Now let's focus on a particular logical falsehood 'F', chosen as a clear case of epistemic possibility (that is, one which is impossible but not obviously so). Then there is an epistemically possible world w which represents that F. Let's also consider a step-by-step logical refutation of 'F': for simplicity, we'll assume the refutation takes the form of a derivation of some explicit contradiction 'A', '$\neg A$' from 'F'.

By applying the principles from the previous paragraph, it follows that a trivially impossible world, representing both that A and that $\neg A$, counts as an epistemically possible world! For each step of the refutation, there corresponds a principle to the effect that, if the premises are true according to an epistemically possible world w, then the premises plus the conclusion are true according to a similar epistemically possible world w'. (I haven't yet said just what these proof-steps might look like: the details will appear in §7.4.) By applying these principles repeatedly, we seem to be forced into counting a world according to which both 'A' and '$\neg A$' are true as an epistemically possible world. But such a world is clearly not epistemically possible.

Moreover, if we accept a full set of classical inference rules, we can infer that everything is epistemically possible. For classical logic supports *ex falso quodlibet*, $A, \neg A \vdash B$; hence by applying the reasoning above, we will reach an epistemically possible world which represents that B, for any 'B' whatsoever. This is absurd. Reasoning contrapositively, if any 'B' is epistemically impossible, then no inconsistent world can count as a epistemically possible world, regardless of how subtly inconsistent it may be. If we accept the linking principles of the form 'if w is an epistemically possible world, then so is w'', then either all ersatz worlds are epistemically possible, thereby trivialising the notion, or else no logically impossible worlds are epistemically possible, thereby lumbering us with logical omniscience. This is a particularly sharp form of the problem of bounded rationality.

Putting the problem in this form draws out what I take to be one of its key features: that it is structurally analogous to the infamous sorites paradox. In a sorites series for a predicate 'F', we are presented with a range of cases and asked to judge of each case whether it is an F. The problem arises when some cases are clear Fs, some are clear non-Fs, but the cases can be arranged in series from the clear Fs to the clear non-Fs in such a way that adjacent cases seem to be the same with respect to *Fness*. For any adjacent pair of cases, if we judge one to be an F, then we will judge the other to be an F also. But then, by applying this principle to each pair of adjacent cases in turn, we will end up judging all cases to be Fs, even though some are clearly non-Fs.

To make this kind of reasoning more concrete, here's an example. Suppose a huge box of very small sweets is bought to a party and guests are invited to help themselves. Taking a sweet or two wouldn't be greedy. And, it seems, taking one extra sweet wouldn't have turned a non-greedy guest into a greedy one. (If you disagree, just suppose the individual sweets are really small: tiny cola pips.) If you want to avoid being greedy, then surely you're safe taking just one extra sweet. But making off with a shoe-box full of the sweets would be very greedy indeed. Yet how can this be, if one extra sweet never makes a difference to whether you're being greedy? We can state the reasoning more formally. We have a general tolerance principle, which says

(6.1) For any number n, if taking exactly n sweets isn't greedy, then taking exactly $n + 1$ sweets isn't greedy either.

Clearly, taking exactly one sweet isn't greedy. Then, instantiating (6.1) with $n = 1$ and applying *modus ponens*, we infer that taking exactly two sweets isn't greedy. We can then repeat the argument (this time, for $n = 2$ in (6.1)), to conclude that taking exactly three sweets isn't greedy. By repeating the argument $n - 1$ times, we conclude that taking exactly n sweets isn't greedy, for any number n we like. Clearly, we will eventually reach a false conclusion, for taking exactly a thousand sweets would be very greedy indeed!

We can block the argument to this absurd conclusion by denying (6.1). But then we are saying that, for some number n, taking exactly n sweets isn't greedy but taking exactly $n + 1$ sweets is. So helping oneself to just one more sweet could turn a non-greedy guest into a greedy one. This 'sharp cut-off principle' is (classically) equivalent to the negation of (6.1), so that denying (6.1) commits us to the existence of a sharp cut-off for 'greedy' in this case. Many philosophers hold that it is absurd to posit sharp cut-offs for vague predicates: surely, they say, it is absurd to think that taking, say, 143 sweets would be greedy, whereas taking 142 would not.

We are in a bind. The tolerance principle (6.1) must be false, yet denying it seems absurd. Philosophers have responded to the puzzle in a number of ways. Some claim that we are rationally committed to tolerance principles such as (6.1). Dummett (1975) holds that competence with vague predicates shows that our language is inconsistent, since he holds that acceptance of the relevant tolerance principle is required for competence with a vague predicate. In a similar way, Eklund (2002) and Sorensen (2001) hold that we are rationally committed to tolerance principles (and hence rationally committed to infinitely many contradictions). Others hold, on the contrary, that 'speakers' acceptance of tolerance principles is quite inessential to vagueness' (Williamson 2007, 120). What everyone agrees on is that the tolerance principles are false and consequently that there is some serious explaining to do somewhere along the line.

Sorensen has a neat take on the problem. For Sorensen, vagueness arises because there are *ungrounded* truths. Usually, truths are grounded in how the world is. But when we progress down a sorites series and hit a borderline (e.g., a number n such that taking n sweets isn't greedy, but taking $n + 1$ is), we encounter truths which are in no way grounded in the way the world is. They are true but lack truthmakers (Sorensen 2001, 165–84). As a consequence, there are true 'threshold' statements, such as 'taking n sweets isn't greedy' (where taking $n + 1$ sweets would be greedy), which are utterly unknowable (Sorensen 2001, 13). Since there is nothing in the world grounding such truths, there is nothing to know, according to Sorensen (2001, 171, 175). So no wonder we find such statements absurd: we have no epistemic access to them whatsoever. They are what Sorensen (1988) calls *blindspots*. (I don't agree with Sorensen's diagnosis, and argue against it in Jago 2013f.)

Williamson (1994) also holds that there exist sharp cut-offs and that truths about them are unknowable. They are unknowable, according to Williamson, because tiny, imperceptible changes in the semantic facts could shift the truth-value of such statements from true to false. Facts of usage chaotically determine the truth-values of such cases and we cannot practically determine the exact outcomes of chaotic systems. Because we cannot know precisely where the sharp cut-offs are for vague predicates, we are not in a position rationally to assert where they are (Williamson 1996). Sharp cut-offs are not absurd, for Williamson, but truths about them are unassertible. This, one might claim, is sufficient to explain our puzzlement surrounding sharp cut-offs. (I'll return to this point in §8.4.)

Supervaluationists such as Dummett (1975), Fine (1975), Mehlberg (1958) and van Fraassen (1966) agree that 'for some n, taking n sweets would be greedy whereas taking one less would not' is true. But they also hold that there is no particular number which witnesses that existential statement: for each particular n, 'taking n sweets would be greedy whereas taking $n - 1$ would not' is not true. (They can make these claims simultaneously because they adopt a logic in which existential statements can be true without witnesses: '$\exists x A$' may be true on a domain even if there is no member of the domain d satisfying '$A[x/d]$'.) Supervaluationists use this feature of their account to explain our puzzlement with cut-off principles (and the corresponding denials of tolerance principles): we can accept the existential generalisation, but none of its instances.

In these and other ways, all theories of vagueness attempt to explain our puzzlement surrounding the tolerance principles (even if they are clearly false). In short, one doesn't solve the sorites merely by denying the tolerance principles. One has to say how tolerance principles could possibly be false (or how there could possibly be sharp cut-offs) and, if there are sharp cut-offs, one needs to explain why the folk (and most philosophers) are so convinced that there aren't any.

These puzzles are very similar to the problem of bounded rationality, in which normative links between epistemic contents seem to clash with the fact that we are not ideal reasoners. Consider these two extreme positions about epistemic content:

THE IDEALISER: As a consequence of the meanings of the logical constants, epistemically possible worlds are closed under logical consequence. Any impossible world is trivially impossible and so not an epistemically possible world. Hence, only logically possible worlds count as epistemically possible worlds. Epistemic space is an ideal space of classical possible worlds.

THE TRIVIALISER: As a consequence of the fact that we are not logically omniscient, closure principles for epistemically possible worlds should be utterly dismissed. There's nothing to them, other than perhaps some psychological quirks. So closure is out and all worlds, however trivially inconsistent, count as epistemically possible worlds. Epistemic space is a trivial space, comprising all worlds whatsoever.

The Idealiser is wrong about epistemic notions for the same reasons that someone who accepts tolerance principles for vague predicates is wrong. She begins by (correctly) noting the strangeness of placing a sharp borderline for 'epistemically possible world' between trivially-related worlds. And she mistakenly infers from this that, if such-and-such worlds are epistemically possible, then trivially-related worlds must be too. She concludes that, if a world w representing both that 'A' and that '$A \to B$' is epistemically possible, then so must be a world w' representing all that w represents plus B. This principle acts just like a tolerance principle for 'epistemically possible world'.

As we saw above, this move (together with similar principles for other basic proof rules) forces the Idealiser to accept that no inconsistent world is epistemically possible. Consequently, she concludes that only the logically possible worlds can count as epistemically possible worlds. Her mistake, as in any sorites argument, is acceptance of these tolerance principles for 'epistemically possible world'. Those principles stand or fall with the closure conditions on epistemically possible worlds. The analogy with sorites cases suggests that we should reject closure principles for epistemically possible worlds (just as we must reject the tolerance principles for vague predicates).

Yet the Trivialiser too is wrong about epistemic notions. She is wrong for the simple reason that, as noted above, one does not solve a sorites paradox merely by denying the relevant tolerance principle. It is clear from the conclusion of a sorites argument that the tolerance principle must be false, but the paradox does not dissolve at that point. In parallel to what I said about tolerance principles above, one has to say how closure principles for contents could possibly be false, given the meanings of the logical constants and given the normative connections that basic inference rules establish between trivially related contents. One must also say why it is that we cannot seem rationally to acknowledge counter-instances to epistemic closure principles, even if we know they must exist. (I'll return to this specific point in §7.3 and §8.4.)

The problem of bounded rationality requires us to find a middle path between these two extremes, between the Idealiser and the Trivialiser. We must deny that epistemically possible worlds are closed under logical consequence, without dismissing the normative importance of the inference rules associated with the logical constants. The normative notion of content for which we are searching is a vague notion, precisely because chains of seemingly uninformative inferences can give rise to informative deductions.

This very tight connection between the sorites and the problem of bounded rationality will be important in what follows. To avoid closure, I must invoke worlds without any internal logical structure.

To avoid triviality, I must deny that all such worlds are epistemically possible. Just which worlds are epistemically possible is not a determinate matter. The task of the next chapter is to make sense of these ideas.

That the problem of bounded rationality is intimately connected with vagueness explains why attempts at a solution such as those discussed in §6.2 and §6.3 fail. They attempt to draw a clear and sharp boundary around particular contents. They hold that it is a determinate matter whether a particular deduction is informative and a determinate matter whether one particular epistemic or doxastic state includes another. But the sorites puzzle requires us to make sense of truth and inference in a vague language: the task is not to reform the language by removing vague predicates. Similarly, solving the problem of bounded rationality requires us to make sense of how some but not all valid inferences are informative, without drawing an artificially sharp line between those that are and those that are not.

Chapter Summary

I began by outlining the problem of bounded rationality (§6.1) and showing why the 'selected worlds' approach (based on paraconsistent logic) does not solve the problem (§6.2). Either it draws arbitrary distinctions between trivial (uninformative) and non-trivial (informative) basic inferences, or else it incorrectly treats every inference whatsoever as being informative. Moreover, the approach is tenable only if some explicitly contradictory worlds are epistemically possible, which is not the case (§6.2).

The urn-models approach (§6.3) takes up the challenge of constructing worlds which are impossible but subtly so: they are never explicitly contradictory. But it is not successful, in part because it draws a determinate sharp distinction between the informative and the uninformative inferences, whereas there is in fact no determinate boundary between the two.

I then drew an analogy between the problem of bounded rationality and the sorites paradox (§6.4) and argued that we should think of epistemic closure principles in much the way we think about tolerance principles for vague predicates. In the next chapter, I set out to make sense of this idea, in terms of a normative but vague space of worlds.

7

Epistemic Space

In this chapter, I set out a response to the problem of bounded rationality. The approach develops the account of worlds constructed in chapter 5 into a normative epistemic space, suitable for analysing epistemic notions. In line with the argument from §6.4, epistemic space incorporates vagueness, so that it is not always determinate whether a given world is included in epistemic space.

7.1 Epistemically Possible Worlds

At the end of the last chapter, I concluded that, to avoid treating notions of epistemic content as being logically closed, I must invoke worlds without any internal logical structure. But to avoid triviality and respect the meanings of the logical constants, I must deny that all such worlds are epistemically possible worlds. The strategy I will pursue is to treat some but not all of the ersatz worlds constructed in §5.6 as epistemically possible worlds. Unlike the strategies of §6.2 and §6.3, I will not single out the relevant worlds by imposing logical closure conditions on what such worlds represent. That is, a world w does not get to be an epistemically possible world in virtue of satisfying conditions of the form

(7.1) If w represents that A, then w also represents that B

where 'B' bears some important logical relation to 'A'. Rather, on the account I'll set out below, a world gets to be an epistemically possible world in virtue of the normative relations it bears to other worlds. It will turn out that whether a given world is epistemically possible is not always a determinate matter. This is just what we should expect, given the points raised in §6.4. Taken together, the epistemically possible worlds and the normative structure between them comprise *epistemic space*.

As I said in §6.2, the basic notion of an epistemically possible world is deeply puzzling. Such a world represents a situation which seems to be a possibility (and which, as far as an agent with no *a posteriori* information is concerned, may well be the actual world). But as we know, to avoid the problem of logical omniscience, some of these epistemically possible worlds must be inconsistent. Such worlds can be ruled out *a priori* as representations of the actual world. So our notion of an epistemically possible world is not the same notion as that discussed by Chalmers (2010), on which epistemically possible worlds capture just the epistemic possibilities which cannot be ruled out *a priori* (i.e., by any amount of *a priori* reasoning).

Our epistemically possible worlds by contrast include worlds which, in Hintikka's words, 'look possible but which contain hidden contradictions' (Hintikka 1975a, 476). Such worlds look possible, despite being *a priori* refutable. They are not easily ruled out as representations of actuality by *a priori* reasoning alone. As Duc (1995, 1997) has it, we are after a notion of an epistemically possible world which allows us to treat agents as being neither logically omniscient nor logically ignorant.

In selecting which worlds (from the total stock constructed in §5.6) are to count as epistemically possible, we want to include what Lewis describes as 'subtly impossible situations', but not 'blatant impossibilities' (Lewis 2004, 176). Lewis goes on to say

> I agree with [Priest] about the many uses to which we could put make-believedly possible impossibilities, if we are willing to use them. The trouble is that all these uses seem to require a distinction between the subtle ones and the blatant ones (very likely context-dependent, very likely a matter of degree) and that's just what I don't understand. (Lewis 2004, 177)

Lewis hits the nail on the head here. To use inconsistent representations for epistemic purposes, they must be subtly inconsistent, and that subtlety is a matter of degree (or at least, it is not always a determinate matter whether an inconsistent representation is subtly impossible). I try to make sense of this idea in this chapter.

Before going further, it is worth getting a little clearer on the target notion of an epistemically possible world. (The following draws on Jago 2009b.) Chalmers, during his discussion of deep epistemic possibilities (2010), does consider hyperintensional notions 'that might be useful in modeling less idealized sorts of reasoners':

> To develop such a conception, we must start with a *non-ideal* notion of deep epistemic possibility. Instead of saying that A is epistemically possible when $\neg A$ cannot be ruled out a priori, we might say that A is epistemically possible when $\neg A$ cannot be ruled out *through reasoning of a certain sort*. (Chalmers 2010, 102)

Chalmers then suggests various options under the rubric 'reasoning of a certain sort'. (He states these options in terms of epistemic necessity but, given the discussion in §8.4, it is doubtful that there are any genuine epistemic necessities.) In terms of epistemic possibility, his options become:

(7.2) It is epistemically possible that A iff it is not obvious *a priori* that $\neg A$;

(7.3) It is epistemically possible that A iff A cannot be disproved (or $\neg A$ cannot be proved) in n steps of logical reasoning;

(7.4) It is epistemically possible that A iff A is cognitively significant.

We might add to Chalmers's list:

(7.5) It is epistemically possible that A iff A is not trivially false;

(7.6) It is epistemically possible that A iff A cannot be ruled out easily by *a priori* reasoning.

I won't discuss these suggestions individually, partly because they are all rather vague and partly because they all point in roughly the same direction (particularly if we replace '*n* steps of logical reasoning' with 'a small amount of logical reasoning' or 'easy logical reasoning'). On these suggestions, a world would count as epistemically possible if and only if nothing it represents is *a priori* obviously or trivially false, or easily disprovable by a small amount of logical reasoning.

These suggestions do not provide us with a definition of 'epistemically possible world', but they do help us to get closer to the target concept. The notions just discussed will guide us in describing a suitable epistemic space. In particular, all these suggestions point to the idea (mentioned above) that an epistemically possible world may permit contradiction, but not obvious contradiction. They may be inconsistent, but only subtly so.

There is one further point in Chalmers's discussion of epistemically possible worlds which is important and which seems to be left out by thinking of epistemically possible worlds as those that cannot easily be ruled out *a priori*. Chalmers holds that epistemic possibility should 'involve some imposition of a rational idealization' and so 'the corresponding notion of deep epistemic necessity should capture some sort of rational *must*' (Chalmers 2010, 65). In characterising epistemically possible worlds in terms of representations which cannot easily be ruled out, we seem to have ignored this important normative dimension.

I agree with Chalmers that epistemic space must respect rational principles, so that the derivative concepts of knowledge and belief capture 'some sort of rational *must*'. For we ascribe knowledge, belief, the ability to form judgements and so on only to agents, that is, systems which we take to be (or which can be interpreted as) rational to some degree. I depart company from Chalmers when he implicitly identifies rational idealisation with the end-point of ideal reasoning processes, that is, with conceptual coherence and logical consistency.

One can impose a criterion of rationality without thereby taking all agents to be ideal reasoners. A coherent, deductively closed set of beliefs may be an ideal of rational enquiry, yet an agent can be deemed rational if she has the ability to reason in accordance with certain logical rules and deploys those abilities as well as the cognitive resources to hand allow. Failures of closure within an agent's knowledge or belief set may be due to a failure of rationality but they may also be due to a lack of cognitive resources. One can hold that the philosophically interesting notion of epistemic space is a rational space, incorporating the normative element of our epistemic concepts, without thereby holding it to be an ideal epistemic space in Chalmers's sense. (Just how to make good on this idea is the topic of §7.2 and §7.4.)

The law frequently invokes the character of the reasonable person and asks, would a reasonable person have acted in this way in similar circumstances? This is a normative concept, in the sense that the accused may be blameworthy when her actions differ significantly from those of the hypothetical reasonable person. Thinking in terms of the reasonable person encapsulates what we expect of a rational agent. Similarly, we have epistemic expectations of agents, which capture what is communally expected of a sincere, rational (although not ideal) agent. We expect such agents to recognise that there are no round squares, that 0 is 0 and not 1, that wholly green objects cannot be wholly red and so on.

This notion of expectation plays an important role in our epistemic concepts, for it is part of our notion of what it is to be an epistemic agent. We can thus think of an epistemically possible world as a representation which an agent may believe in its entirety without thereby falling beneath our epistemic expectations. Although this is a normative notion, it is (partially) dependent on descriptive facts, such as our typical cognitive abilities.

In this way, what our epistemic expectations require of an agent is related to the kinds of *a priori* inference that agents typically find easy, trivial or obvious. We expect agents to detect and reject obvious *a priori* impossibilities, but we do not have the same expectations in the case of subtle impossibilities or in the case of *a posteriori* metaphysical impossibilities. Thus, the contents *that Fermat's Last Theorem is false* and *that Ziggy isn't Bowie*, although impossible, do not exert the same normative force on rational agents as the content *that* $1 + 1 = 3$.

Following these lines of thought, we begin to capture the force of Chalmers's 'rational *must*' whilst avoiding a level of idealisation on which epistemically possible worlds must be logically consistent. These ideas will be fleshed out in §7.2 and §7.4.

7.2   Normative Epistemic Space

Epistemic space is structured by normative principles, even if the worlds that comprise it are not. That is the idea I will pursue in this section (which draws on Jago 2006a and Jago 2009b). My suggestion is that the deductive links set up by the meanings of logical constants establish normative links between worlds, rather than between what is represented at any particular world. We construct epistemic space by using proof rules which capture (or correspond to) the meanings of the logical connectives to structure the set of all worlds. It is the entire space of worlds that thereby gets structured, not the worlds themselves.

Our aim in imposing a structure on our space of worlds is to capture the step-by-step process of constructing a proof. As a first-pass account, and focusing for the time being just on the very simple rule of *conjunction introduction* (from 'A' and 'B', infer '$A \wedge B$'), we structure our space as follows. We find a world w which represents that A and that B but not that $A \wedge B$, and a further world w' just like w, except that w' also represents that $A \wedge B$, and we place an arrow from w to w', as in figure 7.1.

The arrows capture the rational relations between representations established by *conjunction introduction*. Note that the worlds are not closed under *conjunction introduction*. Instead, the normative force of the rule is captured in the arrows between worlds. We think of the normative 'push' of each rule instance in a dynamic way, as an inter-world transition, rather than in the static, intra-world way that we find in classical models.

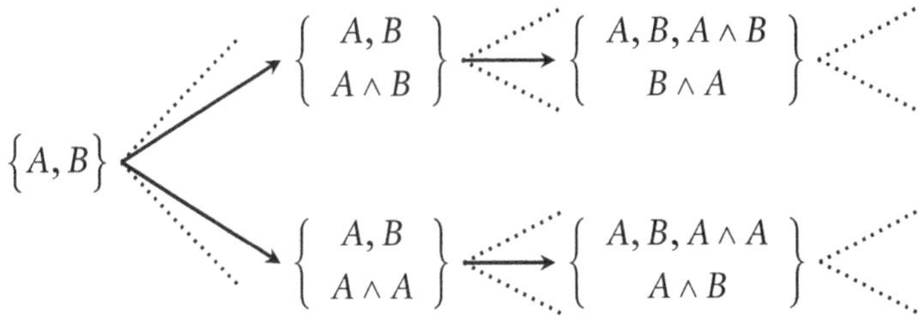

$$\{A,B\} \; \begin{cases} \left\{ \begin{matrix} A,B \\ A \wedge B \end{matrix} \right\} \longleftrightarrow \left\{ \begin{matrix} A,B,A \wedge B \\ B \wedge A \end{matrix} \right\} \\[2em] \left\{ \begin{matrix} A,B \\ A \wedge A \end{matrix} \right\} \longleftrightarrow \left\{ \begin{matrix} A,B,A \wedge A \\ A \wedge B \end{matrix} \right\} \end{cases}$$

Figure 7.1: WORLDS STRUCTURED BY PROOF-RULES

Each arrow represents a single inference to precisely one new conclusion, present at the arrow's target world but absent at its source. Such 'one step' inferences are the kind that are frequently called trivial and uninformative. Arrows thus represent an irreflexive, asymmetrical and intransitive relation. There are many valid inferences (even when focusing only on *conjunction introduction*) which correspond to no single arrow in our structure. For example, the inference $p, q, r \vdash p \wedge (q \wedge r)$ is valid, but there are no corresponding arrows in the structure. Instead, we have chains of worlds-and-arrows, shown in figure 7.2.

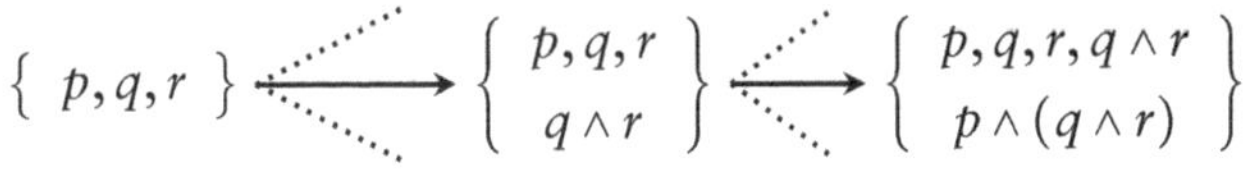

$$\{\, p, q, r \,\} \longleftrightarrow \left\{ \begin{matrix} p, q, r \\ q \wedge r \end{matrix} \right\} \longleftrightarrow \left\{ \begin{matrix} p, q, r, q \wedge r \\ p \wedge (q \wedge r) \end{matrix} \right\}$$

Figure 7.2: CHAINS OF RELATED WORLDS

Things are very simple in this set-up because we have considered only the *conjunction introduction* rule. Obstacles will arise when we consider rules which involve assumption-making or reasoning-by-cases. A further worry is that deductively equivalent proof systems will give us different structures on worlds and hence different answers to the question, 'how are worlds w and u related?' But our choice between deductively equivalent proof systems is arbitrary, in a way that our imposed normative structure should not be. I consider these issues, against the background of modern proof theory, in §7.4.

Before that, I want to get the main idea across. A first-pass approximation of the theory is good enough for this purpose. Let's suppose we have a structure very much like the one just described, but expanded to include other inference rules (with details of how this is done to be filled in). This kind of structure will achieve two related aims.

First, it gives us a handle on the normative relations which hold between representations. The objection against the 'trivial' space of worlds (the unstructured set of all worlds) is that it completely fails to capture these normative relations and hence does not respect the meaning of the logical constants (§6.1, §6.4). Unless these relations are captured, we do not have a genuinely epistemic space at all. Since the structure I've suggested does capture these relations, it allows us to make sense of various epistemic notions of content (which I'll discuss in detail in chapter 8).

Second, it provides us with a way of saying which worlds are more blatantly inconsistent than others. The proof-theoretic structure of epistemic space can be seen as 'unwinding' buried contradictions in a world, thereby transforming subtle contradictions into blatant ones in a step-by-step way. The more steps need to be taken in unwinding the contradiction, the more subtle the original contradiction is. Worlds whose only contradictions (if any) are subtle ones are epistemically possible.

By contrast, contradictory worlds whose contradictions can be unwound into blatant contradictions in just a few steps are themselves fairly blatant and so do not count as epistemically possible worlds. If a world w contains both subtle and blatant contradictions, then the blatant contradictions override the subtle ones, for a single blatant contradiction is sufficient for the blatant incoherence of a situation as a whole.

The epistemically possible worlds are then the worlds which do not quickly unwind into blatantly incoherent worlds. This idea, when spelt out fully in §7.4, will correctly treat 'epistemically possible world' as a vague predicate. It may be indeterminate whether a given world w counts as an epistemically possible world.

A path in epistemic space may look something like the one shown in figure 7.3. In this path, the rightmost world (which represents both that A and that $\neg A$) is explicitly contradictory and hence is a clear case of a world failing to be an epistemically possible world. The other worlds to the right of figure 7.3 are but a few steps away from this world and so are also counted as epistemically impossible. Worlds to the left of figure 7.3 are many steps away from this world and so are clear cases of epistemically possible worlds. In between, we find worlds (in the centre of figure 7.3) which are neither clearly epistemically possible nor clearly epistemically impossible. These are the borderline cases of 'epistemically possible world'.

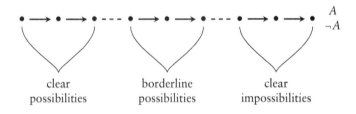

clear
possibilities

borderline
possibilities

clear
impossibilities

Figure 7.3: A PATH IN EPISTEMIC SPACE

Whatever one thinks is the correct semantics for vagueness can be 'plugged in' at this point. If you think that the indeterminate cases are those for which there's no fact of the matter (Tye 1994), then you will partition worlds into three classes: those which are epistemically possible worlds, those which are not epistemically possible worlds, and those for which there is no fact of the matter either way. Many-valued approaches (Smith 2009) instead treat the concept *epistemically possible world* as a matter of degree, so that some worlds are fully epistemically possible, others are fully epistemically impossible, and others still are epistemically possible to some in-between degree. Epistemicists (Sorensen 1985, 2001; Williamson 1994) hold that there is a fact of the matter as to whether w is epistemically possible, but that we cannot know in which way that fact points. I'll say a little more on these options in §7.4. (For overviews of these and other theories of vagueness, see Keefe 2000 or Williamson 1994.)

7.3 Bjerring's Objection

I have sketched the way in which epistemic space will be developed; the details will appear in §7.4. Before that, I need to address a serious objection that has been raised against the approach I am suggesting. Addressing it at this stage will help to refine the concepts we need to develop epistemic space.

The objection, due to Bjerring (2010, 2012), runs as follows. We consider a world w whose representations are not closed under consequence. That is, for some 'C' entailed by premises 'A_1', ..., 'A_n', w represents that $A_1, \ldots, A_n$ but not that C. Now consider a proof P from 'A_1', ..., 'A_n' to 'C'. At least one of the inferences made in that proof cannot be respected by w. According to w, the premises of that inference are true, but the conclusion is not. But then, the objection runs, w is trivially impossible, since something it does not represent is derivable from what it does represent in just one obvious step of reasoning.

In the sketch of epistemic space given in §7.2 (which, remember, is only a first-pass approach), I took *conjunction introduction* as an example and used it to impose a normative structure on worlds. So let's consider Bjerring's objection with respect to this very simple structure. We first assume that a given world w is not closed under *conjunction introduction*. Then there are sentences 'A', 'B' such that, according to w, 'A' is true, 'B' is true, but '$A \wedge B$' is not true. The objection then is that w is clearly not epistemically possible, since we can infer '$A \wedge B$' from what w represents in just one inference step.

To make the objection compelling, we need to know why this latter fact about w shows that w is blatantly not epistemically possible. There are several ways in which Bjerring can make the case. According to the first (and simplest) way, since '$A \wedge B$' is not true according to w, it must be false according to w. Hence it will also be false according to any world w' with an arrow to it from w in epistemic space. But we know that there is an arrow from w to world w', according to which '$A \wedge B$' is true. So w' is a world according to which '$A \wedge B$' is both true and false and this is blatantly, trivially impossible.

A slightly different chain of reasoning would hold that, since w does not represent that $A \wedge B$, w instead represents that $\neg(A \wedge B)$. But then w' (with an arrow from w) will represent both that $A \wedge B$ and $\neg(A \wedge B)$ and, as before, this shows that w' is blatantly trivially impossible.

These lines of reasoning have a hidden premise: that whatever is not true according to a world w is false according to that world. Equivalently: whenever a world does not represent that A, it thereby represents that $\neg A$. But in general, our worlds do not support this premise. Recall from §5.6 that any set of worldmaking sentences constitutes an ersatz world (and any pair of such sets constitutes an ersatz double world). What these worlds represent is a matter of which sentences they include. There are many such sets of sentences which are incomplete: they include neither 'A' nor '$\neg A$'.

Such worlds represent neither that A nor that $\neg A$. If we assume that 'A' is false according to a single world w just in case '$\neg A$' is true according to w, then there are many ersatz worlds according to which some 'A' is neither true nor false. In the case of a double world $w = \langle w^{+}, w^{-} \rangle$, for which it is explicit what is false according to w, some 'A' is neither true nor false according to w just in case 'A' $\notin w^{+}$ and 'A' $\notin w^{-}$. But evidently, there are many such double worlds. Hence this extra premise is not supported by the worlds I am using to construct epistemic space.

There is an alternative way in which Bjerring might run his argument. He might claim that, given my aim to capture normative notions, the kind of move I have just made is illegitimate. The thought is that one can rule out a world by deriving something that is not true according to that world from something that is true according to that world. One would (so the thought runs) thereby show that the world is logically incomplete:

> On one natural understanding, an agent can rule out a partial
> world w by either inferring a contradiction from what holds
> at w, or by inferring that some sentence 'A', which w says is
> indeterminate [i.e., to which it does not assign a truth-value],
> actually is provably true or false according to what holds at w.
> (Bjerring 2012, 26)

The objection is that blatantly incomplete worlds are no better than
blatantly inconsistent worlds. And, as Bjerring shows, in order to
avoid blatantly inconsistent worlds whilst including some subtly
inconsistent worlds in epistemic space, I need to include blatantly
incomplete worlds.

There is, however, an important difference between inconsistent
worlds and incomplete worlds, which is sufficient to diffuse this
objection. To see the difference, we first need to grasp the distinction
between truths *about* a world and truths *according to* a world. I
have described worlds as sets of worldmaking sentences; world w
is one such world. Suppose w contains worldmaking sentence 'A',
which says that Bertie does not exist. Perhaps w contains precisely
2,543,643 other sentences. These are truths about w. But they need
not be truths according to w.

Suppose w contains a sentence containing the property (qua
worldmaking predicate) *being a beagle*. That's a truth about w. Yet
it may be that according to w, there is no such property as *being a
beagle*: w might be a nominalist world, according to which there are
no properties, for example. The sentence in question might say, 'the
property *being a beagle* does not exist'. There is no contradiction
here. 'Tolkien wrote *Lord of the Rings*' is a truth about *Lord of the
Rings*, but 'Tolkien exists' is not true according to *Lord of the Rings*.

Now consider a bad argument against considering any ersatz world
w to be possible:

> w is a set of sentences and so is an abstract object. But I know *a
> priori* that I am not an abstract object; and I know *a priori* that
> the world around me (if there is one) is not an abstract object.
> So I know *a priori* that w is not the actual world. Hence, w is
> not an epistemic possibility.

This argument is no good because it confuses truths about w with truths according to w. This is just the mistake we make (although it is not so blatant in this case) if we claim that an ersatz world w cannot be epistemically possible because it is incomplete. That w is incomplete is a truth about w, not a truth according to w. Indeed, w might without contradiction say of itself, 'I am complete' (even if it is highly incomplete). It need not say that; w might have nothing whatsoever to say on the subject of its (in)completeness. If it does not, then we have no incompleteness-related grounds on which to reject w as an epistemically possible world.

Contrast this with the case of inconsistency. A world may say nothing explicitly about its own consistency or inconsistency. Nevertheless, if it represents both that A and that $\neg A$, we have inconsistency-related grounds on which to reject that world as an epistemic possibility. This is the strongest possible ground we can have for rejecting a world. The argument that we should discard blatantly incomplete worlds, just as we discard blatantly inconsistent worlds, fails.

There is a further way in which Bjerring can argue that incomplete worlds should be discarded on normative grounds:

> If the resulting partial modal space [i.e., including incomplete worlds] is to serve as a proper space for minimally rational agents, worlds cannot be *too* partially described. Plausibly, just as we expect minimally rational agents to rule out blatant logical inconsistencies, so we expect them to accept *obvious* or *self-evident* logical truths. (Bjerring 2012, 26)

Surely, the thought runs, a minimally rational agent automatically knows (e.g.) that $A \vee \neg A$, for any 'A' whatsoever. But once we start down this track, it is hard to know where to stop. It might well be that the inference to '$A \vee \neg A$' from zero premises is one of the simplest that agents can make. Nevertheless, as we have seen, we do not want worlds to be closed under any inference rule (other than $A \vdash A$), and $\vdash A \vee \neg A$ is an inference rule like any other.

Suppose we did accept that worlds are closed under $\vdash A \vee \neg A$, so that every world represents that $A \vee \neg A$ (and hence that every agent knows that $A \vee \neg A$ automatically). What normative grounds do we have for accepting that worlds are closed under that rule, but not closed under *conjunction introduction* or *modus ponens*? These rules are as essential (if not more so) to the meanings of '∧' and '→', respectively, as ⊢ $A \lor \neg A$ is to the meanings of '∨' and '¬'. Yet we cannot accept that worlds are closed under *conjunction introduction* and *modus ponens*. So, to be consistent, we cannot take worlds to be closed under ⊢ $A \lor \neg A$ either.

As a consequence, epistemic space has to contain worlds that are highly incomplete, some of which do not represent that $A \lor \neg A$ for some 'A'. As far as epistemic space is concerned, therefore, it is not a rational requirement on agents that they know or believe every instance of '$A \lor \neg A$'.

There is, to be sure, something counter-intuitive in this result. If an agent fails to know or believe that $A \lor \neg A$ for some 'A', then her epistemic or doxastic state misses out on something trivial. Similarly, if an agent knows or believes that such-and-such, from which 'A' trivially follows and yet she does not know or believe that A, then again her epistemic or doxastic state misses out on something trivial. I'll call such cases, in which an agent fails to know (or believe) some trivial consequence of what she knows (or believes), *epistemic oversights*.

Epistemic oversights are bizarre, but we know they must exist. For every logically non-omniscient agent, there is some knowledge she has which trivially entails something she does not know. Otherwise, her knowledge would be closed under all trivial inference rules and hence deductively closed (since there are sets of deductively complete inference rules, all of which individually concern trivial inferences), contradicting the non-logical-omniscience assumption. An agent might know that $A \to B$ and that A but not that B (for some 'A' and 'B'), for example. That is no more and no less of a rational failing than failing to know that $A \lor \neg A$ (for some 'A').

As a matter of empirical fact, of course, many agents know that $A \lor \neg A$ (for many instances of 'A'). For those agents, worlds which do not represent that $A \lor \neg A$ (for the relevant instances of 'A') are not epistemically accessible, just as worlds which do not represent that Bertie is adorable are not epistemically accessible for agents who know that Bertie is adorable. Neither case is a matter of rational requirements on agents, in the sense that beliefs in '$A \wedge \neg A$' are rationally mandated.

That said, there is something very counterintuitive in ascribing a particular epistemic oversight to an agent. Just try it: say 'Bill knows that if it's raining he'll get wet and Bill knows it's raining, but Bill doesn't know he'll get wet'. That ascription just sounds weird. We're ascribing beliefs to Bill, and thus treating him as a rational agent, whilst at the same time ascribing to him what looks like a rational blooper.

This phenomenon is a serious problem for the view I'm proposing. Bjerring does not mention the problem in this form, but it is very much in the spirit of his attack. It is the sharpest form of objection to my current proposal, but it can be met. My response will have to wait until §8.4 and §8.5, however, once I've given an account of epistemic states and deductive content.

7.4   Capturing Proof Structure

In §7.2, I set out the basic picture of how epistemic space is structured by proof rules and raised two problems. The first problem is that the explanation given in §7.2 of how worlds are related looks to be oversimplified, for reasoning often involves the making and later discharging of assumptions. The second problem is that our choice of proof system seems to be somewhat arbitrary, in a way that the normative structure on worlds should not be. I'll consider each problem in turn.

The first problem amounts to this. It is easy to see how to relate a world which represents that A and that B but not that $A \wedge B$ to a similar world which represents in addition that $A \wedge B$. But not all inferences are as simple as these *conjunction introduction* steps. When we come to rules involving assumptions, or rules for reasoning by cases, it is not so clear how the corresponding structure on worlds should look. The problem, in short, is that worlds represent situations as being the case. They don't represent situations hypothetically being the case, or situations being the case given such-and-such.

To see the problem, consider the Fitch-style natural deduction proof of $B \vdash \neg(A \wedge \neg A)$ shown in figure 7.4. How are we to capture the move from the premise 'B' on line 1 to the assumption '$A \wedge \neg A$' on line 2? Not by a world which represents both that B and that $A \wedge \neg A$, since the latter is merely an assumption, to be cancelled later in the proof.

1	B	premise
2	$A \wedge \neg A$	assumption
3	A	2, $\wedge$E
4	$\neg A$	2, $\wedge$E
5	$\neg(A \wedge \neg A)$	3, 4, *reductio*

Figure 7.4: NATURAL DEDUCTION PROOF OF $B \vdash \neg(A \wedge \neg A)$

The problem is (partly) that the natural deduction notation used above does not explicitly track assumptions in a line-by-line way. We have to look upwards in a proof to see which assumptions are currently operative. This is merely a notational quirk. We can, instead, notate assumptions explicitly, line by line, by writing *sequents*

$$\Gamma \vdash A$$

which can be read as saying that 'A' follows from the set of assumptions Γ. We will then need proof rules to manipulate these sequents. But we also need a way to understand those sequents in terms of worlds. As just noted, worlds do not represent situations in an assumption-like way, so what are we to make of the sentences in Γ on the left-hand side of the sequent '$\Gamma \vdash A$'?

Work in contemporary proof theory (and its philosophy) helps us answer both questions. First, the *sequent calculus* (Gentzen 1934) gives us a system of rules for manipulating sequents (I'll introduce these rules below). Sequent calculi are the proof theorist's systems of choice, for unlike natural deduction, they clearly represent structural proof principles and, unlike axiomatic systems, they make proofs easy to construct. (We don't have to use the sequent calculus to achieve our ends: similar results can be achieved, although less elegantly, with a suitably encoded natural deduction system (Jago 2009c).)

Whilst developing sequent calculi, Gentzen (1934) discovered something very interesting. A very natural intuitionist sequent calculus (which manipulates sequents of the form $\Gamma \vdash A$) becomes a classical proof system if we allow it to contain *multiple-conclusion* sequents, of the form $\Gamma \vdash \Delta$ (where Δ is a set of sentences, which may be empty and may contain more than one sentence). Sentences in Δ behave disjunctively in such sequents: if $A_1, \ldots, A_n \vdash B_1, \ldots, B_m$, then '$A_1 \wedge \cdots \wedge A_n$' entails '$B_1 \vee \cdots \vee B_m$' (so the '$A_i$'s could not all be true whilst the 'B_i's are all false).

These sequents are symmetric, with sets of sentences on both sides of '$\vdash$'. So we need not think of a sequent non-symmetrically, in terms of premises and conclusions. Rather, we can think of '$\Gamma \vdash \Delta$' as stating the incompatibility of the truth of all sentences of Γ with the falsity of all sentences of Δ. Or, in less semantic terms, we can think of '$\Gamma \vdash \Delta$' in terms of the rational incoherence of asserting what's on the left whilst denying what's on the right.

Adopting this viewpoint, the following principles are very natural. First, it would be incoherent both to assert and deny some 'A' simultaneously. Second, repetition of 'A' makes no difference to our coherence or incoherence. Third, the order of our assertions (or denials) makes no difference to our coherence or incoherence. Fourth, asserting or denying less never takes one from coherence to incoherence. If it is rationally coherent to assert each of $\Gamma \cup \{A\}$ whilst denying each of $\Delta \cup \{B\}$, then it is rationally coherent to assert each of Γ and deny each of Δ. Equivalently, coherence can never be restored simply by asserting or denying more.

Fifth, if it is rationally coherent to assert each of Γ whilst denying each of Δ, then either asserting $\Gamma \cup \{A\}$ whilst denying Δ, or asserting Γ whilst denying $\Delta \cup \{A\}$, must be coherent. Equivalently, if it would be incoherent to assert $\Gamma \cup \{A\}$ whilst denying Δ and likewise incoherent to assert Γ whilst denying $\Delta \cup \{A\}$, then it is incoherent to Γ whilst denying Δ. These five principles correspond exactly to the *structural rules* of the sequent calculus shown in figure 7.4.

$$\frac{\quad}{A \vdash A} \text{ IDENTITY} \qquad \frac{\Gamma, A, A \vdash B, B, \Delta}{\Gamma, A \vdash B, \Delta} \text{ CONTRACTION}$$

$$\frac{\Gamma, A, B \vdash C, D, \Delta}{\Gamma, B, A \vdash D, C, \Delta} \text{ EXCHANGE} \qquad \frac{\Gamma \vdash \Delta}{\Gamma, A \vdash B, \Delta} \text{ THINNING}$$

$$\frac{\Gamma, A \vdash \Delta \qquad \Gamma \vdash A, \Delta}{\Gamma \vdash \Delta} \text{ CUT}$$

Figure 7.5: STRUCTURAL RULES

In these rules, I'll call the sequents above the line *upper sequents* and those below the line *lower sequents*. In general, rules may have one or two upper sequents, but always a single lower sequent. In standard presentations of the sequent calculus (see, e.g., Buss 1998), Γ and Δ are either sequences (i.e., lists) of sentences, or *multisets*, in which each element may occur one or more times. (We can treat a multiset Γ as a standard set Δ coupled with a function $\#\# : \Delta \longrightarrow \mathbb{N}$, with $\#\#x$ telling us how many occurrences of x appear in Γ.) The order of sentences matters in a sequence of sentences, but not in a multiset; hence in presentations using multisets, EXCHANGE comes for free.

In addition to the structural rules, we add *logical rules* for the connectives. (I'll focus on the simple case of a propositional language; extension to a first-order language is easy. And I'll focus on classical proof systems, but again, this is not essential. We could even encode non-monotonic inference rules, if we wanted (Jago 2009a).) Rather than introduction and elimination rules, we have *left* and *right* rules for each connective: details below.

The logical rules tell us how to manipulate logically complex sentences in a proof. The structural rules give us ways to jiggle

$$\frac{\Gamma, \neg A \vdash A, \Delta}{\Gamma, \neg A \vdash \Delta} \ \neg\text{L} \qquad \frac{\Gamma, A \vdash \neg A, \Delta}{\Gamma \vdash \neg A, \Delta} \ \neg\text{R}$$

$$\frac{\Gamma, A \vee B, A \vdash \Delta \qquad \Gamma, A \vee B, B \vdash \Delta}{\Gamma, A \vee B \vdash \Delta} \ \vee\text{L}$$

$$\frac{\Gamma \vdash A, B, A \vee B, \Delta}{\Gamma \vdash A \vee B, \Delta} \ \vee\text{R} \qquad \frac{\Gamma, A \wedge B, A, B \vdash \Delta}{\Gamma, A \wedge B \vdash \Delta} \ \wedge\text{L}$$

$$\frac{\Gamma \vdash A, A \wedge B, \Delta \qquad \Gamma \vdash B, A \wedge B, \Delta}{\Gamma \vdash A \wedge B, \Delta} \ \wedge\text{R}$$

$$\frac{\Gamma, A \rightarrow B \vdash A, \Delta \qquad \Gamma, A \rightarrow B, B \vdash \Delta}{\Gamma, A \rightarrow B \vdash \Delta} \ \rightarrow\text{L}$$

$$\frac{\Gamma, A \vdash B, A \rightarrow B, \Delta}{\Gamma \vdash A \rightarrow B, \Delta} \ \rightarrow\text{R}$$

Figure 7.6: LOGICAL RULES

sequents into the right form for further rules to be applied. In this sense, logical rules play an important normative role, whereas structural rules are mere admin. Given that our overall aim is to use proof rules to impose a normative structure on worlds, our interest is in the logical rules only. But we do not want to lose the proving power to which the structural rules standardly contribute.

Accordingly, I will work with a slightly non-standard system, containing only logical rules (shown in figure 7.6) plus a modified IDENTITY. In this system, Γ and Δ in a sequent $\Gamma \vdash \Delta$ will be sets, rather than multisets or sequences of sentences. This renders both CONTRACTION and EXCHANGE unnecessary (that is, both rules are automatically built into our system of rules). Moreover, I will require all sentences appearing in the lower sequent of a rule to appear in all upper sequents as well, so that (reading rules bottom-to-top) sentences are never 'forgotten' in a proof.

In practice, proofs are constructed bottom-up, beginning with the sequent to be proved and working upwards, applying the rules from lower sequent to upper sequent(s). In each case, IDENTITY is our goal. But in the version of the system I've presented, the logical rules require us to carry all sentences with us as we construct the tree from root upwards, and so we will never get to an instance of $A \vdash A$ (unless that's all we start with). So we need to generalise the IDENTITY rule to:

$$\frac{}{\Gamma, A \vdash A, \Delta} \quad \text{IDENTITY}^+$$

A proof of a sequent $\Gamma \vdash \Delta$ is then a tree of sequents generated by these rules, whose root is $\Gamma \vdash \Delta$ and whose leaves are all instances of IDENTITY$^+$. (A leaf in a graph is a vertex (or node) with no outgoing arrow, hence found at the end of each branch.)

In this system (including IDENTITY$^+$), we can dispense with all the structural rules from figure 7.4. Since we are working with sets of sentences, CONTRACTION and EXCHANGE are built in to the system. THINNING is unnecessary, for if we could construct a proof:

$$\frac{\dfrac{A \vdash A}{\vdots}}{\dfrac{\Gamma \vdash \Delta}{\Gamma, B \vdash C, \Delta}}$$

using THINNING, we can also construct a proof

$$\frac{\dfrac{\Gamma, B, A \vdash A, C, \Delta}{\vdots}}{\Gamma, B \vdash C, \Delta}$$

without using THINNING (since the first line is an instance of IDENTITY$^+$). We can also dispense with CUT since, as Gentzen proved, any sequent provable using CUT in the standard system can be proved without it (at the cost of larger proofs).

Our rules are thus IDENTITY$^+$, plus the logical rules in figure 7.6. These rules are all *strong* inference rules, in the sense of Buss (1998). This system is equivalent to the standard sequent calculus: any sequent derivable in one system is derivable in the other. Hence the new system is sound and complete with respect to the truth-table semantics.

How do we go from these rules to our target normative structure on worlds? A sequent $\Gamma \vdash \Delta$ says that asserting (the sentences in) Γ whilst denying Δ would be incoherent. Thus, if $\Gamma \vdash \Delta$ is a valid sequent, then a world according to which each of Γ is true and each of Δ false is incoherent. Double worlds (§5.6) have precisely the structure of explicitly representing such-and-such as being the case and such-and-such as not being the case. This is no coincidence!

Recall from §5.6 that a double world $w = \langle w^+, w^- \rangle$ is a pair of sets of worldmaking sentences (or, if you prefer, a pair of single ersatz worlds). World w represents A as being that case if and only if w^+ represents that A (which is so if and only if 'A^*' $\in w^+$, where 'A^*' is the translation of 'A' into the worldmaking language); and represents B as not being the case iff w^- represents that B (which is so if and only if 'B^*' $\in w^-$). Note that w not representing that A is not the same as w representing that $\neg A$. World w may say nothing whatsoever about whether A, in which case it represents neither that A nor that $\neg A$.

The proof structures established by the sequent calculus, therefore, automatically establish structures on double worlds. Suppose we take 'A', 'B' etc. to range over worldmaking sentences and 'Γ', 'Δ' etc. to range over sets of worldmaking sentences. Then, for every sequent $\Gamma \vdash \Delta$, there is a corresponding double world $w = \langle \Gamma, \Delta \rangle$ according to which all sentences in Γ are true and all in Δ are false. This sequent is valid iff w is logically inconsistent, for $\Gamma \vdash \Delta$ if and only if the combined truth of each 'A' $\in \Gamma$ is logically incompatible with the combined falsity of each 'B' $\in \Delta$.

Since each sequent in each rule instance can be thought of as a double world, each rule instance itself can be thought of as a lower double world, corresponding to the lower sequent, paired with a set of upper double worlds, corresponding to the upper sequent or sequents. (This is exactly the form that the structure on epistemic space will take: see the definition of relation T below.) Thus, we can re-write each of our sequent rules so that they have the form:

$$\frac{u}{w} \quad \text{or} \quad \frac{u \quad v}{w}$$

A rule of the former form tells us that if u is inconsistent, then w is inconsistent (and hence, if w is consistent, then so is u). A rule of the later form tells us that if both u and v are inconsistent, then w is inconsistent (and hence, if w is consistent, then so is at least one of u and v).

Proofs are tree-shaped diagrams built from these rules. We can use this fact to impose a proof-like structure on our worlds, by replacing rules of the kind shown above with tree diagrams:

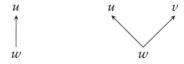

Note how the arrows follow sequent rules from bottom to top. This is the consistency-preserving direction: if w is consistent, then u (in the left diagram) and at least one of u and v (in the right diagram) is consistent too. (This is also the order in which, in practice, proofs are constructed.)

In this way, given double worlds $w_i = \langle \Gamma_i, \Delta_i \rangle$, we transform a proof of the form:

$$\cfrac{\Gamma_4 \vdash \Delta_4 \quad \cfrac{\cfrac{\Gamma_7 \vdash \Delta_7}{\Gamma_5 \vdash \Delta_5}}{\Gamma_2 \vdash \Delta_2} \quad \cfrac{\Gamma_6 \vdash \Delta_6}{\Gamma_3 \vdash \Delta_3}}{\Gamma_1 \vdash \Delta_1}$$

into the structure on double worlds shown in figure 7.7. I'll call these tree diagrams *world graphs*. Now recall that a proof of $\Gamma \vdash \Delta$ is a tree of sequents whose root is $\Gamma \vdash \Delta$ and whose leaves are all instances of

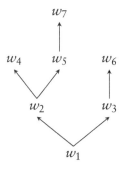

Figure 7.7: A WORLD GRAPH

IDENTITY$^+$. Such instances correspond to worlds $\langle w^+, w^- \rangle$ where w^+ and w^- overlap on some sentence 'A' (i.e., $w^+ \cap w^- \neq \varnothing$). Call such worlds *terminals*. A world graph then corresponds to a proof when all its leaves are terminals. So I'll call a world graph whose leaves are all terminals a *world proof*.

Given the soundness of our rules and the way world proofs are constructed from rule instances, for any world proof P, the double world $w = \langle w^+, w^- \rangle$ at the root of P is logically inconsistent (and so the sequent $w^+ \vdash w^-$ is valid). Consistent worlds, therefore, are never found at the root of (or anywhere else in) a world proof. Conversely, for any world w, if w is logically inconsistent then, given the completeness of the proof rules and the way world proofs are constructed by rule instances, there is a world proof P with w at its root. The intuitive idea (made precise below) is then that worlds associated with small world proofs are fairly blatantly inconsistent, whereas worlds associated with very large world proofs only are subtly inconsistent. We take the latter worlds (along with all those worlds not associated with any world proof), but not the former worlds, to be epistemically possible.

The details of this approach need to be made more precise: I'll get to them below. Before that, I need to address the second problem raised at the start of this section, concerning the arbitrariness of our choice of proof system. Had we used some other (deductively equivalent) proof system, we would have imposed a different structure on worlds. This alternative structure might treat some world w, deemed epistemically impossible by our structure, as being epistemically possible (or vice versa). This arbitrariness will then spread throughout our account of epistemic contents.

In responding to the worry, all we have at our disposal are facts about the nature of worlds and facts about the meanings of the logical connectives. If these do not pin down a unique structure on worlds, then the arbitrariness objection will bite hard. I'll argue, however, that these facts alone uniquely pin down the sequent system I've just described.

Let us begin with facts about the nature of worlds. Worlds are pairs of sets of worldmaking sentences, $\langle \Gamma, \Delta \rangle$. So, whatever proof system we use, its rules must take inputs of that form. But pairs of sets of sentences are by definition multi-conclusion sequents and hence our proof system must be a multi-conclusion sequent system. Moreover, it must be a system whose rules act on sets (rather than sequences or multi-sets) of sentences. This much is fixed purely by the nature of worlds.

Sequent systems which act on sets of sentences do not include the 'weak' structural rules CONTRACTION, EXCHANGE or THINNING. What remains to be done, therefore, is to determine (i) the form of the identity axioms, (ii) the logical rules, and (iii) the presence or absence of cut. For (i), we need only the normative principle that worlds which represent that it is both the case and not the case that A (for some 'A') are trivially a priori impossible. In terms of world-proofs, this means that any such world can be a leaf node of a proof. This fixes the form of the identity axioms as the IDENTITY$^+$ rule, used above.

For (ii), we rely on the fact that the connectives have their standard classical meanings. For a proof system to be complete with respect to these meanings, we need at least two rules for each connective, one acting on the left of sequents and one acting on their right. What's on the left of a sequent w captures what is the case, according to w, and what's on the right captures what fails to be the case, according to w. Now consider the case of conjunctions in general. If it is the case that $A \wedge B$ then it is the case both that A and that B; and if it is not the case that $A \wedge B$ then either it is not the case that A or not the case that B. That is precisely what the rules ∧L and ∧R say. This is the sense in which these rules, and only these rules, are determined by the meaning of '∧'. The same goes for the other left and right rules listed above and the meanings of the corresponding connectives. These rules and only these rules are determined by the meaning of those connectives.

The only remaining point to settle is the presence or absence of CUT. This point is crucial, since including CUT will greatly affect proof length. CUT allows us to relate worlds w, u, and v where w doesn't feature some C as a subsentence of any sentence, u represents that C is not the case, and v represents that C is the case. This kind of rule isn't determined purely by the meanings of the connectives in the sense given above, since there is no connective involved. So, given that relations between worlds are allowed only when they're determined by the meanings of connectives, we should adopt a system without CUT.

I've argued that, given just those facts about the nature of worlds and the meaning of the connectives, we can uniquely pin down the proof system described above. (Well, not quite. In the rules above, all sentences appearing in the lower sequent also appear in the upper sequents. This isn't mandated by the nature of worlds or by the meanings of the connectives. But this does not matter, because dropping this requirement would not affect proof size.)

Note that I am not arguing here that the sequent system set out above is superior to others qua proof system. The claim is merely that, given our task of imposing a normative structure on worlds which is mandated by the meanings of the logical constants, the above system is the correct choice.

I've presented a proof system, argued that it is the correct choice for our purposes and briefly sketched how it translates into world-proofs. The final task is to combine all possible world-proofs into a single normative structure on worlds. Because world proofs are branching diagrams, we need some way of tracking which branches in the total structure belong to the same proof and which do not. One way to do this is using AND-OR diagrams, in which we link together arrows that belong to the same proof. A small portion of this AND-OR structure might look like figure 7.8. We obtain world proofs from an

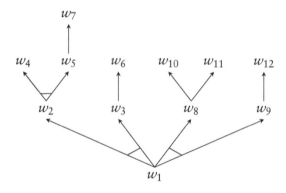

Figure 7.8: AN AND-OR STRUCTURE CONTAINING WORLD PROOFS

AND-OR diagram by taking sub-trees of it, so that we never split up arrows that have been linked together. Thus, the AND-OR structure in figure 7.8 contains the world proof shown in figure 7.7. It also contains the world proof:

$$w_8 \longrightarrow w_{11}$$

but it does not contain the world proof

$$w_1 \longrightarrow w_3 \longrightarrow w_6$$

as this breaks up the joined arrows $w_1 \longrightarrow w_2$ and $w_1 \longrightarrow w_3$.

Now let's formalise all of this. To capture a rule, it is easier to relate the lower world to the *set* of the upper worlds, rather than to each of the upper worlds individually. If W_d is the set of all double worlds, we use a relation $T \subseteq W_d \times 2^{W_d}$, defined as the set of all pairs $\langle w, \{u\} \rangle$ plus all pairs $\langle w, \{u, v\} \rangle$ for which there are rule instances, respectively:

$$\frac{u}{w} \quad \text{and} \quad \frac{u \qquad v}{w}$$

In this way, the AND-OR structure shown in figure 7.8 on double words is captured by the following T-transitions:

$$w_1 \xrightarrow{T} \{w_2, w_3\} \qquad w_1 \xrightarrow{T} \{w_8, w_9\} \qquad w_2 \xrightarrow{T} \{w_4, w_5\}$$

$$w_3 \xrightarrow{T} \{w_6\} \qquad w_5 \xrightarrow{T} \{w_7\} \qquad w_8 \xrightarrow{T} \{w_{10}\}$$

$$w_8 \xrightarrow{T} \{w_{11}\} \qquad w_9 \xrightarrow{T} \{w_{12}\}$$

We can easily recapture world proofs from this T-structure. The set of world graphs $\mathcal{G}_T$ given by T is defined as follows: $G \in \mathcal{G}_T$ if and only if G is a rooted directed acyclic graph with vertices $V_G \subseteq W_d$ and edges $E_G \subseteq W_d^2$, restricted so that $\langle w, u \rangle \in E_G$ only if:

$$\exists X \subseteq W_d(\langle w, X \rangle \in T \ \& \ u \in X \ \& \ \forall x(x \in X \leftrightarrow \langle w, x \rangle \in E_G))$$

In a world graph G, each vertex has zero, one or two children. Leaves are vertices with zero children. G is a world proof iff all its leaves are terminals. The *size* of G, $|G|$, is the number of non-leaf vertices it contains (which corresponds to the number of inference tokens captured by G, since each instance of IDENTITY$^+$ is excluded from the count). Let $\mathcal{G}_w = \{G \mid G \text{ is a world proof whose root is } w\}$.

We can now totally order the double worlds in W_d using the sizes of their associated world proofs. First, we set

$$\#w = \begin{cases} \min\{\,|G| \mid G \in \mathcal{G}_w\} & \text{if } \mathcal{G}_w \neq \emptyset \\ \omega & \text{otherwise} \end{cases}$$

Next, we set $w \preceq u$ iff $\#w \leq \#u$. Terminal worlds (those w such that $w^- \cap w^+ \neq \emptyset$) are $\preceq$-minimal elements, associated with world proofs of size 0. These are the worlds which are most blatantly inconsistent of all. Worlds not at the root of any world proof are $\preceq$-maximal. These are the consistent worlds.

All other worlds are inconsistent, but not all inconsistent worlds are on a par. Intuitively, $\preceq$ orders worlds by how blatantly inconsistent they are, with more blatantly inconsistent worlds lower in the order than less blatantly inconsistent ones. When $w \leq u$, the inconsistencies in u are buried at least as deep as those in w. So, if one accepts w as an epistemically possible world, then one should also accept u as being epistemically possible.

This does not yet give us an account of which worlds are epistemically possible and so we have not yet delineated the boundaries of epistemic space. But we have constrained it with the $\leq$ ordering: whenever we include a world w in epistemic space, we must also include worlds u for which $w \leq u$. The remaining problem is to say where the boundary falls. This is not a problem specific to bounded rationality concerns: it crops up when we deal with any vague predicate. This is the point (as mentioned in §7.2) at which we 'plug in' whatever we think is the correct view of vagueness.

If vague cases are cases for which there is no fact of the matter either way, then we should partition the worlds into three classes: those that are epistemically possible, those that are not, and those for which there is no fact of the matter either way. This partition is constrained by $\leq$ as follows: if w is an epistemically possible world, then so are all u such that $w \leq u$; if w is not an epistemically possible world, then neither is any u such that $u \leq w$; and if there is no fact of the matter regarding w_1 and w_2, and $w_1 \leq w_2$, then there is no fact of the matter regarding any u such that $w_1 \leq u \leq w_2$.

Epistemicists, by contrast, will partition worlds into just two classes: the epistemically possible worlds and the epistemically impossible worlds, again constrained by $\leq$ in the obvious way. Many-valued accounts will assign a degree of truth $\delta_w \in [0,1]$ to 'w is an epistemically possible world', constrained so that $\delta_w \leq \delta_u$ iff $w \leq u$. (I gave an account along these lines in Jago 2009b.) On this degree-theoretic view, epistemic space has fuzzy boundaries and can be treated as a fuzzy set of worlds. (A fuzzy set X is a pair consisting of a classical set Y and a function from Y to $[0,1]$, known as the *membership function*, assigning to each member of Y a degree of membership in X. In the case of epistemic space, the underlying set is W_d, the set of all double worlds and the membership function is δ.)

Whichever approach to vagueness we adopt, we resolve the vagueness in 'epistemically possible world' in just the same way we resolve the vagueness in 'small number' (in the context of thinking of the size of proof-trees), so that a world w is an epistemic possibility just in case #w is not a small number. This approach then links up well with the intuitive guide notions of epistemic possibility (7.2)–(7.6) discussed in §7.1. Since small values for #w correspond to small proofs showing w to be inconsistent (and hence impossible), the epistemically possible worlds are the ones that represent no obvious or trivial *a priori* impossibilities discoverable through a small amount of logical reasoning.

7.5   Absurdity Revisited

In the account of epistemic space just presented, worlds are related together by the logical inference rules. We can think of the normative links between worlds as gradually 'unwinding' those subtle contradictions, until they become explicit. There is a loose end to consider, however: what if one does not agree that a world according to which some '*A*' is both true and false is absurd? I have been assuming that contradictions are absurd and hence that blatant contradictions are blatantly absurd. Worlds which represent that something both is and is not the case are epistemically impossible if any world is. Call this the *key principle of epistemic content*. If someone denies this principle, then she will not agree that we have succeeded in relating subtle absurdities to blatant ones.

I have in mind those philosophers who hold either that true contradictions are possible, or that there actually are true contradictions. They will complain that I have assumed from the outset that contradictions are *a priori* absurd, hence not possible, and that without this (in their eyes, unwarranted) assumption, my account will collapse.

Dialethists such as Priest (1979, 1987, 2002) hold that some contradictions are not only possible truths, but are actual truths.

Perhaps the main motivation for this view is the (strengthened) liar paradox, which focuses on a sentence

(λ) this sentence is not true.

If λ has a classical truth-value and if the inference rules for 'true' and 'false' work in the way we expect them to, then we can infer that λ is both true and false. Using the usual rules for negation and conjunction, we can then infer that '$\neg\lambda$' is true (since λ is false) and hence that the explicit contradiction '$\lambda \wedge \neg\lambda$' is true. The dialethist motivates her position by claiming that this is the simplest response to the liar paradox (Priest 1987). (For more background and discussion of the dialethist approach to the liar, see the papers in Beall 2003, 2007 and Priest et al. 2004.)

On the view I have developed, worlds that represent explicit contradictions are paradigmatically epistemically impossible. This feature is captured in the IDENTITY$^+$ rule. This rule allows such explicitly contradictory worlds to be the leaves of world-proofs. In effect, this means that no world is more epistemically impossible than an explicitly contradictory world.

As a consequence, no such explicitly contradictory world is ever part of an epistemic content, for such contents comprise only epistemically possible worlds. Moreover, when one entertains a belief, or forms an assumption, what one thereby believes or assumes is an epistemic content. Consequently, on my view, explicit contradictions are literally unbelievable; one cannot even entertain their truth as assumptions or hypotheses.

The problem is that (it is claimed) people do believe in true contradictions. Dialethists believe that the liar is both true and not true. And even non-dialethists can entertain this belief, if only to attempt to show why it is wrong. But I claim that none of this is possible. As I seriously suggesting that, for the past 40 years or so, Graham Priest's professed philosophical beliefs are in fact completely empty? (Williamson (2007, chapter 4) runs an objection along these lines.) No, I'm not suggesting that. Priest is indisputably one of the world's leading experts on the logic and philosophy of truth, negation, the liar and surrounding areas. That he is so involves his beliefs. So, on anyone's view, Priest must have substantial, contentful beliefs in these areas.

To reconcile this fact with the theoretical framework I've developed, we first need to consider the kind of logical concepts the dialethist deploys. She will say 'the liar is both true and false', but does not accept that this assertion entails every other sentence. She denies that 'A' and '$\neg A$' together entail arbitrary sentences: $A, \neg A \vdash B$. But this sequent is proved in just two steps using the (classical) rules from §7.4:

$$\frac{A, \neg A \vdash A, B}{A, \neg A \vdash B} \quad \begin{array}{l} \text{IDENTITY}^+ \\[4pt] \neg\text{L} \end{array}$$

So the dialethist cannot accept the $\neg$L rule. Her notion of negation differs from the classical one. Let's call her concept *negation**. Semantically, *negation** functions in accordance with the paraconsistent rules set out in §6.2.

Much of Priest's efforts over the years have been devoted to showing that paraconsistent logical systems containing *negation** in place of classical negation are mathematically and conceptually coherent. I agree. One can entertain beliefs and assumptions about paraconsistent logical systems, just as one can about intuitionistic systems. They are beliefs involving *negation**, which I would express using 'not*'.

In particular, when a dialethist uses the term 'the liar', she refers to a content involving *negation**, which I might express as 'this sentence is not* true'. She asserts of it that it is both true and not* true. Both that content and what she asserts of it are genuine epistemic contents, non-empty sets of deeply epistemically possible worlds and hence are the kind of content that one may believe or entertain as an assumption.

Priest (and other dialethists) agree with me that their relevant beliefs involve *negation** rather than classical negation. But they do not agree that their use of the English 'not' differs from the standard use, which I take to mean *classical negation*. (Williamson (2007, chapter 4) too argues that one may differ significantly from others in the inferences one is prepared to draw using a word such as 'not' and yet still mean the same as those others by it. I disagree: in at least some cases, certain inferences are essentially tied up with the concept in question. I am claiming that the concept of negation (as expressed by 'not' in English) and the rules ¬L and ¬R provide one such case. I return to this point below.) Insofar as this particular disagreement concerns what a word of English means, one may have contentful beliefs either way. So again, I am not forced to say that the dialethist's beliefs are empty of content.

I've argued that the key principle that explicit contradictions (expressed using 'not' and cognates) are epistemically contentless is compatible with there being contentful dialethist beliefs. This defends the key principle against what seemed to be a strong empirical challenge. But it does not provide any positive justification for the key principle. Can any be found?

It is tempting to say that no justification can be given. To give a justification, one must engage in a debate in which both sides are genuine epistemic possibilities, thereby undermining the very claim we are attempting to justify. If this is the case, then I must dogmatically defend the key principle. This position is similar to the one Lewis adopts on the law of non-contradiction. He notes that his refusal to question non-contradiction's validity 'may seem dogmatic':

> And it is; I am affirming the very thesis that Routley and Priest have called into question—contrary to the rules of debate—I decline to defend it. Furthermore, I concede that it is indefensible against their challenge. They have called so much into question that I have no foothold on undisputed ground. (Lewis 1982, 101)

I think we can improve on the 'dogmatic' position. First, note that the key principle concerns explicitly contradictory contents involving *classical negation*. It does not say anything about contents formed from conjunction and negation*. Indeed, I've allowed that the latter kinds of contents are epistemically contentful and hence believable. Everyone, dialethists included, can accept that certain contents formed from conjunction and classical negation are not epistemically contentful. Indeed, this is why dialethists often claim that classical negation is defective. My opponent should not reject the key principle. Rather, she should claim that classical negation does not play a central normative role in our epistemic practises.

On the approach I've developed, our epistemic practices are captured by imposing normative relations on worlds, interpreted as representing that such-and-such is the case and that so-and-so is not the case. The dialethist will read this last 'not' in terms of negation*. Accordingly, she will not feel any repulsive epistemic force from worlds $\langle\{\ldots, A, \ldots\}, \{\ldots, A, \ldots\}\rangle$. (These are the worlds that correspond to the IDENTITY$^+$ rule.) But, if my account is to get off the ground, it is essential that such worlds have this repulsive normative force.

The focus of the debate has now shifted from the acceptability of the key principle to the correct interpretation of the 'not' in 'world w represents that such-and-such is not the case'. The question is whether 'not' in English is interpreted as classical negation or the dialethist's negation*. The crucial difference in practical use between classical negation and negation* is that the former, but not the latter, excludes the truth of the content it operates on. Interpreted dialethically, 'not A' does not exclude 'A', for both may be true simultaneously.

In communicating with one another (and in particular in expressing our beliefs), we need ways of indicating what contents we accept (or assert) and what we reject (or deny). We could do this by, say, putting a thumb up or down as we speak. But we don't do this. Instead, we interpret a good deal of speech as assertion and so we require a way of marking rejection of a content by asserting some other related content. As it happens, we do this by using 'no' and 'not'.

We mark rejection of 'A' by asserting 'not A'. Since rejection of some content precludes the simultaneous acceptance of that same content, 'not' must mean *classical negation* and not *negation**. (The dialethist denies that 'not' has the function of relating assertions to denials in this way (Berto 2008). She is thereby making an empirical mistake about the way we in fact use 'not'.)

In sum, we can adopt the key principle and still attribute contentful beliefs (invoking negation*) to dialethists. We have good reason to think that our uses of 'not' function to exclude the truth of what is negated and hence that 'not' is used as classical negation. Worlds that break this rule, by representing that some *A* both is and is not the case, are thus trivially impossible, just as the key principle says.

Chapter Summary

I began by clarifying the target notion of an *epistemically possible world* (§7.1). Worlds in epistemic space are structured by the normative links given by basic inference rules (§7.2). This normative structure 'unwinds' the contradictions found in logically impossible worlds in a step-by-step way. A world is epistemically possible, and hence appears in epistemic space, if and only if any contradictions found in it are not unwound into trivial contradictions in just a small number of steps (§7.2). It is then indeterminate just which worlds are epistemically possible.

In response to Bjerring's objection (§7.3), I argued that worlds are judged to be epistemically possible (or impossible) on the basis of what they represent as being the case. They are judged to be epistemically impossible when they are trivially inconsistent, but not when they are trivially incomplete. Trivial incompleteness in epistemic space is unavoidable. This leads to the problem of epistemic oversights (to which I will return in §8.4).

The normative structure on worlds in epistemic space is given by considering a variant of the sequent calculus, with double worlds playing the role of sequents (§7.4). Finally, I defended the key principle that explicitly contradictory worlds are epistemically impossible if any are and indicated how this approach is compatible with the dialethist's beliefs being contentful (§7.5).

8

Epistemic Content

In this chapter, I use the epistemic space developed in chapter 7 to construct various epistemic notions of content, including the content of valid but non-trivial deductions. I give formal models of knowledge and belief states in which accessibility relations are indeterminate and prove that epistemic oversights are always indeterminate cases of knowledge. I then discuss hyperintensions and epistemic closure and consider the question of whether the impossible worlds approach I have been developing is trivial.

8.1 Epistemic Contents

In the previous chapter, I constructed a normative epistemic space of worlds, structured by proof rules. This space is highly structured and accordingly, it allows us to construct highly structured notions of content. It is these notions of content that are in play when we discuss knowledge, belief, cognitive information and cognitive significance, including the information given by valid deductions. I'll refer generically to these as epistemic contents.

The basic notions of epistemic content are derived from the standard possible-worlds account. As a first-pass approximation, epistemic contents are sets of epistemically possible worlds. These contents capture a notion of epistemic information in the sense that they rule out various would-be possibilities. Thus, epistemic contents are far more fine-grained than the corresponding possible-worlds notion of content (for there are epistemically possible worlds far more fine-grained than any metaphysically or logically possible world). But (as we shall see) epistemic contents are also structured by normative principles, just as epistemic space is. Epistemic contents are derived from regions of epistemic space and so they inherit epistemic space's normative structure.

The simplest notion of epistemic content we can construct is a region of epistemic space, that is, a set of epistemically possible worlds. On this simple view, the epistemic content of 'A' (relative to some context of utterance) is the set of all epistemically possible worlds which represent that A. Epistemic contents thus inherit the vagueness of 'epistemically possible world'. Epistemic contents have indeterminate membership, for w is found in the epistemic content of 'A' iff (i) w represents that A and (ii) w is epistemically possible. Since it may be indeterminate whether w is epistemically possible, it may also be indeterminate whether w is in the content of 'A'. (Just how this vagueness in content is modelled depends, once again, on one's preferred account of vagueness (§7.4).)

We do well to enrich this notion of content, in several directions. In one direction, we can move from epistemically possible worlds to *centred* epistemically possible worlds, which specify an agent and a time at the 'centre' of the world. We can think of a centred epistemically possible world as a triple $\langle w, i, t \rangle$, where w is a regular epistemically possible world, i is an agent and t a time. Centred epistemically possible worlds help us to account for the content of indexical sentences (those including 'I', 'now' and so on). Since indexicals are not my concern here, I won't say any more about centred epistemically possible worlds. It would be easy to adapt what I say below about (non-centred) worlds to incorporate centred worlds.

A further direction in which the basic notion of epistemic content can be enriched is by considering an account symmetrical between what is true and what is false according to a world. To do so, we pay attention not only to the worlds according to which 'A' is true, but also to the worlds according to which 'A' is false. Such sets give us the *positive* and *negative* contents for '*A*', denoted '$|A|^+$' and '$|A|^-$', respectively. Epistemic contents are then positive content-negative content pairs, $\langle |A|^+, |A|^- \rangle$. This is the notion of content I'll adopt.

In general, a negative content $|A|^-$ is not identical to the positive content $|\neg A|^+$ and we do well to be sensitive to this difference. Since we allow highly incomplete worlds to be epistemically possible, the positive content of a sentence as trivial as '$A \vee \neg A$' is far from universal. There are many epistemically possible worlds not included in that positive content. Yet the negative content $|A \vee \neg A|^-$ is empty, for worlds associated with a world proof of size 1 are not epistemically possible. Although '$A \vee \neg A$' fails to be true according to all epistemically possible worlds, it is not false according to any of them. This fact allows us to recapture the idea that sentences such as '$A \vee \neg A$' are trivial and uninformative (see §8.2 below). To do so, we will need to pay attention to negative as well as positive contents.

As well as defining contents as (pairs of) sets of epistemically possible worlds, we can define more complex relational structures on epistemic space and use these to account for the epistemic and doxastic states of agents. This is the idea of analysing such states in terms of epistemic accessibility relations, familiar from epistemic logic, as discussed in §1.2. I'll say how these structures work and address some problems that arise with them in §8.4 below.

Before going further, I should mention a serious problem that remains for the theory of epistemic content. I'll then spend the rest of this chapter discussing various notions of epistemic content in more detail and showing how these notions can be used to respond to the problem.

The basic problem, touched upon in §7.3, is that the structure on epistemic space respects one kind of normative relation between worlds, but does not seem to respect another. The respected normative constraint is the one that excludes blatantly impossible worlds from counting as epistemic possibilities. The normative constraint that appears not to be respected is the one which links incomplete worlds to slightly more complete worlds. A world which represents nothing but that $A \wedge B$ seems suspect; shouldn't it also represent that A and that B? As a consequence of such worlds, the content of '$A \wedge B$' is not included in the content of 'A', as it would be if contents were sets of classical possible worlds only. So the normative link between '$A \wedge B$' and 'A' is not one of content-inclusion.

As discussed in §7.3, the issues here are subtle. A world which represents only that $A \wedge B$ does not thereby represent 'A' as being false; it says nothing explicitly about whether A. But it does say something implicitly about whether A, since it says that $A \wedge B$. What should we make of this?

My stance is that, since we are interested in non-ideal notions of content, the distinction between representing both that A and that B on the one hand, and representing that $A \wedge B$ on the other, is unavoidable (see §7.3). The same goes for other trivially related sentences. Nevertheless, the account should acknowledge that the content of '$A \wedge B$' is intimately related to the contents of 'A' and 'B'. Similarly, we would like to acknowledge that, although worlds may represent that $A \wedge B$ but not that A, there is nevertheless a strong sense in which the inference from '$A \wedge B$' to 'A' is trivial and uninformative. And again, although we have to acknowledge epistemic oversights in a non-ideal agent's epistemic state (§7.3), we should be able to capture the intuition that there's something very strange in saying that an agent knows that A and that $A \rightarrow B$, but not that B.

The task for the remainder of this chapter, therefore, is to develop notions of epistemic content which respect these intuitions, as far as possible, whilst avoiding ideal contents (of the kind served up by the classical possible-worlds approach). I'll begin in §8.2 with an analysis of the content of valid deductions. This will provide us with a distinction between informative (i.e., contentful) and uninformative inferences, which will serve us well when discussing an agent's epistemic states in §8.4.

8.2 The Content of Deduction

The aim in this section (which draws on Jago 2013c) is to account for the intuitive idea that some (but not all) valid deductions are informative. The data to be accommodated are that some valid inferences are capable of extending our knowledge and hence should count as informative and non-trivial (§6.1); yet not all valid deductions are informative. It is highly implausible to claim that the deductive move from '$A \wedge B$' to 'A' is non-trivial and informative, in the way that a proof of Gödel's second incompleteness proof is non-trivial and informative. So it is no good to say that a proof of Gödel's second incompleteness theorem is informative because each tiny step in the proof is informative. Nor is it any good to locate the proof's informativeness at some particular step of the proof, since that merely pushes the problem further back: what makes that particular step of the proof informative?

In line with the approach adopted in chapter 1 and in §8.1 above, informativeness is a matter of ruling out various would-be possibilities (i.e., epistemically possible worlds). Hence, a valid deduction is informative if and only if the move from its premises to its conclusion throws out some epistemically possible worlds. I will speak of the content of a valid deduction $\Gamma \vdash A$, meaning the information we can obtain in performing that deduction, so that $\Gamma \vdash A$ is informative if and only if its content is non-empty.

The positive content of set of sentences Γ is the set of worlds according to which each 'A' $\in \Gamma$ is true and the negative content of Γ is the set of worlds according to which some 'A' $\in \Gamma$ is false:

$$|\Gamma|^+ = \bigcap_{\text{'}A\text{'}\in\Gamma} |A|^+ \quad \text{and} \quad |\Gamma|^- = \bigcup_{\text{'}A\text{'}\in\Gamma} |A|^-$$

A first attempt to capture the content of the deduction $\Gamma \vdash A$ is to consider the difference between the combined positive content of the premises Γ and the positive content of the conclusion 'A' (as in §6.2):

(8.1) $|\Gamma|^+ - |A|^+$

This is the set of all worlds according to which the premises, but not the conclusion, are true. Thinking dynamically, we think of this notion of content by first narrowing down epistemic space to the (positive) content of the premises. If 'A' is true throughout this region, then it would be uninformative to infer 'A' from Γ. If there are worlds in this region according to which 'A' is not true (that is, if $|\Gamma|^+ - |A|^+$ is non-empty) then the inference $\Gamma \vdash A$ is deemed informative.

The problem with this notion of content, however, is that it deems far too many inferences informative. This is a consequence of allowing highly incomplete (but not blatantly inconsistent) worlds to be epistemically possible. Suppose that Γ is consistent (or at least, not blatantly inconsistent) and 'A' $\notin \Gamma$. Then there is an epistemically possible world w such that $w^+ = \Gamma$ (so that Γ is the set of truths according to w), according to which 'A' is not true. Then $w \in |\Gamma|^+ - |A|^+$, hence $\Gamma \vdash A$ is deemed a contentful, informative inference, for any such Γ. As a consequence, $p, q \vdash p$ is deemed uninformative, yet $p \wedge q \vdash p$ and $p, q \vdash p \wedge q$ are deemed informative (where 'p' and 'q' are logically primitive sentences). Moreover, although $p, q \vdash p \wedge q$ is deemed informative, $p, \neg p \vdash p \wedge \neg p$ is not. These are consequences any decent notion of the content of deduction should avoid.

What we need to test, in order to find out whether the inference $\Gamma \vdash A$ is informative, is whether the combined truth of Γ is trivially incompatible with the falsity of 'A'. If they are trivially incompatible, then the inference is uninformative and the corresponding content is empty. So we analyse the content of the deduction $\Gamma \vdash A$ as:

(8.2) $$|\Gamma|^+ \cap |A|^-$$

The previous notion of content (8.1) failed because the worlds in $|\Gamma|^+ - |A|^+$ are not required to take a stand on whether A: they may say nothing either way as to whether A. But the analysis of content in (8.2) forces worlds to take a stand. If $|\Gamma|^+ \cap |A|^-$ is empty, then any world according to which the premises are true and the conclusion is false is not epistemically possible and hence there is no information to be gained by inferring 'A' from Γ. (Note that, restricting to classical possible worlds, (8.1) and (8.2) are equivalent.) This is the notion of the content of deduction with which I will work.

On this notion of content, truly trivial deductions are deemed contentless and hence uninformative, just as we want. For example, suppose that '$A \to B$' and 'A' are true and 'B' is false according to world w. Then there is a world proof with w at its root, which we can represent as:

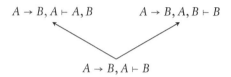

This graph has size 1 (since it contains just one non-leaf node), hence $\#w \leq 1$. Since epistemically possible worlds are associated only with relatively large world proofs (so that, for such worlds u, $\#u$ is relatively high), w is not epistemically possible. Hence the content of a *modus ponens* step '$A \to B$', 'A' to 'B', defined as $|A \to B|^+ \cap |A|^+ \cap |B|^-$, is empty. In this way, single *modus ponens* steps are correctly treated as being trivial and uninformative.

Not all valid deductions are treated as being uninformative, however. Suppose that worlds w for which $\#w \geq m$ are epistemically possible. Then the deduction

$$p_1, p_1 \to p_2, p_2 \to p_3, \ldots, p_{n-1} \to p_n \vdash p_n$$

is contentful when $n > m$. Its content consists of epistemically possible worlds according to which 'p_1' and each '$p_i \to p_{i+1}$' ($i < n$) is true and 'p_n' is false. We can verify that there exist such epistemically possible worlds as follows. Let w be such that $w^+ = (\bigcup_{i<n}\{\text{'}p_i \to p_{i+1}\text{'}\}) \cup \{\text{'}p_1\text{'}\}$ and $w^- = \{\text{'}p_n\text{'}\}$. The shortest world proof with w at its root corresponds to $n - 1$ applications of $\to$L, hence $\#w = n - 1 \geq m$ and so, by assumption, w counts as a scenario. There are then infinitely many epistemically possible worlds according to which 'p_1' and each '$p_i \to p_{i+1}$' ($i < n$) are true and 'p_n' is false: to construct one, we simply extend w^+ or w^- (or both) in a way that does not allow for a world proof smaller than the one just considered to be constructed. We thus have an account of content on which some but not all valid inferences are informative.

A worry mentioned in §8.1 above is that, on this account, the meanings of logical constants are not captured simply as content-inclusion relationships, as they are on the classical possible worlds account. On the latter account, we would have:

$$(8.3) \qquad |A \wedge B|^+ \subseteq |A|^+ \quad \text{and} \quad |A \to B|^+ \cap |A|^+ \subseteq |B|^+$$

These inclusion relationships capture (one aspect of) the meaning of '∧' and '→'. But, as we have seem, these inclusion relationships cannot be accepted without closing worlds under *conjunction elimination* and *modus ponens*.

Since agents are not logically omniscient with respect to these rules, it follows that (8.3) is false, at least as far as epistemic contents are concerned. (There may be other useful notions of content which do satisfy (8.3). But these notions are not the ones we need for analysing epistemic notions such as knowledge, belief or information.) The worry is that, without (8.3) in play, we have no way to capture at the level of content the normative link between '$A \wedge B$' and 'A', or between '$A \to B$', 'A' and 'B'.

This worry can be met by showing that these normative links can be captured at the level of content; indeed, they can be captured using inclusion relations between contents. Here's how. On the set of all epistemically possible worlds W_e, $|A|^{-c}$ (the set-theoretic complement of $|A|^-$, defined as $W_e - |A|^-$) contains all those worlds which do not represent that A is not the case. The classical possible worlds framework identifies $|A|^{-c}$ with $|A|^+$, since a classical possible world does not represent that it is not the case that A if and only if it does represent that A. Thus, on a domain of classical possible worlds, $|A|^+ \subseteq |B|^+$ holds iff $|A|^+ \subseteq |B|^{-c}$ holds and so the inclusion relationships in (8.3) are equivalent to:

$$(8.4) \qquad |A \wedge B|^+ \subseteq |A|^{-c} \quad \text{and} \quad |A \to B|^+ \cap |A|^+ \subseteq |B|^{-c}$$

On the totality of epistemic space, $|A|^{-c}$ is not identified with $|A|^+$, since an epistemically possible world may say nothing about whether A. Hence epistemic space draws a distinction between (8.1) and (8.2), whereas the classical space of worlds does not. Moreover, although epistemic space does not verify the inclusion relationships in (8.3), it does verify those in (8.4).

To see why this is so, suppose $|A \wedge B|^+ \nsubseteq |A|^{-c}$. Then, by definition, there is some epistemically possible world according to which '$A \wedge B$' is true but 'A' is false. But then w is at the root of the world proof of size 1, represented in figure 8.1.

$$A \wedge B, A, B \vdash A$$

$$\uparrow$$

$$A \wedge B \vdash A$$

Figure 8.1: WORLD PROOF FOR $A \wedge B \vdash A$

Hence $\#w \leq 1$ and so w is not an epistemically possible world: contradiction. A similar argument shows that $|A \to B|^+ \cap |A|^+ \subseteq |B|^{-c}$.

This is one way in which this epistemic notion of content captures the meanings of '$\wedge$' and '$\to$', by relating the content of '$A \wedge B$' to the content of 'A' and by relating the contents of '$A \to B$' and 'A' to the content of 'B'. The same goes for the other connectives: $|A|^+ \subseteq |A \vee B|^{-c}$, for example, corresponding to the trivial rule of *disjunction introduction*, $A \vdash A \vee B$. Similar results hold for trivial combinations of connectives. Since '$A \vee \neg A$' is trivially valid, $B \vdash A \vee \neg A$ is a trivial inference for any 'A'. This is captured at the level of content by the fact that $|B|^+ \subseteq |A \vee \neg A|^{-c}$.

Indeed, for any set of epistemically possible worlds X, we have $X \subseteq |A \vee \neg A|^{-c}$. This is because worlds according to which '$A \vee \neg A$' is false are not epistemically possible, since such worlds are associated with a world proof of size 2, as in figure 8.2. Since such worlds are not epistemically possible (since determinately, 2 is small), $|A \vee \neg A|^- = \varnothing$ and hence $|A \vee \neg A|^{-c}$ is the set of all epistemically possible worlds.

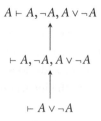

$$A \vdash A, \neg A, A \vee \neg A$$

$$\uparrow$$

$$\vdash A, \neg A, A \vee \neg A$$

$$\uparrow$$

$$\vdash A \vee \neg A$$

Figure 8.2: WORLD PROOF FOR $\vdash A \vee \neg A$

It follows that $X \subseteq |A \vee \neg A|^{-c}$ for any set of epistemically possible worlds X and so $|B|^+ \subseteq |A \vee \neg A|^{-c}$ for any 'A' whatsoever.

In summary, we have an account of content which counts some but not all valid deductions as informative. In particular, completely trivial inferences are treated as contentless and hence uninformative. In the next section, I'll pursue these ideas further and investigate a relation which captures the trivial consequences of a set of premises.

8.3   Trivial Consequences

In the previous section, I investigated a notion of content on which trivial deductions are contentless. Such deductions $\Gamma \vdash A$ correspond to content-inclusion relations of the form $|\Gamma|^+ \subseteq |A|^{-c}$. In this section (which draws on Jago 2013e), I take this idea further, by formalising a system of *trivial consequence* which captures these content-inclusion relationships.

The inclusion relationships $|\Gamma|^+ \subseteq |A|^{-c}$ investigated in the previous section are defined relative to a fixed class of worlds: the class of all epistemically possible worlds. As such, these inclusion relationships give us a kind of *modal entailment* from Γ to 'A'. (In a classical setting, Γ modally entails 'A' relative to worlds W when all worlds $w \in W$ which represent that Γ also represent that A. Our examples do not quite fit this pattern. Our examples hold when, for any epistemically possible world according to which the Γs are true, 'A' is not false.) Logical entailments, by contrast, are defined over a class of models, each of which may contain many worlds. My aim here is to treat trivial consequence as a logical entailment relation. Accordingly, I'll need to work with a class of models of epistemic space.

I will fix on a formal object language $\mathcal{L}$ which, for simplicity, will be a set of logically primitive sentences $\mathcal{P}$ closed under '$\neg$', '$\wedge$', '$\vee$' and '$\rightarrow$'. (Extension to quantified languages is simple.) I will work with structures $E = \langle W, V^+, V^-, \# \rangle$, where W is a set of arbitrary entities (thought of as fine-grained worlds), V^+ and V^- are *labelling functions* of type $W \longrightarrow 2^{\mathcal{L}}$, assigning a set of sentences to each world in W and $\#$ is a ranking function of type $W \longrightarrow \mathbb{N} \cup \{\omega\}$, assigning an ordinal number to each world in W. We think of $V^+ w$ and $V^- w$ as the sets of truths and falsehoods according to w, respectively. The rank of E is the smallest $\#w$ such that $w \in W$, that is, $\min\{\#w \mid w \in W\}$.

(The entities in W need not be the double worlds of §5.6. They are the 'worlds' of formal structures. They can be any entity whatsoever, as far as the semantics is concerned. It might be more accurate to call them 'points'. It will not hurt to call them 'worlds', so long as we keep this clarification in mind.)

We are interested in structures in which the ranking function $\#$ used here corresponds to the $\#$ function from §7.4. (I'm re-using the '$\#$' symbol on purpose, for the function used in the formal models here is intended to mimic the function defined on double worlds in §7.4.) Consider the set of sequent rules from §7.4, but now defined over our object language $\mathcal{L}$, rather than over the worldmaking language. A proof in this system (that is, a tree constructed in accordance with the rules and with an instance of IDENTITY$^+$ at each of its leaves) is *associated with* $w \in W$ iff the sequent $V^+ w \vdash V^- w$ is at the root of the tree. Mimicking §7.4, the size of a proof is the number of its non-leaf nodes. We are then interested in the class of models $\mathcal{E}$ for which $\#w$ is the size of the smallest proof associated with w, if there is one, and ω otherwise. (This restriction on $\#$ mimics the definition of $\#$ in §7.4.) I'll call the models $E \in \mathcal{E}$ *spaces*.

Each space $E \in \mathcal{E}$ has a rank, which intuitively tells us just how trivial the most trivially impossible world in E is. If E has rank 0, for instance, then E contains worlds according to which some sentence is both true and false (that is, for some w in E, $V^+w \cap V^-w \neq \varnothing$). If E's rank is large, by contrast, then intuitively, no world in E is trivially impossible. We can think of each space $E \in \mathcal{E}$ as giving a sharpening of 'epistemic space', qua set of all epistemically possible worlds. There will be some range of integers (those that are not small) which give admissible sharpenings of 'epistemic space'. We will use these sharpenings to reason about the properties of epistemic space. I will, however leave the notion of 'admissible sharpening' as an informal notion. For formal purposes, I'll consider all spaces $E \in \mathcal{E}$.

We now have the materials needed to define a logical consequence relation to capture the trivial consequences of a set of premises. Given a space $E \in \mathcal{E}$, a *pointed space* is a pair $\langle E, w \rangle$, where $w \in W$ in E. The rank of $\langle E, w \rangle$ is the rank of E. Say that $E, w \Vdash A$ iff $A \in V^+w$ in E and $E, w \dashv A$ iff $A \in V^-w$ in E. For a pointed space E, we define $E \Vdash \Gamma$ iff $E \Vdash A$ for each 'A' $\in \Gamma$ and $E \dashv \Gamma$ iff $E \dashv A$ for at least one 'A' $\in \Gamma$.

Definition 8.1 (Trivial consequence) With respect to any integer $n \in \mathbb{N}$, $A \in \mathcal{L}$ is a trivial consequence of $\Gamma \subseteq \mathcal{L}$, $\mathrm{triv}_n(\Gamma, A)$, if and only if, for all pointed epistemic spaces $E \in \mathcal{E}$ of rank $r > n$, $E \Vdash \Gamma$ only if $E \dashv A$.

As a definition of consequence, this definition is rather unusual: the clause has '$E \dashv A$' where we would usually have '$E \Vdash A$'. Trivial consequence is not about truth-preservation; rather, a trivial consequence holds when the truth of the premises guarantee falsity avoidance for the conclusion across appropriate models.

Theorem 8.1 triv_n has the following properties, for all $n \in \mathbb{N}$:

(a) $\mathrm{triv}_n \subset \mathrm{triv}_{n+1}$, that is, if $\mathrm{triv}_n(\Gamma, A)$ then $\mathrm{triv}_{n+1}(\Gamma, A)$.

(b) triv_n is monotonic: if $\mathrm{triv}_n(\Gamma, A)$ and $\Gamma \subseteq \Delta$ then $\mathrm{triv}_n(\Delta, A)$.

(c) $\mathrm{triv}_n(\Gamma, A)$ only if Γ classically entails A.

(d) triv_n is reflexive.

(e) $\text{triv}_0(\Gamma, A)$ if and only if $A \in \Gamma$.

(f) For $n \geq 1$, triv_n is non-transitive and does not satisfy CUT: it is not the case that if $\text{triv}_n(\Gamma, A)$ and $\text{triv}_n(\Gamma \cup \{A\}, B)$ then $\text{triv}_n(\Gamma, B)$.

Proof: For (a), suppose that $\text{triv}_n(\Gamma, A)$ and that pointed model M has a rank $r > n + 1$ s.t. $M \Vdash \Gamma$. Then for all M' of rank $r > n$ s.t. $M' \Vdash \Gamma$, $M' \nVdash A$. Hence $M \nVdash A$, and so $\text{triv}_{n+1}(\Gamma, A)$. For (b), suppose $\text{triv}_n(\Gamma, A)$, $\Gamma \subseteq \Delta$ and $M \Vdash \Delta$. Then $M \Vdash \Gamma$ and so, by definition, $M \nVdash A$. Hence $\text{triv}_n(\Delta, A)$. For (c), suppose Γ does not classically entail A. Then there is no closed tree in our sequent system with $\Gamma \vdash A$ at its root. Let $M^w = \langle \{w\}, \varnothing, V^+, V^-, \text{Id}, \dots, \text{Id} \rangle$ where $V^+w = \Gamma$, $V^-w = \{A\}$ and Id is the identity function, so that $M^w \Vdash \Gamma$ and $M^w \nVdash A$. Since $\#w = \omega$, M^w has rank ω and hence $\neg\text{triv}_n(\Gamma, A)$ for any $n \in \mathbb{N}$. (c) follows by contraposition.

For (d), we have $\text{triv}_0(\{A\}, A)$. By (b), if $A \in \Gamma$ then $\text{triv}_0(\Gamma, A)$ and, by (a), $\text{triv}_n(\Gamma, A)$ for any $n \in \mathbb{N}$. Hence triv_n is reflexive for each $n \in \mathbb{N}$. For (e), the 'if' follows from reflexivity. For the 'only if', suppose $A \notin \Gamma$ and let $M^w = \langle \{w\}, \varnothing, V^+, V^-, \text{Id}, \dots, \text{Id} \rangle$ where $V^+w = \Gamma$ and $V^-w = \{A\}$. Then $M^w \Vdash \Gamma$ and $M^w \nVdash A$. Since $A \notin \Gamma$, $\#w > 0$, hence M^w has a rank $r > 0$, hence $\neg\text{triv}_1(\Gamma, A)$.

For (f), note that triv_0 trivially satisfies CUT. So suppose $n > 0$ and let $\Gamma_n = \{p_1 \wedge (p_2 \wedge \cdots \wedge (p_{n+1} \wedge p_{n+2}) \cdots)\}$. Then $\text{triv}_n(\Gamma, p_{n+1} \wedge p_{n+2})$ and $\text{triv}_n(\Gamma \cup \{p_{n+1} \wedge p_{n+2}\}, p_{n+2})$, but $\neg\text{triv}_n(\Gamma, p_{n+2})$. For a counterexample, let $M^w = \langle \{w\}, \varnothing, V^+, V^-, \text{Id}, \dots, \text{Id} \rangle$ where $V^+w = \Gamma$ and $V^-w = \{p_{n+2}\}$. We have $M^w \Vdash \Gamma$ and $M^w \nVdash p_{n+2}$. Since $\#w = n + 1$, M^w has rank $n + 1$ and so $\neg\text{triv}_n(\Gamma, p_{n+2})$. Hence, for $n > 1$, triv_n does not satisfy CUT. Since CUT is a form of transitivity, the argument that triv_n is non-transitive is similar.   ∎

So long as n is not too small, the trivial consequences include all the inferences usually called trivial (on the use of 'trivial' that does not apply to all valid inferences). Table 8.1 gives some examples, showing the minimal value of n for which triv_n holds. Let's consider one example from the table: $\text{triv}_2(A \vee B, \neg A, B)$. To see why it

$\mathrm{triv}_1(\{A \wedge B\}, A)$	$\mathrm{triv}_1(\{A, B\}, A \wedge B)$
$\mathrm{triv}_1(\{A\}, A \vee B)$	$\mathrm{triv}_2(\{A \vee B, \neg A\}, B)$
$\mathrm{triv}_1(\{A \rightarrow B, A\}, B)$	$\mathrm{triv}_3(\{A \rightarrow B, \neg B\}, \neg A)$
$\mathrm{triv}_5(\{\neg(A \wedge B)\}, \neg A \vee \neg B)$	$\mathrm{triv}_5(\{\neg(A \vee B)\}, \neg A \wedge \neg B)$

Table 8.1: SOME TRIVIAL CONSEQUENCES

is not the case that $\mathrm{triv}_1(A \vee B, \neg A, B)$, consider the space $E = \langle\{w\}, V^+, V^-, \#\rangle$ such that $V^+ w = \{`A \vee B\text{'}, `\neg A\text{'}\}$ and $V^- = \{`B\text{'}\}$. Then $\#w = 2$ and hence the pointed space $\langle E, w \rangle$ is of rank 2. $\langle E, w \rangle \Vdash A \vee B$, $\langle E, w \rangle \Vdash \neg A$ and $\langle E, w \rangle \dashv\vert B$, hence $\neg\mathrm{triv}_1(A \vee B, \neg A, B)$.

Above, I said that we can think of each n within some admissible range as a sharpening of 'epistemic space'. In this range, triv_n gives us sharpenings of 'trivial consequence'. Thus, an inference from Γ to 'A' is determinately trivial iff $\mathrm{triv}_n(\Gamma, A)$ for all n in the range, determinately non-trivial iff $\neg\mathrm{triv}_n(\Gamma, A)$ for all n in the range and it is indeterminate whether the inference is trivial otherwise. (As I said above, I will not incorporate this machinery into our formal semantics: I will leave is as an informal notion.)

In the next section, I turn from the content of deduction to concepts of knowledge and belief. I'll show how to model epistemic and doxastic states on the epistemic space developed so far and discuss the problem of epistemic oversights (§7.3). The trivial consequence relation developed in this section will play a role in the solution.

8.4   Knowledge and Belief States

My approach to modelling epistemic and doxastic states takes its cue from the standard epistemic logic approach (§1.2). To recap, we model agent i's epistemic states by imposing an epistemic accessibility relation R_i on worlds (which must all be epistemically possible worlds). R_i relates epistemically possible worlds to epistemically possible worlds. World w represents that agent i knows that A if and only if all worlds epistemically accessible from w for i (that is, all worlds u such that $R_i wu$) represent that A.

The knowledge of different agents is represented using a different accessibility relation R_i for each agent i. To ensure that knowledge is always factive, each relation R_i is reflexive. Doxastic states can be modelled in a similar way, using doxastic accessibility relations R_i^δ for each agent i, which are non-reflexive (since belief is not factive) and which relate worlds only to epistemically possible ones. World w represents that agent i believes that A if and only if all worlds doxastically accessible from w for i (that is, all worlds u such that $R_i^\delta wu$) represent that A.

This is how logically possible worlds represent knowledge and belief. Since it is logically impossible for what an agent knows to be false, there must be a logically impossible world according to which some agent knows something false. Similarly, agent i's knowing that A logically entails that A is epistemically possible for i (and hence epistemically possible simpliciter). So, if it is epistemically impossible that A, then it is logically impossible to know that A. Hence there must be a logically impossible world according to which some agent knows something that's epistemically impossible.

The simplest way to accommodate these facts is to allow logically impossible worlds to represent agents' knowledge in an arbitrary way (just as logically impossible worlds represent that A in an arbitrary way for other logically complex sentences 'A'). So, just as in §5.6, double worlds w are pairs of arbitrary sets of worldmaking sentences $\langle w^+, w^- \rangle$. We now add the extra requirement that a world w is logically possible only if (i) '$K_i A$' $\in w^+$ if and only if, for all worlds u such that $R_i wu$, 'A' $\in u^+$; and (ii) '$K_i A$' $\in w^-$ if and only if there is some world u such that $R_i wu$ and 'A' $\in u^-$. (Similarly for '$B_i A$', in terms of R_i^δ.) Worlds which fail this test are logically impossible. They may represent both that '$K_i A$' is true and that 'A' is false, for example.

Since it is sometimes indeterminate whether a given world is epistemically possible, it is sometimes indeterminate whether R_i holds between worlds w and u. As a consequence, it is sometimes indeterminate whether agent i knows that A. Suppose it is indeterminate whether there is any world R_i accessible from w which does not represent that 'A'. This will be the case when all clear epistemically possible worlds such that $R_i w u$ represent that A and, for some world v which does not represent that A, it is indeterminate whether $R_i w v$. If v is R_i-accessible from w, then i does not know that A, according to w. If there is no such world v, then i does know that A, according to w. Hence it is indeterminate whether w represents that i knows that A. (This is not a representation of indeterminacy: w does not say that '$K_i A$' is indeterminate. Rather, it is indeterminate whether world w says that $K_i A$.)

This is just what we should expect, given that epistemic states are very much like the epistemic contents of sentences. If we fix on a particular epistemically possible world w, the set of worlds that are R_i-accessible from w is indeterminate in membership, just as epistemic contents are indeterminate in their membership. We can define a *projection function* $f_i \subseteq W_d \times 2^{W_d}$ for each agent i, so that $f_i w = \{u \mid R_i w u\}$. (Strictly speaking, this should be 'f_{R_i}', which by convention I abbreviate to 'f_i'.) For each world w, $f_i w$ is the set of worlds R_i-accessible from w. Then for logically possible worlds w, $f_i w$ gives us the content of agent i's epistemic state at world w. Agent i knows that A, according to such worlds w, just in case $f_i w \subseteq |A^+|$. For logically impossible worlds u, $f_i u$ doesn't tell us anything, since epistemic states are arbitrary amongst the logically impossible worlds.

This is not the end of the story, however, for there remains a serious objection to this account of knowledge: the problem of epistemic oversights from §7.3. The worry is that, by allowing highly incomplete worlds in epistemic space, we seem to deny agents knowledge that they should have in virtue of being rational agents. For on the account I have given, an agent may not know some trivial consequence of what she knows (and similarly, may not believe some trivial consequence of what she believes). These are epistemic oversights.

I argued in §7.3 that epistemic oversights are here to stay. If an agent is not logically omniscient, then her knowledge is not deductively closed. So, for any deductively complete set of inference rules, her knowledge is not closed under all of those rules. But for some such sets of rules, all of the rules concern trivial inferences (standard natural deduction, sequent calculus or axiomatic systems are such cases). Therefore, the agent's knowledge is not closed under some trivial rule of inference: she knows the premises of (some instance of) the rule, from which the conclusion trivially follows, and yet she does not know the conclusion. She has an epistemic oversight, in other words. This conclusion follows independently of my account of epistemic states. Epistemic oversights are not an unwanted artefact of a theory; rather, they are genuine features of our epistemic lives, for which an adequate theory must account.

So I disagree with Bjerring on what the problem is. He says that 'just as we expect minimally rational agents to rule out blatant logical inconsistencies, so we expect them to accept obvious or self-evident logical truths' (Bjerring 2012, 26). By contrast, I hold that blatant inconsistencies '$A \wedge \neg A$' are not believable, yet it is perfectly possible to fail to know or believe trivial truths (and, more generally, trivial consequences of one's knowledge or beliefs).

The problem, as I see it, is that ascriptions of particular epistemic oversights to an agent are highly counterintuitive. Making those ascriptions feels wrong. Indeed, making such ascriptions is wrong. There is, I claim, a rational prohibition on making such ascriptions, even when they express a true content. In the remainder of this section and §8.5, I explain why this is so.

To begin with, let's consider sorites cases (§6.4) once again. Consider our party guests taking some number of sweets from a box. The greedy guests are those who take many sweets, but there seems to be no precise number we can give to answer the question, 'what is the minimum number of sweets a guest could take and thereby be greedy?' Philosophical theories of vagueness disagree on whether any particular number answers the question. If vagueness consists in 'no fact of the matter' cases, then there is simply no fact of the matter to answer the question. Epistemicists radically disagree:

on their view, there is a precise number which answers the question, but we cannot possibly know which number is it.

Despite these differences, all theories agree that (for any particular number n), if n is the correct answer to the question, then it is indeterminate that n is the correct answer and hence 'n is the correct answer' is not something we can genuinely know. The picture is something like this. Suppose n is the right answer to the question, 'what is the minimum number of sweets a guest could take and thereby be greedy?' Nevertheless, had things (including the meanings of words like 'greedy') been ever so slightly different, too slightly for us to notice any change in meaning, perhaps $n + 1$ or $n - 1$ would have been the correct answer. Given that we cannot discriminate epistemically between these three possibilities (in which n, or $n + 1$, or $n - 1$ is the right answer), we cannot know that n is the correct answer (even assuming it is). We can know that the answer is in the vicinity of n: we know that taking, say, 3 sweets isn't greedy, whereas taking 1,000 is. But we can have only inexact knowledge of where the cut-off point is (Williamson 1992).

Since we cannot know whether the correct answer to the question 'what is the minimum number of sweets a guest could take and thereby be greedy?' is $n - 1$, n, $n + 1$ or some other nearby value, there is something wrong with asserting the answer to be n. For one should assert only what one knows, or at least, what one has good reason to believe. In asserting 'n is the minimum number of sweets a guest could take and thereby be greedy', one is thereby claiming some evidence in favour of n in answer to the question, but one cannot have such evidence. In all cases of vagueness, we simply aren't at liberty to assert precisely in borderline cases, even if we happen (purely by chance) to hit on the truth.

This phenomenon of *unassertibility at the borderline* can help us explain why it sounds so strange to assert that agent i does not know some trivial truth or does not know some trivial consequence of what she knows. I am committed to the existence of such epistemic oversights. But, I will argue, there are no determinate instances. Whenever 'A' is a trivial(ish) truth, either agent i knows that A or else it is indeterminate whether i knows that A: it is never determinate that i does not know that A. More generally, if 'A' follows easily from what agent i determinately knows, then either i also knows that A, or else it is indeterminate whether i knows that A. There is never a case in which i determinately knows such-and-such, from which it it easily follows that A, such that it is determinate that i does not know that A. The task now is to explain why this is so.

It might be thought that the kind of indeterminacy in knowledge just mentioned is a direct result of the vagueness of epistemic space, revealed in the fact that it is often indeterminate whether a given world is found in epistemic space. But this is not so: the problem of epistemic oversights (that is, of an agent not knowing easy consequences of what she knows) occurs even if we restrict our attention only to worlds which are determinately epistemically possible. As discussed in §7.3 and §8.1, the problem is the result of the presence of highly incomplete worlds in epistemic space, and a world may be highly incomplete and yet determinately epistemically possible. (The vagueness of epistemic space does play a role in the vagueness of knowledge, but not as directly as just suggested.)

Instead, indeterminacy in knowledge of the kind required arises because of indeterminacy in epistemic accessibility relations. This can happen even amongst clear epistemically possible worlds. As we saw above, it may be that it is indeterminate whether u is epistemically accessible from w for agent i (i.e., whether $u \in f_i w$) because it is indeterminate whether u is an epistemically possible world. But it may also be indeterminate whether $u \in f_i w$ even when u is a clear epistemic possibility.

Each set $f_i w$ is a kind of content and so should behave in the same ways as the contents described in §8.1. (Because worlds in epistemic space may be highly incomplete, not every such content can be expressed using sentences of the language, even if we allow infinite disjunctions.) Suppose that $f_i w \subseteq |A|^+ \cap |B|^+$, $f_i w \nsubseteq |A \wedge B|^+$, so that $w \Vdash \mathsf{K}_i A$ and $w \Vdash \mathsf{K}_i B$ but $w \nVdash \mathsf{K}_i(A \wedge B)$. As we saw in §8.2, the epistemic content of '$A \wedge B$' is not identical to the combined content of 'A' and 'B', but it is very closely related: there is no world in epistemic space according to which 'A' and 'B' are true but '$A \wedge B$' is false and no world according to which '$A \wedge B$' is true but either 'A' or 'B' is false.

In the terminology introduced in §8.3, '$A \wedge B$' is a trivial consequence of 'A' and 'B' together: $\mathrm{triv}_n(\{A, B\}, A \wedge B)$ for all $n \geq 1$. Likewise, $\mathrm{triv}_n(\{A \wedge B\}, A)$ and $\mathrm{triv}_n(\{A \wedge B\}, B)$ for all $n \geq 1$. In intuitive terms, these trivial consequences tell us that epistemic concepts do not draw a determinate distinction between the content of '$A \wedge B$' and the combined contents of 'A' and 'B'. So the accessibility relations in our models should not draw determinate distinctions between 'A'-and-'B'-worlds and '$A \wedge B$'-worlds.

My aim in the next section is to develop these ideas further. I'll specify restrictions on epistemic accessibility relations, such that they do not draw determinate distinctions between trivially related contents. Combined with the fact that we may not rationally assert indeterminate truths, this will allow a response to the problem of epistemic oversights.

8.5   Indeterminate Epistemic Accessibility

In the previous section, I sketched a response to the problem of epistemic oversights. Epistemic oversights always concern indeterminate cases of knowledge; indeterminate truths are not rationally assertible; and so we may never rationally attribute a particular oversight to an agent. For this response to work, I noted, we require indeterminacy in epistemic accessibility relations (as well as in the boundaries of epistemic space itself), so that accessibility relations never draw determinate distinctions between contents immediately related by trivial inferences.

To satisfy ourselves that the account works as it should, we will need to be able to prove that there is never a case in which agent i determinately knows such-and-such, from which it trivially follows that A, such that it is determinate that i does not know that A. That is the aim of this section (which draws on Jago 2013e).

To do this, it will be necessary to work with the formal models of epistemic space, the spaces $E \in \mathcal{E}$, from §8.2. I will expand these models to include epistemic accessibility relations (or rather, the corresponding projection functions) and use them to prove that the desired relationship between triviality and determinate knowledge holds. The 'real' epistemic accessibility relations on 'real' epistemic space will conform to the structural features given in the definitions below. So we can think of the expanded epistemic models as artificial sharpenings of epistemic space, complete with epistemic accessibility relations.

First, we expand the logical object language $\mathcal{L}$ from §8.2 to include a determinacy operator '$\triangle$', where '$\triangle A$' abbreviates 'it is determinate that A is the case'. We can introduce an indeterminacy operator '$\triangledown$' by definition:

$$\triangledown A =_{\mathrm{df}} \neg \triangle A \wedge \neg \triangle \neg A$$

with '$\triangledown A$' read as 'it is indeterminate whether A is the case'. In the model theory, I will work with projection functions f_i (§8.4), rather than accessibility relations R_i, where $f_i w$ gives the set of worlds that are epistemically accessible from world w for agent i. (Recall from §8.4 that, given an accessibility relation R_i, we set $f_i w = \{u \mid R_i wu\}$ and, given a projection function f_i, we can define $R_i = \{\langle w, u \rangle \mid u \in f_i w, w \in W\}$. Working with projection functions is merely a convenient notational change.) Relative to $\mathcal{L}$ (which, I am assuming, is fixed throughout), we define models and related notions as follows.

Definition 8.2 (Epistemic model) An epistemic model for k agents is a tuple $M = \langle W^P, W^I, V^+, V^-, \#, f_1, \ldots, f_k \rangle$, where W^P and W^I are sets of worlds (thought of as sets of possible and impossible worlds, respectively), V^+, V^- and $\#$ are as in §8.3 and each f_i is an epistemic projection function. Let $W^{\cup} = W^P \cup W^I$. The rank of M is $\min\{\#w \mid w \in W^{\cup}\}$.

In the formal spaces in §8.3, I didn't need to distinguish between possible and the impossible worlds. But here it helps to draw the distinction, since logical entailment will be defined relative to the possible worlds only.

Given any accessibility projection function f_i in M and any sentence 'A' $\in \mathcal{L}$, we define f_i^A, the 'A'-variant of f_i, as follows:

Definition 8.3 ('A'-variant of f_i)

$$
f_i^A w = \begin{cases} \begin{pmatrix} (f_i w \cap \{w \mid \text{'}A\text{'} \in V^+ w\}) \\ \cup\,(f_i w \cap W^P) \end{pmatrix} & \text{if } f_i w \subseteq \{w \mid \text{'}A\text{'} \notin V^- w\} \\ f_i w & \text{otherwise} \end{cases}
$$

Let $f_i^{\mathcal{L}} = \{f_i\} \cup \{f_i^A \mid \text{'}A\text{'} \in \mathcal{L}\}$.

Definition 8.4 (Alternative sequences) For an epistemic model M as above, the set α_M of *alternative sequences* over M is:

$$
\alpha_M = \{\langle g_1 \cdots g_k\rangle \mid g_i \in f_i^{\mathcal{L}}, i \leq k\}
$$

I will use the notation '$\vec{g}$' to denote sequences of functions, and '$\vec{g}^i$' to denote the ith function of the sequence $\vec{g}$. Thus, if $\vec{g} = \langle f_i \cdots f_k\rangle$ then $\vec{g}^i = f_i$.

In a model M, we can think of α_M as setting out the grey area for epistemic accessibility and of each alternative sequence $\vec{g} \in \alpha_M$ as a sharpening of 'epistemic accessibility' for that model. On this account, models are defined relative to a particular sharpening $\langle f_1 \cdots f_k\rangle$, from which all the others in α_M are generated. We can think of $\langle f_1 \cdots f_k\rangle$ as the sharpening that gets things right: it tells us what's true (simpliciter), whereas what's determinately true is a matter of what is true on all alternatives in α_M. This allows for a classical definition of truth, on which $M \Vdash A$ or $M \Vdash \neg A$ for all (pointed) models M.

(Alternatively, we could give a supervaluationist-style treatment by defining models relative to a set of alternative sequences and define truth (simpliciter) as truth on all alternatives. Then it will always be the case that $M \Vdash A \vee \neg A$ but not always the case that $M \Vdash A$ or $M \Vdash \neg A$. Theorem 8.3, the main result of this section, holds on either approach.)

Definition 8.5 ($\vec{g}$-truth and $\vec{g}$-falsity) Given an epistemic model M as above and an alternative sequence $\vec{g} \in \alpha_M$, we define $\vec{g}$-relative truth and falsity in M, $\Vdash_{\vec{g}}$ and $\dashv\vert_{\vec{g}}$, as follows. (M is implicit in each clause.) For possible worlds $w \in W^P$:

$$w \Vdash_{\vec{g}} p \quad \text{iff} \quad p \in V^+ w$$

$$w \Vdash_{\vec{g}} \neg A \quad \text{iff} \quad w \nVdash_{\vec{g}} A$$

$$w \Vdash_{\vec{g}} A \wedge B \quad \text{iff} \quad w \Vdash_{\vec{g}} A \text{ and } w \Vdash_{\vec{g}} B$$

$$w \Vdash_{\vec{g}} A \vee B \quad \text{iff} \quad w \Vdash_{\vec{g}} A \text{ or } w \Vdash_{\vec{g}} B$$

$$w \Vdash_{\vec{g}} A \to B \quad \text{iff} \quad w \nVdash_{\vec{g}} A \text{ or } w \Vdash_{\vec{g}} B$$

$$w \Vdash_{\vec{g}} K_i A \quad \text{iff} \quad u, \vec{g} \Vdash_{\vec{g}} A \text{ for all } u \in \vec{g}^i w$$

$$w \Vdash_{\vec{g}} \triangle A \quad \text{iff} \quad w \Vdash_{\vec{h}} A \text{ for all } \vec{h} \in \alpha_M$$

$$w \dashv\vert_{\vec{g}} A \quad \text{iff} \quad w \nVdash_{\vec{g}} A$$

For impossible worlds $w \in W^I$:

$$w \Vdash_{\vec{g}} A \quad \text{iff} \quad A \in V^+ w$$

$$w \dashv\vert_{\vec{g}} A \quad \text{iff} \quad A \in V^- w$$

Definition 8.6 (*n*-entailment) A pointed model is a pair $M' = \langle M, w \rangle$ where M is as above and $w \in W^P$ in M. We define truth relative to M' as:

$$M' \Vdash A \quad \text{iff} \quad M, w \Vdash_{\langle f_1 \cdots f_n \rangle} A$$

where $f_1, \ldots, f_n$ are all the epistemic projection functions in M. $M' \Vdash \Gamma$ iff $M' \Vdash A$ for each 'A' $\in \Gamma$. For any $n \in \mathbb{N}$, logical *n*-entailment is then defined as follows: $\Gamma \vDash_n A$ iff, for every pointed model M of rank $\geq n$, $M \Vdash \Gamma$ only if $M \Vdash A$.

It is then easy to see that $\vDash_n$ extends classical entailment and that our previous definition of triv_n (§8.3) can be put equivalently in terms of our new epistemic models:

Theorem 8.2 For any $n \in \mathbb{N}$:

(a) If Γ classically entails A, then $\Gamma \vDash_n A$.

(b) $\text{triv}_n(\Gamma, A)$ iff, for all epistemic models M of rank $r > n$, all worlds $w \in W^\cup$ in M and all $\vec{g} \in \alpha_M$, if $M, w \Vdash_{\vec{g}} B$ for each $B \in \Gamma$ then $M, w \nvdash\vert_{\vec{g}} A$.

Proof: For (a), suppose $\Gamma \nvDash_n A$. Then there is an epistemic model M, world $w \in W^P$ in M and alternative $\vec{g} \in \alpha_M$ such that $w \Vdash_{\vec{g}} B$ for all $B \in \Gamma$ but $w \nVdash_{\vec{g}} A$. Let $v : \mathcal{P} \longrightarrow \{true, false\}$ be a classical valuation such that $vp = true$ iff 'p' $\in V^+w$ in M. Now extend v for '$\neg$', '$\wedge$', '$\vee$' and '$\rightarrow$' in the usual (classical) way. We show that vC satisfies each 'C' $\in \Gamma \cup \{$'$\neg A$'$\}$ by induction on the complexity of 'C'. If 'C' $:=$ 'p', then 'p' $\in V^+w$ hence $vp = true$. Now assume that, for all 'D' $\in \Gamma \cup \{$'$\neg A$'$\}$ of lower complexity than 'C', $vD = true$ iff $w \Vdash_{\vec{g}} D$. If 'C' $:=$ '$\neg C_1$' then $w \Vdash_{\vec{g}} \neg C_1$, hence $w \nVdash_{\vec{g}} C_1$ and, by hypothesis, $vC_1 = false$. Then $vC = true$. If 'C' $:=$ '$C_1 \wedge C_2$', then $w \Vdash_{\vec{g}} C_1$ and $w \Vdash_{\vec{g}} C_2$ and, by hypothesis, $vC_1 = vC_2 = true$, hence $v(C_1 \wedge C_2) = true$. The '$\vee$' and '$\rightarrow$' cases are similar. Hence $\Gamma \nvDash_n A$ only if $\Gamma \cup \{$'$\neg A$'$\}$ is classically satisfiable; (a) follows by contraposition.

For (b), 'only if' direction: assume that $\mathrm{triv}_n(\Gamma, A)$ and $M, w \Vdash_{\vec{g}} B$ for each 'B' $\in \Gamma$, where M has rank $r > n$. By theorem 8.1(c), Γ classically entails 'A' and so, by (a), $\Gamma \vDash_n A$. So if $w \in W^P$ in M, $M, w \Vdash_{\vec{g}} A$. If $w \in W^I$, on the other hand, let $E = \langle W^I, V^+, V^-, \# \rangle$, where W^I, V^+, V^- and # are taken from M. Then $\langle E, w \rangle \Vdash \Gamma$ and E has whatever rank M has. By definition 8.1, $\langle E, w \rangle \nVdash A$. This gives us '$A$' $\notin V^-w$ in M and hence $M, w \nVdash_{\vec{g}} A$.

'If' direction: assume the r.h.s. of the theorem and that

$$\langle \langle W_1, V^+, V^-, \# \rangle, w \rangle \Vdash \Gamma$$

where $w \in W_1$ and $\langle W_1, V^+, V^-, \# \rangle$ is any epistemic space of rank $r > n$. Let $M = \langle W^P, W_1, V^+, V^-, \#, \vec{g} \rangle$ for some W^P and $\vec{g}$. Then M too has rank r and, by definition 8.5, $w \Vdash_{\vec{g}} C$ iff 'C' $\in V^+w$. So $M, w \Vdash_{\vec{g}} \Gamma$ and hence, by our assumption, $M, w \nVdash_{\vec{g}} A$. Then, by definition 8.5, 'A' $\notin V^-A$ and so $\langle \langle W_1, V^+, V^-, \# \rangle, w \rangle \nVdash A$. By definition 8.1, it follows that $\mathrm{triv}_n(\Gamma, A)$.   ■

This result tells us that the extra structure I have added to spaces $E \in \mathcal{E}$ to obtain epistemic models M does not interfere with the trivial consequence relation. We could have defined the triv_n relation in terms of epistemic models, rather than in terms of epistemic spaces, and the definitions would have been equivalent. It is important to note, however, that triv_n is sensitive to all pairs $\langle M, w \rangle$ where $w \in W^\cup$ in M, and not just those for which $w \in W^P$. This contrasts with the logical n-entailments, which are sensitive only to possible worlds $w \in W^P$.

I now turn to the main result of this section, relating trivial consequence, knowledge and (in)determinacy:

Theorem 8.3 For any $n \in \mathbb{N}$, if $\text{triv}_n(\Gamma, A)$ then $\{\triangle \mathsf{K}_i B \mid \text{'}B\text{'} \in \Gamma\} \vDash_n \neg\triangle\neg\mathsf{K}_i A$ (Jago 2013e).

Proof: Assume that $\text{triv}_n(\Gamma, A)$ and, for all 'B' $\in \Gamma$, $\langle M, w \rangle \Vdash \triangle \mathsf{K}_i B$, where $M = \langle W^P, W^I, V^+, V^-, \#, \vec{f} \rangle$ and $w \in W^P$. Then for all 'B' $\in \Gamma$ and all $\vec{g} \in \alpha_M$, $M, w \Vdash_{\vec{g}} \mathsf{K}_i B$. Hence $M, u \Vdash_{\vec{g}} B$, for all $u \in \vec{g}_i w$ and all 'B' $\in \Gamma$. Given $\text{triv}_n(\Gamma, A)$ and theorem 8.2(b), it follows that $M, u \nVdash_{\vec{g}} A$, for all $u \in \vec{g}_i w$ and all $\vec{g} \in \alpha_M$. This guarantees that $f_i w \subseteq \{v \mid \text{'}A\text{'} \notin V^- v\}$ and so, by definition 8.3:

$$f_i^A w = (f_i w \cap \{v \mid \text{'}A\text{'} \in V^+ v\}) \cup (f_i w \cap W^P)$$

Then, for every world $u \in f_i^A w$ and alternative $\vec{h} \in \alpha_M$ such that $\vec{h}_i = f_i^A$, $M, u \Vdash_{\vec{h}} A$. Since $w \in W^P$, this gives us $M, w \Vdash_{\vec{h}} \mathsf{K}_i A$, hence $M, w \nVdash_{\vec{f}} \triangle\neg\mathsf{K}_i A$ and so $M, w \Vdash_{\vec{f}} \neg\triangle\neg\mathsf{K}_i A$. It follows that $\langle M, w \rangle \Vdash \neg\triangle\neg\mathsf{K}_i A$ and so $\{\triangle \mathsf{K}_i B \mid \text{'}B\text{'} \in \Gamma\} \vDash_n \neg\triangle\neg\mathsf{K}_i A$. ∎

Corollary 8.4 For any $n \in \mathbb{N}$:

(a) If $\text{triv}_n(\Gamma, A)$ then $\{\text{'}\triangle\mathsf{K}_i B\text{'} \mid \text{'}B\text{'} \in \Gamma\} \cup \{\text{'}\neg\mathsf{K}_i A\text{'}\} \vDash_n \triangledown\mathsf{K}_i A$.

(b) If $n > 1$, then $\vDash_n \neg\triangle\neg\mathsf{K}_i(A \vee \neg A)$ and $\neg\mathsf{K}_i(A \vee \neg A) \vDash_n \triangledown\mathsf{K}_i(A \vee \neg A)$.

Proof: For (a), suppose $\text{triv}_n(\Gamma, A)$. Then by theorem 8.3, $\{\triangle\mathsf{K}_i B \mid B \in \Gamma\} \vDash_n \neg\triangle\neg\mathsf{K}_i A$ and, since $\triangle B \vDash_n B$, $\neg\mathsf{K}_i A \vDash_n \neg\triangle\mathsf{K}_i A$. Hence $\{\triangle\mathsf{K}_i B \mid B \in \Gamma\} \cup \{\neg\mathsf{K}_i A\} \vDash_n \triangle\neg\mathsf{K}_i A \wedge \neg\triangle\neg\mathsf{K}_i A$ and, by definition of '$\triangledown$', $\{\triangle\mathsf{K}_i B \mid B \in \Gamma\} \cup \{\neg\mathsf{K}_i A\} \vDash_n \triangledown\mathsf{K}_i A$. For (b), suppose $(A \vee \neg A) \in V^- w$ in some space E. Then $\#w \leq 2$ and so E has a rank $r \leq 2$. Hence for any pointed space E' of rank $r > 2$, $E' \nVdash A \vee \neg A$ and so, for all

$n > 1$, $\text{triv}_n(\varnothing, A \vee \neg A)$. By theorem 8.3, $\vDash_n \neg \triangle \neg K_i(A \vee \neg A)$ and, by (a), $\neg K_i(A \vee \neg A) \vDash_n \triangledown K_i(A \vee \neg A)$ for all $n > 1$.   ∎

These results are a very pleasing feature of the theory. We think of each $n \in \mathbb{N}$ as a sharpening of 'trivial consequence' and 'epistemic space'. Some (informally specified) range of n gives the admissible sharpenings and what is (in fact) determinately true is what is true on all of those sharpenings. Theorem 8.3 then tells us that, however we sharpen these notions, if the inference from Γ to 'A' is trivial, then determinate knowledge of Γ entails that the agent does not determinately lack knowledge that A.

If 'A' is a trivial consequence of what agent i knows, then it is never determinate that i fails to know that A. Equivalently (as the corollary says), if agent i does not know some trivial consequence 'A' of what she knows, then it is indeterminate whether she knows that A. So, on the account proposed, there are no determinate epistemic oversights. Equivalently, if an agent has a particular epistemic oversight, then it is indeterminate whether she has that particular oversight.

Since what is indeterminate is not rationally assertible, it is then never rational to assert that agent i has a particular epistemic oversight. If an agent is not logically omniscient, then we can be sure that she suffers from some epistemic oversight. Indeed, it is determinate that real-world agents are not logically omniscient and hence determinate that real-world agents suffer from epistemic oversights. But we can never say what they are. Whenever we focus on a particular trivial consequence 'A' of agent i's knowledge, it is never rational to assert that she does not know that A. Epistemic oversights are elusive, just as counterexamples to tolerance principles for vague predicates are.

8.6   Hyperintensions and Senses

In this section, I show how the fine-grained contents discussed so far in this chapter can be used to make good sense of informative, cognitively significant identity statements. This requires assigning epistemic contents to sub-sentential terms (such as names and predicates), as well as to sentences as a whole.

In §1.4, I discussed how Frege (1892) used his notion of the sense of a term to explain puzzles about informative identity statements. The puzzle is to explain how a true identity statement '$a = b$' can be informative, or cognitively significant. Frege's answer was: because the senses associated with the names 'a' and 'b' differ. Senses are the bearers of cognitive significance and hence informativeness. But senses, as Frege uses them, are rather mysterious entities. The mystery shrouding what senses are is lifted by identifying Frege's senses with Carnap's intensions: functions from worlds to extensions (§1.4).

The problem with intensions is that they are not hyperintensional. They can explain the cognitive significance of a true identity statement '$a = b$' only if that statement is a contingent truth. For if it is necessary, then for all possible worlds w, the extension of 'a' at w is identical to the extension of 'b' at w, and hence 'a' and 'b' have the same intension. If proper names are rigid designators, then '$a = b$' is a necessary truth whenever 'a' and 'b' are (actually) co-referring proper names (Kaplan 1989a,b; Kripke 1980). The intensions assigned to 'a' and 'b' are therefore identical if the worlds in question are metaphysically possible worlds.

If we define intensions relative to all logically possible worlds (allowing some logically possible but metaphysically impossible worlds), then the intensions of the proper names 'a' and 'b' may differ. Alternatively, we could make use of *two-dimensional semantics* to differentiate between metaphysically equivalent but logically non-equivalent terms (Chalmers 2004, 2006a,b; Davies and Humberstone 1980; Stalnaker 2004). Neither approach can differentiate between logically or mathematically equivalent descriptions, however.

Consider the following description of a number:

$$\lim_{x \to \infty} \frac{\pi x}{\left(\dfrac{x}{\ln x}\right)}$$

where π is the *prime counting function*, defined so that πx is the number of primes $p \le x$ (for any $x \in \mathbb{R}$). Call this description 'd'. The number described by d turns out to be 1. The statement of this identity,

$$\lim_{x \to \infty} \frac{\pi x}{\left(\dfrac{x}{\ln x} \right)} = 1$$

is the prime number theorem, first proved (independently) by Hadamard and de la Vallée Poussin in 1896. So the intension of description d is the constant function from logically possible worlds to the number 1, as is the intension of the numeral '1'. Yet the prime number theorem is informative and non-trivial. It was an important discovery in number theory and both Hadamard's and de la Vallée Poussin's original proofs of it are long and complex.

We remedy the situation by replacing intensions with *hyperintensions*: functions from epistemically possible worlds to extensions. Hyperintensions allow us to distinguish semantically between mathematically equivalent descriptions, such as d and '1'. Hyperintensions have a finer grain than intensions because they are defined over the larger class of all epistemically possible worlds, which includes some (but not all) logically impossible worlds. When restricted to the class of logically possible worlds, hyperintensions behave just as intensions do (in fact, they become identical to intensions).

We can then use hyperintensions to interpret Fregean senses, in their role as bearers of cognitive significance. Hyperintensions do a better job than intensions of capturing this aspect of Fregean senses. Indeed, Frege (in some places) allows that equivalent expressions may differ in their sense. He writes:

> wherever the coincidence of *Bedeutung* is not self-evident, we have a difference in sense. Thus the sense of '$2^3 + 1$' is also different from the sense of '3^2' even though we have the *Bedeutung* is the same, because a special act of recognition is required in order to see this. (Frege 1980, 152–3).

> I say of the designations '3 + 1', '1 + 3', '2 + 2', '2 × 2', that they have the same *Bedeutung* but different senses. (Frege 1969, 241)

The sign '16 – 2' is a proper name of a number. '17 – 3' designates the same number, but '17 – 3' does not have the same sense as '16 – 2'. (Frege 1979, 232)

In these passages, Frege is allowing that mathematical truths are sometimes non-trivially informative. (It is worth noting that Frege is inconsistent on this point. In a letter to Husserl from 1906 (Frege 1979, 69–70), he says that equivalent contents express the same thought.)

(It is worth noting, however, that '3 + 1' and '1 + 3' (for example) do not differ determinately in sense. Just as anyone who knows the meaning of '∧' cannot determinately fail to know that '$A \wedge B$' and '$B \wedge A$' agree in truth-value, so anyone who knows the meaning of '+' cannot determinately fail to know that '$x + y$' and '$y + x$' agree in truth-value, for any x and y. '3 + 1 = 1 + 3' should be treated as a trivial truth. This is the result given by the epistemic space approach I developed above, suitably expanded to incorporate quantifiers and the Peano axioms for basic arithmetic. As '3 + 1 = 1 + 3' in an instance of the commutativity axiom for '+', hence a trivial logical truth, it is not false according to any epistemically possible world. Then $|3 + 1 = 1 + 3|^-$ is empty and so the inference (from zero premises) to '3 + 1 = 1 + 3' is contentless (§8.2, §8.3). Because of this, it is never determinate and hence never assertible that a particular agent fails to know that 3 + 1 = 1 + 3 (§8.5).)

Carnap's intensions cannot capture these fine-grained hyperintensional distinctions between mathematically equivalent designators. Hyperintensions defined on epistemic space provide a better interpretation of Fregean senses than Carnap's intensions. One may object that senses are supposed to be non-linguistic entities. I respond to objections of this kind in §8.8. In short, contents defined on epistemic space are (in the relevant sense) non-linguistic, for they are constructed from non-linguistic reality.

I have been arguing that, if one wants to use Frege's notion of sense to analyse knowledge and belief ascriptions and to explain puzzles of cognitive significance (as Frege did), then we should think of those senses as hyperintensions, defined on epistemic space. I am not suggesting that a hyperintensions-based account fulfils other aspects of Frege's theory of language. Hyperintensions do not play a role in determining the reference of a term. (Indeed, the reference of a predicate 'F' must be fixed before we can assign a hyperintension to 'F'.)

Nor does the hyperintensional account of content I have proposed require that terms within the scope of 'knows that' or 'believes that' switch their reference, from their conventional designation to their conventional sense, as they do on Frege's account (§1.4). Indeed, the Fregean doctrine that 'Bertie' in 'I know that Bertie is adorable' does not refer to Bertie is one of the main reasons for rejecting the Fregean account as a whole. This particular doctrine is no part of the theory I have been suggesting. We can take the best parts of the Fregean view and leave the problematic assumptions behind.

So far in this chapter, I have discussed various epistemic notions of content which can be defined on epistemic space. In the remaining two sections, I'll address two issues that arise as a consequence of using fine-grained impossible worlds in the account. The first concerns epistemological scepticism (§8.7); the second concerns a worry that accounts given in terms of fine-grained impossible worlds are trivial (§8.8).

8.7   Epistemic Closure

In this section, I turn from developing the theory of epistemic content to discussing the idea that knowledge is closed under known implication. This is the principle that (as a first pass), if one knows that what one knows implies that A, then one thereby knows that A.

The principle plays an important role in philosophical discussions of external world scepticism. It is relevant here because I have given an account of epistemic states which makes use of impossible worlds which are not closed under logical consequence. The denial of logical closure principles on what worlds represent has been a central theme of my approach to hyperintensionality. However, as I shall argue below, we should not be fooled into thinking (as others have thought) that the denial of closure gives us a way to respond to scepticism.

Closure under known implication (as a first pass and in its simplest single-premise form) states that:

(8.5) If agent *i* knows that *A* and knows that '*A*' implies '*B*', then she knows that *B*.

The exact force of 'implies' is usually left unspecified, but we may take it to mean whatever '→'-sentences express (so that the closure principle concerns agents who know that *A* and that *A* → *B*).

(The principle is sometimes called 'closure under known entailment', but this is a misnomer as applied to sceptical issues. The implication in sceptical arguments is usually from an everyday proposition, such as 'I have two hands', to the denial of a sceptical scenario, such as 'I am not a brain in a vat'. This implication isn't a logical entailment, since it isn't a logical truth that brains in vats lack hands.)

This principle has received attention because of its relation to scepticism. I know that, if I am currently typing on my laptop, then I'm not in some devilish sceptical scenario (I'm not having some super-realistic dream whilst really in bed, I haven't been reduced to a brain hooked up to a hallucination-machine by an evil scientist, or anything like that). Given how troubling sceptical scenarios are for philosophers, that's a big 'if'. The antecedent seems correspondingly hard to know. For if I know the antecedent then, given (8.5), I know that I'm not currently in a sceptical scenario (I'm not a brain in a vat, or whatever). So, if (8.5) is accepted, the following arguments can be made:

DOGMATIST: You know that if you're currently typing, then you're not in a radical sceptical scenario. But clearly, you know that you're currently typing (since that's obvious), so you know that you're not in a radical sceptical scenario. Problem solved!

SCEPTIC: You know that if you're currently typing, then you're not in a radical sceptical scenario. But you don't know that you're not in a radical sceptical scenario. How could you know that, given that everything would seem just the same to you if you were in a radical sceptical scenario? So you don't know that you're currently typing.

Both of these positions seem wrong. If the sceptic is right, then I know very little at all: I know certain *if . . . then* information, but I never get to know that I'm typing, or that I have hands. That seems unacceptable. Nevertheless, the dogmatist seems no better off, since her reason for holding that we do know we're not in a sceptical scenario trades on the premise (that I know I'm currently typing) which the sceptic denies. How can she dogmatically insist that I know so much about my situation in the world, when the sceptic has strong arguments (or at least, arguments that have worried many good philosophers) to the contrary?

Because of this seeming impasse, the option of denying (8.5) becomes more attractive. Both Dretske (1970) and Nozick (1981) make this move. Suppose you park in the car park and walk around the corner, out of sight. Five minutes later, do you know where your car is? Of course! It would be absurd to think that you lose your knowledge of where your car is as soon as you lose sight of it. Do you know that eager car-thieves haven't stolen your car in the intervening five minutes? Some feel less confident in answering *yes* to this question. After all, if your car had been stolen the moment you were out of sight, then you wouldn't be any the wiser. Things would look to you just as they look now; so on what basis could you know that your car hasn't been stolen?

Here's the rub: if you don't know that your car hasn't been stolen, how can you know that it's still in the car park? After all, you know that if it is in the car park, then it hasn't been stolen. Dretske and Nozick, however, hold that you can know that your car is in the car park (because that's where you left it), even if you don't know that it hasn't been stolen (because things wouldn't seem any different if it had been stolen). They do this by denying (8.5).

How can this move be justified? On Nozick's truth-tracking

account of knowledge (Nozick 1981), one knows that *A* iff one's true belief that *A* is such that, had it been false that *A*, one would not have believed that *A*, and had it been true that *A*, then one would have believed that *A*. On this account, you know where your car is (having parked it in the car park five minutes ago), since if it were not in the car park it would be wherever you parked it instead, in which case you wouldn't have believed the car is in the car park.

In possible-worlds terms: the closest worlds in which your car is not in the car park are those worlds where you parked it elsewhere and in which your beliefs reflect this. Worlds in which the car has been stolen, or taken by aliens, or in which you parked elsewhere but still believed you parked in the car park, are further removed from the actual world. But you don't know that the car hasn't been stolen: if it had, you would still believe that the car hasn't been stolen. Hence, on Nozick's account, you can know that *A*, know that *A* → *B*, and yet not know that *B*. This fact gives Nozick a neat response to the sceptic. He can grant her premise (that one does not know that one is not in a sceptical scenario) and yet deny her conclusion. If Nozick is right, then scepticism has been contained: it does not challenge our knowledge of everyday matters.

Given how much emphasis I have placed on worlds not being closed under *modus ponens* (or under any inference rule bar *A* ⊢ *A*), it might seem that I am on Dretske's and Nozick's side here. On my view, there are many worlds which represent that *A*, that *A* → *B* but not that *B*. Some of these worlds can be epistemically accessible to an agent (although never determinately so, §8.5). Hence, on the account I gave in §8.4, there will be agents who know that *A*, that *A* → *B*, but not that *B* (although not determinately so). So I certainly allow for failures (in indeterminate cases only, but failures nevertheless) of (8.5).

Yet I do not side with Dretske and Nozick against the sceptic. Rejecting (8.5) is necessary but not sufficient for their anti-sceptical case. Indeed, given what I have said about failures of logical omniscience, I hold that everyone, sceptic included, should reject (8.5). Although (8.5) is not a statement of the problem of logical omniscience, there is no reason to suppose that (8.5) holds in general, given that agents are not logically omniscient. A logically omniscient agent has epistemic oversights somewhere in her epistemic state and some of these gaps concern simple inferences (such that she knows the premises but not the conclusion). It would be highly implausible to suppose that *modus ponens* inferences never constitute one of these oversights.

There are weaker principles which are both sufficient for the sceptic's argument and much more plausible than (8.5), however. What matters, from the sceptic's point of view, is that you cannot (given your current situation) come to know that you are not in a sceptical scenario. An agent who does not know that she is not a brain in a vat because she has never formed a belief either way (perhaps she has never considered the matter; perhaps the concept *brain in a vat* is not part of her repertoire) will singularly fail to impress our sceptic.

Confronted with such an agent, our sceptic will reply (with justification):

> Fine! But let's tell the agent about the sceptical scenario and let her form a belief that her case isn't like that. Let her think really hard and bring all her current evidence to bear on the matter. Still, no matter how hard she thinks, she just can't come to know that she's not in such a situation. Her belief falls short of knowledge, because things would seem just the same to her even if she were in a sceptical situation.

So the existence of agents who falsify (8.5) because they haven't thought about the potential conclusion 'B', or because they don't have the cognitive resources to derive 'B' from '$A \to B$' and 'A' (perhaps because of other, more important cognitive tasks they are undertaking), makes no impact on the sceptical argument.

What would constitute a challenge to the sceptic's argument is an agent who knows that A and that $A \to B$ but, no matter how hard she reflects on this knowledge and no matter what cognitive resources she brings to bear on the matter (whilst retaining her knowledge that

A and that $A \to B$), she simply cannot come to know that B. But I, like many others, find such cases highly implausible. I find the following (weaker) epistemic closure condition hard to resist:

(8.6) If an agent knows that A and that $A \to B$, then she is in a position to know that B: if she competently deduces and hence comes to believe that B from these bits of her knowledge (whilst retaining what she knows), she thereby knows that B.

Hawthorne (2005, 29) and Williamson (2000a, 117) endorse similar epistemic closure principles.

Nothing I have said about epistemic space gives us any reason to reject (8.6). The construction of epistemic space I have given simply does not furnish us with anti-sceptical tools. Nor should it: whether the sceptic is ultimately correct is a matter of what we should say about concepts such as *evidence* and *justification*. If these are given a suitably externalist treatment, then the sceptic can be challenged. If not, then the sceptic's case looks strong. The construction of epistemic space needs to be viable either way; and so it is no objection that it does not provide us with anti-sceptical tools.

Since I find (8.6) highly plausible, I reject Dretske's and Nozick's response to scepticism. When considering sceptical arguments, it does no serious harm to assume that knowledge is closed under known implication (or even that the agents in question are logically omniscient). Nevertheless (and just for the record), we do know much about the world around us, contrary to the sceptic's claims. Perhaps the way to make this claim is via a contextualist account of knowledge (Lewis 1996); perhaps not (Williamson 2000a). The construction of epistemic space is neutral on this question, as it should be.

8.8   Is the Approach Trivial?

I will end by considering a general objection to the approach to content that I have given, and which might be raised against any

semantic account which uses very fine-grained impossible worlds.
(Here I draw on Jago 2013b.) The objection goes roughly as follows:

> We want to assign a content to a sentence 'A'. We first
> try assigning a set of possible worlds as the content, but
> we soon see that this is too coarse-grained. So we finesse
> the approach and assign a set of possible and impossible
> worlds to 'A'. These worlds are sets of sentences, and
> a world w is in the content of 'A' if and only if that
> world is a set containing 'A'. But then we come full
> circle: the 'content' assigned to 'A' is none other than
> 'A' itself, with a bit of set-theoretic machinery thrown
> in for good measure. Clearly, this 'content' can tell us
> nothing about the meaning of 'A'. We asked a question
> about the meaning of 'A' and what we get back by way
> of answer, more or less, is 'A' itself!

(I have heard objections of this form several times in discussion,
although I have not seen it in print. It seems to me to be a genuine
problem for some hyperintensional theories and so it is worth
addressing here, to show why it does not affect the view I have
presented.)

There are a couple of worries expressed here, one to do with
defining content in terms of linguistic entities and one to do with the
granularity of contents thus assigned. These distinct worries might
be expressed as follows.

WORRY 1: A sentence 'A' is assigned a content, which is a set of
worlds (or a pair of sets of worlds), which themselves are sets
(or pairs of sets) of sentences. So ultimately, the content of 'A'
is given in terms of further sentences, much like a translation of
'A' into some other language. But a translation of 'A' can tell us
what 'A' means (or what its content is) only if we have a prior
grasp of the meanings (or content) of the sentences used to
translate 'A'. Ultimately, we have to step beyond the linguistic
realm of translations and assign meanings and contents non-
linguistically, by correlating the sentence with the non-linguistic
world.

WORRY 2: A sentence 'A' is assigned a content, which is the set of worlds which represent that A (or a pair of sets of worlds, representing that A is the case and that A is not the case, respectively). But these worlds are so fine-grained that the content thus assigned does not even include the content of '$A \vee B$', or of other trivial consequences of 'A'. So the granularity of contents is just the granularity of sentences. Each sentence of the language has its own unique content. So why not just let the content of 'A' be the singleton $\{'A'\}$? Of course, if we did that, the theory would unquestionably not be an adequate account of content. But how is the present proposal any better?

Both worries need to be taken seriously. A weak response to worry 1 goes as follows. We are interested in modelling the contents of sentences (and of epistemic and doxastic states, and of thoughts in general). We do this in terms of worlds. It really doesn't matter what those worlds are; all that matters is their formal properties. As in modal logic, it doesn't matter what we take the worlds to be. All that matters is the logics obtained by imposing various constraints on the semantics, and we can investigate all of this without being concerned one jot with the metaphysical nature of worlds.

This response does have some merit and it is indeed often a good idea to keep logical and metaphysical issues separate when investigating modal, intensional and hyperintensional concepts. But at some point, those with curious minds want to know, what is content? It is part of an answer to say that contents have such-and-such structure, but this is only part of the answer. Similarly, it is one thing to know that the natural numbers have an ω-structure, but that on its own does not tell us what numbers are. So I agree that an account of content (that is, of what contents are) should make contact with the non-linguistic world.

What worry 1 misses, however, is that the account of content I have put forward in this chapter does make contact with the non-linguistic world. Worlds are constructed from sets of worldmaking sentences, but those sentences are themselves constructed from worldly entities. The worldmaking sentence representing that Bertie is adorable contains properties whose combination is uniquely possessed by Bertie, plus the property of *being adorable*. As a consequence, Bertie-contents will involve properties whose combination is uniquely possessed by Bertie. This is the very real and direct sense in which those contents are about Bertie himself.

Worry 2 is more subtle. If the objection is that the account I've given assigns contents which are too fine-grained, then we need to hear more from the objector about what is the correct granularity to assign to contents. Suppose, for example, she says it is the coarse granularity provided by metaphysical or logical equivalence (that is, the granularity of sets of metaphysically or logically possible worlds).

This in itself is no argument against my view; it is just another theory of content, one that I argued against in chapter 2. She will need responses to the problem of logical omniscience, the problem of deduction and the problem of bounded rationality in general. (In §2.5 and §2.6, I argued that the best responses on behalf of the possible worlds approach, those of Stalnaker and Lewis, fail.) So I take it that, if worry 2 is to be a genuine worry, it shouldn't be put by arguing that contents in fact have a coarser grain than on my account.

Perhaps the genuine worry contained in worry 2 is that, on my view, a sentence '*A*' is assigned a content in terms of itself, or in terms of the singleton {'*A*'}, with some set-theoretic distractions thrown in. But this is clearly a misinterpretation of my proposal. '*A*' (a sentence of the object language, English, say) is not assigned a content in terms of '*A*' or {'*A*'}, but rather in terms of (sets of) worldmaking sentences. Hence it is not true that each object language sentence is assigned a content which ultimately consists of itself, plus some set-theoretic smoke and mirrors.

What is important is whether an account of content can answer the problem of bounded rationality. To do this, it must provide contents which are neither logically ideal, in the sense of never distinguishing between equivalent contents, nor logically trivial, in the sense of failing to capture logical relationships between contents. The crucial question is how a theory of content should capture these normative, logical relationships without imposing implausible closure conditions on contents. Answering this question has been my project in chapters 6 onwards.

Chapter Summary

Epistemic contents are constructed from regions of epistemic space. We assign positive and negative contents, $|A|^+$ and $|A|^-$, to a sentence or utterance that expresses *that A* (§8.1). The content of a valid deduction is what is ruled out by inferring the conclusion from the premises: the set of worlds according to which the premises are all true but the conclusion is false (§8.2). When this set is non-empty, the deduction is contentful and hence informative; otherwise, it is trivial and uninformative. Some but not all inferences are deemed informative, on this view. Basic inferences such as *modus ponens* and *disjunction introduction* are deemed trivial, but inferences constructed from repeated applications of them can be informative. The triv_n relation, which can be thought of as a non-transitive logical entailment relation, captures trivial consequences of a set of premises (§8.3).

Knowledge and belief states are given by epistemic and doxastic accessibility relations (or projection functions) on epistemic space (§8.4). Since epistemic contents are indeterminate in membership, accessibility relations do not determinately discriminate between trivially logically related contents. *Epistemic accessibility* is a vague relation, even amongst the determinate epistemically possible worlds.

As a consequence, one is never in a rational position to ascribe an epistemic oversight to an agent (§8.4). I formalised these ideas and proved that particular epistemic oversights always concern indeterminate cases of knowledge: an agent never determinately fails to know some trivial consequence of what she determinately knows (§8.5). Despite initial appearances, this account of knowledge does not provide any support to the closure-denier's response to external-world scepticism (§8.7).

Epistemic contents allow us to make good sense of hyperintensional Fregean senses (§8.6). They allow us to adopt Frege's solution to the problem of informative identity statements, without having to accept Frege's unappealing doctrine of reference switching in (hyper)intensional contexts. Finally, I responded to some worries that impossible-world accounts of content are trivial (§8.8).

Appendix

Modal Epistemic Logic

In this appendix, I briefly go over some of the technical details of (classical) modal epistemic logic, which was introduced informally in §1.2.

Each agent under discussion is assigned an integer $1, \ldots, n$. The language of modal epistemic logic, $\mathcal{L}$, is the smallest set containing the logically primitive sentences $\mathcal{P} = \{\text{`}p_1\text{'}, \ldots, \text{`}p_n\text{'}\}$ and closed under '$\neg A$', '$A \wedge B$', '$A \vee B$', '$A \rightarrow B$', '$A \leftrightarrow B$' and, for each $i \leq n$, '$K_i A$' and '$B_i A$'.

An epistemic-doxastic model M for $\mathcal{L}$ (for n agents) is a $2n + 2$-tuple

$$\langle W, R_1, \ldots, R_n, R_1^\delta, \ldots, R_n^\delta, V \rangle$$

where W is a set of points (thought of as possible worlds), each $R_{i \leq n} \subseteq W \times W$ is an epistemic accessibility relation between worlds, each $R_{i \leq n}^\delta \subseteq W \times W$ is a doxastic accessibility relation between worlds, and $V : W \longrightarrow 2^{\mathcal{P}}$ is the *labelling function*, assigning a set of primitive sentences to each world. Truth-according-to-a-world, '$M, w \Vdash A$', is defined as follows (leaving M implicit in each clause):

$w \Vdash p$	iff	$p \in Vw$
$w \Vdash \neg A$	iff	$w \nVdash A$
$w \Vdash A \wedge B$	iff	$w \Vdash A$ and $w \Vdash B$
$w \Vdash A \vee B$	iff	$w \Vdash A$ or $w \Vdash B$
$w \Vdash A \rightarrow B$	iff	$w \nVdash A$ or $w \Vdash B$

$$w \Vdash A \leftrightarrow B \quad \text{iff} \quad \text{either } (w \Vdash A \text{ and } w \Vdash B)$$
$$\text{or } (w \nVdash A \text{ and } w \nVdash B)$$
$$w \Vdash \mathsf{K}_i A \quad \text{iff} \quad \text{for all } u, R_i w u \text{ only if } u \Vdash A$$
$$w \Vdash \mathsf{B}_i A \quad \text{iff} \quad \text{for all } u, R_i^{\delta} w u \text{ only if } u \Vdash A$$

For a set of sentences Γ, $M \Vdash \Gamma$ iff $M \Vdash A$ for all 'A' $\in \Gamma$.

An epistemic-doxastic frame $\mathcal{F}$ for n agents is a model without a valuation: a $2n+1$-tuple $\langle W, R_1, \ldots, R_n, R_1^{\delta}, \ldots, R_n^{\delta} \rangle$. A frame captures epistemic and doxastic structure, but does not capture what is true according to the worlds. M is based on $\mathcal{F}$ when adding some valuation V to $\mathcal{F}$ results in M. For a frame $\mathcal{F}$, Γ $\mathcal{F}$-entails 'A', $\Gamma \vDash_{\mathcal{F}} A$, iff, for all models M based on $\mathcal{F}$ and all worlds $w \in W$ in M, $M, w \Vdash \Gamma$ only if $M, w \Vdash A$. $\mathcal{F}$-validity is $\mathcal{F}$-entailment from $\varnothing$, written $\vDash_{\mathcal{F}} A$. Entailment and validity (simpliciter) are $\mathcal{F}$-entailment and $\mathcal{F}$-validity for all frames $\mathcal{F}$.

The following axiomatisation is sound and complete on the frame of all epistemic-doxastic models:

(A0) All truth-functional tautologies.

(A1) $\vdash \mathsf{K}_i(A \to B) \to (\mathsf{K}_i A \to \mathsf{K}_i B)$

(A2) $\vdash \mathsf{B}_i(A \to B) \to (\mathsf{B}_i A \to \mathsf{K}_i B)$

$$(\text{MP}) \quad \frac{\vdash A \to B \quad \vdash A}{\vdash B} \qquad\qquad (\text{N}) \quad \frac{\vdash A}{\vdash \mathsf{K}_i A} \qquad \frac{\vdash A}{\vdash \mathsf{B}_i A}$$

This is the smallest normal modal logic **K** (named after Kripke (1959, 1963a,b)) containing the 'K_i' and 'B_i' operators. The presence of more than one modal operator makes it a *multi-modal* logic.

By imposing conditions on the R_i and R_i^{δ} relations in a frame, we obtain stronger logics. Many axiom schemes correspond to frame-conditions in the following sense. Axiom scheme S corresponds to frame-condition C just in case, if logic L is sound and complete on frame $\mathcal{F}$, then logic $L + A$ is sound and complete on the frame $\mathcal{F}$ restricted to C (see, e.g., van Benthem 1983):

Axiom name	Axiom scheme	Frame condition
T	$K_i A \to A$	R_i is reflexive
	$B_i A \to A$	R_i^δ is reflexive
4	$K_i A \to K_i K_i A$	R_i is transitive
	$B_i A \to B_i B_i A$	R_i^δ is transitive
5	$\neg K_i A \to K_i \neg K_i A$	R_i is euclidian
	$\neg B_i A \to B_i \neg B_i A$	R_i^δ is euclidian
KB	$K_i A \to B_i A$	$R_i^\delta \subseteq R_i$

Restricting to the 'K_i' operators only, adding the T axiom to logic **K** gives multi-modal **KT**. In a similar way, the (multi-modal) logics **K4**, **K5**, **KT4** and **KT5** are obtained by adding the relevant axiom or axioms to **K**. **KT4** is Lewis and Langford's logic **S4** (Lewis and Langford 1932); **KT5** (= **KT45**) is **S5**. **KT5** is sound and complete on partition models, in which each R_i is an equivalence relation.

There has been a good deal of debate over whether the 4 and 5 axioms are acceptable (for either the K_is or the B_is). Hintikka (1962) argued that the 4 axiom is acceptable for knowledge but the 5 axiom is not. Some authors (particularly those in computer science) adopt the 5 axiom as a pragmatic measure (since it greatly reduces the complexity of the resulting logic). But the 5 axiom is far too strong for our ordinary concept of knowledge (Stalnaker 2006). There are also strong reasons for rejecting the 4 axiom (Williamson 1992), both in the case of knowledge and of belief. I didn't assume either axiom in this book.

For more background on modal logic, see Chellas 1980 or Hughes and Cresswell 1996. For some of the more modern developments in modal logic (particularly in relation to epistemic logic in computer science), see Blackburn et al. 2002.

A Little History

The possible world semantics for knowledge and belief ascriptions was first introduced by Hintikka (1962). Hintikka's work appeared around the same time as Kripke's (1959; 1963a; 1963b) use of possible worlds semantics in alethic modal logic, the logic of possibility and necessity, which contains the 'necessarily' operator '□' in place of knowledge operators 'K_i'. Hintikka developed his ideas further in the papers in *Models for Modalities* (1969) and *The Intentions of Intentionality and Other New Models for Modalities* (1975b). Lenzen (1978) surveys work in this early period of modal epistemic logic.

In the 1980s, interest in modal epistemic logic spread to computer science, artificial intelligence, game theory and economics. The *TARK* (Theoretical Aspects of Reasoning about Knowledge) conferences, beginning in 1986, helped to spread ideas relating to modal epistemic logic across disciplinary boundaries. Many important papers in epistemic logic were published in this period, including Fagin and Vardi 1986, Vardi 1986, Halpern 1987, Fagin and Halpern 1988, Fagin et al. 1990, Halpern and Moses 1990 and Halpern et al. 1995. Much of the ideas developed during this period are discussed in Fagin, Halpern, Moses and Vardi's collaborative *Reasoning About Knowledge* (Fagin et al. 1995).

Since then, much of the focus in the epistemic logic community has been on merging epistemic and doxastic logic with *dynamic logic* and with game theory. This results in *dynamic doxastic logic* (Segerberg 1995, 2001) and *dynamic epistemic logic* (van Ditmarsch et al. 2003a,b, 2007). These approaches study how actions affect knowledge and beliefs. Of particular interest are *public announcements* to a group of agents and how these affect the agents' individual knowledge and the common knowledge of the group (Baltag et al. 1998).

Bibliography

Aczel, P. (1988). *Non-Well-Founded Sets*. CSLI Lecture Notes Vol. 14. Stanford: CSLI Publications.

Adams, R. (1974). Theories of actuality. *Noûs* 8(3): 211–31.

—— (1981). Actualism and thisness. *Synthese* 49(1): 3–41.

Armstrong, D. (1997). *A World of States of Affairs*. Cambridge: Cambridge University Press.

—— (2004). *Truth and Truthmakers*. Cambridge: Cambridge University Press.

Baltag, A., Moss, L. and Solecki, S. (1998). The logic of public announcements, common knowledge, and private suspicions. *Proceedings of the 7th conference on theoretical aspects of rationality and knowledge*, pp. 43–56. San Francisco: Morgan Kaufmann.

Barker, S. and Jago, M. (2012). Being positive about negative facts. *Philosophy and Phenomenological Research* 85(1): 117–38.

Beall, J. (2003). *Liars and Heaps: New Essays on Paradox*. Oxford: Oxford University Press.

—— (2006). True, false and paranormal. *Analysis* 66(2): 102–13.

—— (2007). *Revenge of the Liar: New Essays on the Paradox*. Oxford: Oxford University Press.

Belnap, N. (1977). A useful four-valued logic. In J. Dunn and G. Epstein (eds). *Modern Use of Multiple-valued Logic*, pp. 5–37. Dordrecht: D. Reidel.

Berto, F. (2008). Ἀδύνατον and material exclusion. *Australasian Journal of Philosophy* 86(2): 165–90.

—— (2010). Impossible worlds and propositions: Against the parity thesis. *Philosophical Quarterly* 60(240): 471–486.

—— (2012). Impossible worlds. In E. N. Zalta (ed.), *The Stanford Encyclopedia of Philosophy*, winter 2012 edition, http://plato.stanford.edu/entries/impossible-worlds/.

Bird, A. (2007). *Nature's Metaphysics: Laws and Properties*. Oxford: Oxford University Press.

Bjerring, J. (2010). *Non-Ideal Epistemic Space*. PhD thesis, RSSS, Australian National University.

—— (2012). Impossible worlds and logical omniscience: an impossibility result. *Synthese*, doi 10.1007/s11229-011-0038-y.

Black, R. (2000). Against quidditism. *Australasian Journal of Philosophy* 78(1): 87–104.

Blackburn, P., de Rijke, M. and Venema, Y. (2002). *Modal Logic*. New York: Cambridge University Press.

Bolzano, B. (1834). *Lehrbuch der Religionswissenschaft: ein Abdruck der Vorlesungshefte eines ehemaligen Religionslehrers an einer katholischen Universität*. Sulzbach: J. E. v. Seidelschen.

Bremer, M. (2003). Is there an analytic limit of genuine modal realism? *Mind* 112(445): 79–82.

Bricker, P. (1987). Reducing possible worlds to language. *Philosophical Studies* 52(3): 331–55.

Brogaard, B. and Salerno, J. (2013). Remarks on counterpossibles, *Synthese* 190(4): 639–60.

Buss, S. (1998). An introduction to proof theory, in S. Buss (ed.). *Handbook of Proof Theory*, pp. 3–78. Amsterdam: Elsevier.

Cameron, R. (2009). What's metaphysical about metaphysical necessity? *Philosophy and Phenomenological Research* 79(1): 1–16.

Carnap, R. (1947). *Meaning and Necessity*. Chicago: University of Chicago Press.

Casati, R. and Varzi, A. (1994). *Holes and Other Superficialities*. Cambridge, MA: MIT Press.

Chalmers, D. (2004). Epistemic two-dimensional semantics. *Philosophical Studies* 118(1): 153–226.

—— (2006a). The foundations of two-dimensional semantics. In M. Garcia-Carpintero and J. Macia (eds). *Two-Dimensional Semantics: Foundations and Applications*, pp. 55–140. New York: Oxford University Press.

—— (2006b). Two-dimensional semantics. In E. Lepore and B. Smith (eds). *The Oxford Handbook to Philosophy of Language*, pp. 574–606. Oxford: Oxford University Press.

—— (2010). The nature of epistemic space. In A. Egan and B. Weatherson (eds). *Epistemic Modality*, pp. 60–107. Oxford: Oxford University Press.

Chellas, B. (1980). *Modal logic: an Introduction*. Cambridge: Cambridge University Press.

Church, A. (1951). A formulation of the logic of sense and denotation, in P. Henle, H. Kallen and S. Langer. *Structure, Method, and Meaning*, pp. 3–24. New York: The Liberal Arts Press.

—— (1973). Outline of a revised formulation of the logic of sense and denotation (part I). *Noûs* 7(1): 24–33.

—— (1974). Outline of a revised formulation of the logic of sense and denotation (part II). *Noûs* 8(2): 135–156.

Cohen, S. (1998). Contextualist solutions to epistemological problems: Scepticism, Gettier, and the lottery. *Australasian Journal of Philosophy* 76(2): 289–306.

Corazza, E. (2002). Description-names. *Journal of Philosophical Logic* 31(4): 313–25.

Cresswell, M. (1973). *Logics and Languages*. London: Methuen.

Crimmins, M. (1992). *Talk About Belief*. Cambridge, MA: MIT Press.

—— and Perry, J. (1989). The prince and the phone booth: Reporting puzzling beliefs. *Journal of Philosophy* 86: 685–711.

Davidson, D. (1968). On saying that. *Synthese* 19(1–2): 130–146.

—— (1985). *Inquiries into Truth and Interpretation*. Oxford: Oxford University Press.

Davies, M. and Humberstone, L. (1980). Two notions of necessity. *Philosophical Studies* 38(1): 1–30.

Dennett, D. (1987). *The Intentional Stance*. Cambridge, MA: MIT Press.

DeRose, K. (1992). Contextualism and knowledge attributions. *Philosophy and Phenomenological Research* 52(4): 913–29.

—— (1995). Solving the skeptical problem. *The Philosophical Review* 104(1): 1–52.

des Rivieres, J. and Levesque, H. J. (1686). The consistency of syntactical treatments of knowledge. *Computational Intelligence* 4(1): 31–41.

Divers, J. (1999). A genuine realist theory of advanced modalizing. *Mind* 108(430): 217–240.

—— (2002). *Possible worlds*. London: Routledge.

—— and Melia, J. (2002). The analytic limit of genuine modal realism. *Mind* 111(441): 15–36.

—— and —— (2003). Genuine modal realism limited. *Mind* 112(445): 83–86.

—— and —— (2006). Genuine modal realism: Still limited. *Mind* 115(459): 731–40.

Donnellan, K. (1966). Reference and definite descriptions. *Philosophical Review* 75: 281–304.

Dowe, P. (2001). A counterfactual theory of prevention and 'causation' by omission, *Australian Journal of Philosophy* 59: 216–26.

—— (2009). Absences, possible causation, and the problem of non-locality. *The Monist* 92: 24–41.

Dretske, F. (1970). Epistemic operators. *Journal of Philosophy* 67(24): 1007–23.

—— (1981). The pragmatic dimension of knowledge. *Philosophical Studies* 40(3): 363–78.

Duc, H. (1997). Reasoning about rational, but not logically omniscient, agents. *Journal of Logic and Computation* 5: 633–648.

—— (1995). Logical omniscience vs. logical ignorance. In C. Pinto-Ferreira and N. Mamede (eds.), *Progress in artificial intelligence: 7th Portuguese conference on artificial intelligence*, LNAI vol. 990, pp. 237–248. Berlin: Springer.

Dummett, M. (1975). Wang's paradox. *Synthese* 30(3): 301–24.

—— (1978a). The justification of deduction. In his *Truth and other enigmas*, pp. 166–85. Cambridge, MA: Harvard University Press.

—— (1978b). *Truth and Other Enigmas*. Cambridge, MA: Harvard University Press.

—— (1991). *The Logical Basis of Metaphysics*. Cambridge, MA: Harvard University Press.

—— (1993). *The Seas of Language*. Oxford: Oxford University Press.

Dunn, J. (1966). *The Algebra of Intentional Logics*. PhD thesis, University of Pittsburgh.

—— (1976). Intuitive semantics for first-degree entailments and coupled trees, *Philosophical Studies* 29(3): 149–68.

—— (1986). Relevance logic and entailment. In F. Guenthner and D. Gabbay (eds.), *Handbook of Philosophical Logic* vol. 3, pp. 117–224. Dordrecht: Reidel.

Eberle, R. (1974). The logic of believing, knowing, and inferring. *Synthese* 26(3–4): 356–82.

Edgington, D. (1986). Do conditionals have truth conditions? *Crítica: Revista Hispanoamericana de Filosofía* 18(52): 3–39.

—— (1995). On conditionals. *Mind* 104(414): 235–329.

Eklund, M. (2002). Inconsistent languages. *Philosophy and Phenomenological Research* 64(2): 251–75.

Ellis, B. and Lierse, C. (1994). Dispositional essentialism. *Australasian Journal of Philosophy* 72(1): 27–45.

Evans, G. (1982). *The Varieties of Reference*. Oxford: Clarendon Press.

Fagin, R. and Halpern, J. (1988). Belief, awareness and limited reasoning. *Artificial Intelligence* 34: 39–76.

Fagin, R., Halpern, J., Moses, Y. and Vardi, M. (1995). *Reasoning About Knowledge*. Cambridge, MA: MIT press.

Fagin, R., Halpern, J. and Vardi, M. (1990). A nonstandard approach to the logical omniscience problem. In R. Parikh (ed.), *Proceedings of the Third Conference on Theoretical Aspects of Reasoning About Knowledge*, pp. 41–55. San Francisco: Morgan Kaufmann.

Fagin, R. and Vardi, M. (1986). Knowledge and implicit knowledge in a distributed environment: preliminary report. In J. Halpern (ed.), *Proceedings of the 1986 Conference on Theoretical Aspects of Reasoning About Knowledge*, pp. 187–206. San Francisco: Morgan Kaufmann.

Field, H. (1977). Logic, meaning, and conceptual role. *Journal of Philosophy* 74(7): 379–409.

Fine, K. (1975). Vagueness, truth and logic. *Synthese* 30(3): 265–300.

—— (1982). First-order modal theories III—facts. *Synthese* 53(1): 43–122.

Frege, G. (1879). *Begriffsschrift, eine der Arithmetischen Nachgebildete Formelsprache des reinen Denkens*. Halle: Louis Nebert.

—— (1884). *Die Grundlagen der Arithmetik: eine Logisch Mathematische Untersuchung über den Begriff der Zahl*. Breslau: W. Koebner.

—— (1892). Über sinn und bedeutung. *Zeitschrift für Philosophie und Philosophische Kritik* 100: 25–50.

—— (1893). *Grundgesetze der Arithmetik*, vol. 1. Jena: Hermann Pohle.

—— (1903). *Grundgesetze der Arithmetik*, vol. 2. Jena: Hermann Pohle.

—— (1956). The thought: A logical inquiry. *Mind* 65(259): 289–311.

—— (1969). On Herr Peano's Begriffsschrift and my own. In B. McGuinness (ed.), *Collected Papers on Mathematics, Logic, and Philosophy*, pp. 243–48. Oxford: Blackwell.

—— (1979). *Posthumous Writings of Gottlob Frege*. Chicago: University of Chicago Press.

—— (1980). *Philosophical and Mathematical Correspondence*. Chicago: University of Chicago Press.

Gentzen, G. (1934). Untersuchungen über das logische schließen. *Mathematische zeitschrift* 39: 176–210.

Gettier, E. (1963). Is justified true belief knowledge? *Analysis* 23(6): 121–3.

Goodman, J. (2004). A defense of creationism in fiction. *Grazer Philosophische Studien* 67(1): 131–55.

Grant, J., Kraus, S. and Perlis, D. (2000). A logic for characterizing multiple bounded agents. *Autonomous Agents and Multi-Agent Systems* 3(4): 351–87.

Hall, N. (2004). Two concepts of causation. In J. Collins, N. Hall and L. Paul (eds.), *Causation and Counterfactuals*, pp. 181–204. Cambridge, MA: MIT Press.

Halpern, J. (1987). Using reasoning about knowledge to analyze distributed systems, *Annual Review of Computer Science* 2: 37–68.

—— and Moses, Y. (1990). Knowledge and common knowledge in a distributed environment environment. *Journal of the ACM* 37(3): 549–87.

——, —— and Vardi, M. (1995). Algorithmic knowledge. In R. Fagin (ed.), *Theoretical Aspects of Reasoning about Knowledge: Proceedings of the Fifth Conference, TARK 1994*, pp. 255–66. San Francisco: Morgan Kaufmann.

Harman, G. (1987). (Non-solipsistic) conceptual role semantics. In E. LePore (ed.), *New Directions in Semantics*. London Academic Press.

Hawthorne, J. (2005). The case for closure. In M. Steup and E. Sosa (eds.), *Contemporary Debates in Epistemology*, pp. 26–43. Oxford: Blackwell.

Hayes, P. and McCarthy, J. (1969). Some philosophical problems from the standpoint of artificial intelligence. *Machine Intelligence* 4: 463–502.

Heller, M. (1998). Property counterparts in ersatz worlds. *Journal of Philosophy* 95(6): 293–316.

Henkin, L. (1961). Some remarks on infinitely long formulas. *Infinitistic Methods: Proceedings of the Symposium on Foundations of Mathematics*, pp. 167–183. New York: Pergamon Press.

Hintikka, J. (1962). *Knowledge and Belief: an Introduction to the Logic of the Two Notions*. Ithaca, NY: Cornell University Press.

—— (1969). *Models for Modalities: Selected Essays*. Dordrecht: D. Reidel.

—— (1970). Surface information and depth information. In J. Hintikka and P. Suppes (eds.), *Information and Inference*, pp. 263–97. Dordrecht: D. Reidel.

—— (1973a). *Logic, Language-Games and Information: Kantian Themes in the Philosophy of Logic*. Oxford: Clarendon Press.

—— (1973b). Surface semantics and its motivation. In H. Leblanc (ed.), *Truth, Syntax and Modality*. Amsterdam: North-Holland.

—— (1975a). Impossible possible worlds vindicated. *Journal of Philisophical Logic* 4: 475–84.

—— (1975b). *The Intentions of Intentionality and Other New Models for Modalities*. Dordrecht: D. Reidel.

Horwich, P. (1990). *Truth*. Oxford: Blackwell.

—— (1995). Meaning, use and truth. *Mind* 104(414): 355–68.

—— (2004). A use theory of meaning. *Philosophy and Phenomenological Research* 68(2): 351–72.

Hughes, G. and Cresswell, M. (1996). *A New Introduction to Modal Logic.* New York: Routledge.

Humberstone, L. and Meyer, R. K. (2007). The relevant equivalence property. *Logic Journal of IGPL* 15(2): 165–81.

Jago, M. (2006a). Imagine the possibilities: Information without overload. *Logique et Analyse* 49(196): 345–71.

—— (2006b). *Logics for Resource-Bounded Agents.* PhD thesis, University of Nottingham.

—— (2007). Hintikka and Cresswell on logical omniscience. *Logic and Logical Philosophy* 15(4): 325–54.

—— (2009a). Epistemic logic for rule-based agents. *Journal of Logic, Language and Information* 18(1): 131–58.

—— (2009b). Logical information and epistemic space. *Synthese* 167(2): 327–41.

—— (2009c). Resources in epistemic logic. In J.-Y. Béziau and A. Costa-Leite (eds.), *Dimensions of Logical Concepts*, Vol. 55, pp. 11–33. Campinas: Coleção CLE.

—— (2011). Setting the facts straight. *Journal of Philosophical Logic* 40: 33–54.

—— (2012). Constructing worlds. *Synthese* 189(1): 59–74.

—— (2013a). Against Yagisawa's modal realism. *Analysis* 73(1): 10–17.

—— (2013b). Are impossible worlds trivial? Forthcoming in V. Puncochar and P. Svarny (eds). *The 2012 Logica Yearbook 2012.* London: College Publications.

—— (2013c). The content of deduction. *Journal of Philosophical Logic* 42(2): 317–34.

—— (2013d). Impossible worlds. Forthcoming in *Noûs.*

—— (2013e). The problem of rational knowledge. Forthcoming in *Erkenntnis.*

—— (2013f). The problem with truthmaker-gap epistemicism. *Thought* 1(4): 320–9.

Jeffrey, R. (1983). *The Logic of Decision.* Chicago: University of Chicago Press.

Kaplan, D. (1975). How to Russell a Frege-Church. *Journal of Philosophy* 72(19): 716–29.

—— (1978). Dthat. In P. Cole (ed.). *Syntax and Semnatics*, vol. 9, pp. 221–53. New York: Academic Press.

—— (1989a). Afterthoughts. In J. Almog, J. Perry and H. Wettstein (eds.), *Themes From Kaplan*, pp. 565–614. Oxford: Oxford University Press.

—— (1989b). Demonstratives. In J. Almog, J. Perry and H. Wettstein (eds). *Themes from Kaplan*, pp. 481–563. Oxford: Oxford University Press.

Keefe, R. (2000). *Theories of Vagueness.* Cambridge: Cambridge University Press.

King, J. (1995). Structured propositions and complex predicates. *Noûs* 29(4): 516–35.

King, J. (1996). Structured propostions and sentence structure. *Journal of Philosophical Logic* 25(5): 495–521.

Konolige, K. (1986). *A Deduction Model of Belief.* San Francisco: Morgan Kaufman.

Kratzer, A. (1986). Conditionals. In A. Farley, P. Farley and K. McCollough (eds.), *Papers from the Parasession on Pragmatics and Grammatical Theory*, pp. 115–35. Chicago: Chicago Linguistics Society.

Kripke, S. (1959). A completeness theorem in modal logic. *Journal of Symbolic Logic* 24(1): 1–14.

—— (1963a). Semantical analysis of modal logic I: normal modal propositional calculi. *Zeitschrift für Mathematische Logik und Grundlagen der Mathematik* 9: 67–96.

—— (1963b). Semantical considerations on modal logic. *Acta Philosophica Fennica* 16: 83–94.

—— (1977). Speaker's reference and semantic reference. *Midwest Studies in Philosophy* 2(1): 255–76.

—— (1980). *Naming and Necessity.* Oxford: Blackwell.

Lakemeyer, G. (1986). Steps towards a first-order logic of explicit and implicit belief. In J. Halpern (ed.), *Proceedings of the 1986 Conference on Theoretical Aspects of Reasoning About Knowledge*, pp. 325–40. San Francisco: Morgan Kaufmann.

Lakemeyer, G. (1987). Tractable meta-reasoning in propositional logics of belief. *Proceedings of the Tenth International Joint Conference on Artificial Intelligence*, vol. 1, pp. 401–08. San Francisco: Morgan Kaufmann.

Lakemeyer, G. (1990). A computationally attractive first-order logic of belief. *Proceedings of JELIA 90*, pp. 333–47. Heidelberg: Springer.

Lenzen, W. (1978). Recent work in epistemic logic. *Acta Philosophica Fennica* 30(1): 1–219.

Levesque, H. J. (1984). A logic of implicit and explicit belief. *Proceedings of the Fourth National Conference on Artificial Intelligence*, pp. 198–202. AAAI Press.

Lewis, C. and Langford, C. (1932). *Symbolic Logic*. New York: The Appleton-Century Company.

Lewis, D. —— (1968). Counterpart theory and quantified modal logic. *Journal of Philosophy* 65(5): 113–26.

—— (1970). How to define theoretical terms. *Journal of Philosophy* 67(13): 427–46.

—— (1971). Counterparts of persons and their bodies. *Journal of Philosophy* 68(7): 203–11.

—— (1973). *Counterfactuals*. Cambridge, MA: Harvard University Press.

—— (1982). Logic for equivocators. *Noûs* 16(3): 431–41.

—— (1983). New work for a theory of universals. *Australian Journal of Philosophy* 61: 347–77.

—— (1986). *On the Plurality of Worlds*. Oxford: Blackwell.

—— (1990). Noneism or allism? *Mind* 99(393): 23–31.

—— (1996). Elusive knowledge. *Australasian Journal of Philosophy* 74(4): 549–67.

—— (2004). Letters to Priest and Beall. In B. Armour-Garb, J. Beall and G. Priest (eds.), *The Law of Non-Contradiction: New Philosophical Essays*, pp. 176–7. Oxford: Oxford University Press.

—— and Lewis, S. (1970). Holes. *Australasian Journal of Philosophy* 48(2): 206–12.

Linsky, B. and Zalta, E. (1994). In defense of the simplest quantified modal logic. *Philosophical Perspectives* 8: 431–58.

—— and —— (1996). In defense of the contingently concrete. *Philosophical Studies* 84: 283–94.

Loewer, B. and Lepore, E. (1989). You can say that again. *Midwest Studies in Philosophy* 14: 338–56.

Lycan, W. (1994). *Modality and Meaning*. Dordrecht: Kluwer.

Martin-Löf, P. (1975). An intuitionistic theory of types: predicative part. In H. Rose and J. Shepherdson (eds.), *Logic Colloquium '73*, pp. 73–118. Amsterdam: North Holland.

McDaniel, K. (2004). Modal realism with overlap. *Australasian Journal of Philosophy* 82(1): 137–52.

Mehlberg, H. (1958). *The Reach of Science*. Toronto: University of Toronto Press.

Meinong, A. (1904). Über gegenstandstheorie. In A. Meinong (ed.), *Untersuchungen zur Gegenstadstheorie und Psychologie*, pp. 1–50. Leipzig: Barth.

Melia, J. (2001). Reducing possibilities to language. *Analysis* 61(1): 19–29.

Miller, G. and Johnson-Laird, P. (1976). *Language and Perception*. Cambridge, MA: MIT Press.

Molnar, G. (2000). Truthmakers for negative truths. *Australasian Journal of Philosophy* 78(1): 72–86.

Moore, R. C. and Hendrix, G. (1979). Computational models of beliefs and the semantics of belief sentences. *SRI Technical Note 187*. Menlo Park: SRI International.

Morreau, M. and Kraus, S. (1998). Syntactical treatments of propositional attitudes. *Artificial Intelligence* 106: 161–77.

Morse, A. (1965). *A Theory of Sets*. New York: Academic Press.

Mulligan, K., Simons, P. and Smith, B. (1984). Truth-makers. *Philosophy and Phenomenological Research* 44(3): 287–321.

Mumford, S. (2003). *Dispositions*. New York: Oxford University Press.

—— (2007). Negative truth and falsehood. *Proceedings of the Aristotelian Society* 107(1): 45–71.

Naylor, M. (1986). A note on David Lewis's realism about possible worlds. *Analysis* 46(1): 28.

Nolan, D. (1997). Impossible worlds: A modest approach. *Notre Dame Journal of Formal Logic* 38(4): 535–72.

Nozick, R. (1981). *Philosophical Explanations*. Cambridge, MA: Harvard University Press.

Parsons, J. (2006). Negative truths from positive facts? *Australasian Journal of Philosophy* 84(4): 591–602.

Peirce, C. S. (1992). *Reasoning and the Logic of Things: The Cambridge Conferences Lectures of 1898*. Cambridge, MA: Harvard University Press.

Prawitz, D. (1971). Ideas and results in proof theory. In J. Fenstad (ed.), *Proceedings of the 2nd Scandinavian Logic Symposium (Oslo 1970)*, pp. 235–308. Amsterdam: North Holland.

—— (1973). Towards a foundation of a general proof theory. In P. Suppes, L. Henkin, A. Joja, and Gr. C. Moisil (eds.), *Logic, Methodology, and Philosophy of Science IV*, pp. 225–50. Amsterdam: North Holland.

Priest, G. (1979). Logic of paradox. *Journal of Philosophical Logic* 8: 219–41.

—— (1987). *In Contradiction: A Study of the Transconsistent*. Martinus Nijhoff, Dordrecht.

—— (1997). Sylvan's box. *Notre Dame Journal of Formal Logic* 38: 573–82.

—— (2002). Paraconsistent logic: essays on the inconsistent. In D. Gabbay and F. Guenthner (eds.) *Handbook of Philosophical Logic*, vol. 6, pp. 287–393. Dordrecht: Kluwer.

—— (2005). *Towards Non-Being*. Oxford: Clarendon Press.

—— (2008). *An Introduction to Non-Classical Logic: from If to Is*. Cambridge: Cambridge University Press.

——, Beall, J. and Armour-Garb, B. (2004). *The Law of Non-Contradiction: New Philosophical Essays*. New York: Oxford University Press.

Quine, W. (1951). Two dogmas of empiricism. *Philosophical Review* 60(1): 20–43.

—— (1960). *Word and Object*. Cambridge, MA: MIT Press.

—— (1969). *Ontological Relativity and Other Essays*. New York: Columbia University Press.

Quine, W. —— and Ullian, J. (1970). *The Web of Belief*, 2nd edn. New York: Random House.

Rantala, V. (1975). Urn models. *Journal of Philosophical Logic* 4: 455–74.

Read, S. (1995). *Thinking About Logic*. Oxford: Oxford University Press.

Rescher, N. and Brandom, R. (1980). *The Logic of Inconsistency*. Oxford: Blackwell.

Restall, G. (2004a). One way to face facts. *Philosophical Quarterly* 54(216): 420–26.

—— (2004b). Relevant and substructural logics. In D. Gabbay and J. Woods (eds.), *Handbook of the History of Logic: Logic and the Modalities in the Twentieth Century*, vol. 7, pp. 289–398. Amsterdam: Elsevier.

Richard, M. (1990). *Propositional Attitudes*. Cambridge: Cambridge University Press.

Ripley, D. (2012). Structures and circumstances: two ways to fine-grain propositions. *Synthese* 189(1): 97–118.

Robinson, D. (1993). Epiphenomenalism, laws and properties. *Philosophical Studies* 69(1): 1–34.

Rodriguez-Pereyra, G. (2002). *Resemblance Nominalism: a Solution to the Problem of Universals*. New York: Oxford University Press.

Rosen, G. (1990). Modal fictionalism. *Mind* 99(395): 327–54.

Routley, R. (1989). Philosophical and linguistic inroads: Multiply intensional relevant logics. In J. Norman and R. Routley (eds.), *Directions in Relevant Logic*, pp. 269–304. Dordrecht: Kluwer.

Russell, B. (1902/1967). Letter to Frege. In J. van Heijenoort (ed.), *From Frege to Gödel*, pp. 124–5. Cambridge, MA: Harvard University Press.

—— (1903). *The Principles of Mathematics*. Cambridge: Cambridge University Press.

—— (1905). On denoting. *Mind* 14: 479–93.

Salmon, N. (1986). *Frege's Puzzle*. Cambridge, MA: MIT Press/Bradford Books.

—— (1998). Nonexistence. *Noûs* 32: 277–319.

—— (2005). *Metaphysics, Mathematics, and Meaning*. New York: Oxford University Press.

Schnieder, B. (2007). Mere possibilities: A Bolzanian approach to non-actual objects. *Journal of the History of Philosophy* 45(4): 525–50.

Schroeder-Heister, P. (1991). Uniform proof-theoretic semantics for logical constants (abstract). *Journal of Symbolic Logic* 56: 1142.

Segerberg, K. (1995). Belief revision from the point of view of doxastic logic. *Logic Journal of IGPL* 3(4): 535–53.

—— (2001). The basic dynamic doxastic logic of AGM. *Frontiers in Belief Revision* 22: 57–84.

Sequoiah-Grayson, S. (2008). The scandal of deduction. *Journal of Philosophical Logic* 37(1): 67–94.

Sharlow, M. F. (1988). Lewis's modal realism: a reply to Naylor. *Analysis* 48(1): 13–15.

Shoemaker, S. (1980). Causality and properties. In P. van Inwagen (ed.), *Time and Cause: Essays presented to Richard Taylor*, pp. 109–35. Dordrecht, Reidel.

Sider, T. (2002). The ersatz pluriverse. *Journal of Philosophy* 99(6): 279–315.

—— (2003). *Four-Dimensionalism: an Ontology of Persistence and Time*. New York: Oxford University Press.

Skolem, T. (1922). Einige bemerkungen zur axiomatischen begründung der mengenlehre. In *Proceedings of the Fifth Scandinavian Mathematical Congress, Helsinki*, pp. 217–232. Reprinted in J. Fenstad (ed., 1970), *Selected Works in Logic, pp. 137–52*. Oslo: Universitetsforlaget.

Skyrms, B. (1981). Tractarian nominalism. *Philosophical Studies* 40(2): 199–206.

Smith, N. (2009). *Vagueness and Degrees of Truth*. Oxford: Oxford University Press.

Soames, S. (2002). *Beyond Rigidity: the Unfinished Semantic Agenda of Naming and Necessity*. Oxford: Oxford University Press.

—— (2005). Naming and asserting. In Z. G. Szabó (ed.), *Semantics versus Pragmatics*, pp. 356–82. Oxford: Oxford University Press.

Sorensen, R. (1985). An argument for the vagueness of 'vague'. *Analysis* 45(3): 134–37.

—— (1988). *Blindspots*. New York: Oxford University Press.

—— (2001). *Vagueness and Contradiction*. Oxford: Oxford University Press.

Stalnaker, R. (1968). A theory of conditionals. In N. Rescher (ed.), *Studies in Logical Theory*, pp. 98–112. Oxford: Blackwell.

—— (1976a). Possible worlds. *Noûs* 10(1): 65–75.

—— (1976b). Propositions. In A. MacKay and D. Merrill (eds.), *Issues in the Philosophy of Language*, pp. 79–91. New Haven: Yale University Press.

—— (1984). *Inquiry*. Cambridge, MA: MIT Press.

—— (1991). The problem of logical omniscience I. *Synthese* 89: 425–40.

—— (1999). The problem of logical omniscience II. In his *Context and Content: Essays on Intentionality in Speech and Thought*, pp. 255–73. Oxford: Oxford University Press,

—— (2004). Assertion revisited: On the interpretation of two-dimensional modal semantics. *Philosophical Studies* 118(1): 299–322.

—— (2006). On logics of knowledge and belief. *Philosophical Studies* 128(1): 169–99.

Swoyer, C. (1982). The nature of natural laws. *Australasian Journal of Philosophy* 60(3): 203–23.

Thomasson, A. (1999). *Fiction and Metaphysics*. Cambridge: Cambridge University Press.

Twardowski, K. (1894). *Zur Lehre vom Inhalt und Gegenstand der Vorstellungen: eine Psychologische Untersuchung*. Wein: Hölder.

Tye, M. (1994). Sorites paradoxes and the semantics of vagueness. *Philosophical Perspectives* 8: 189–206.

van Benthem, J. (1983). *Modal Logic and Classical Logic*. Napoli: Bibliopolis.

—— (2011). *Logical Dynamics of Information and Interaction*. Cambridge: Cambridge University Press.

—— and Martinez, M. (2008). The stories of logic and information. In J. van Benthem and P. Adriaans (eds.), *Handbook of the Philosophy of Information*, pp. 217–80. Amsterdam: Elsevier.

van Ditmarsch, H., Hoek, W. and Kooi, B. (2003). Concurrent dynamic epistemic logic. In V. Hendricks, K. Jørgensen and S. Pedersen (eds.), *Knowledge Contributors*, Synthese Library Series vol. 322, pp. 105–43. Amsterdam: Kluwer Academic Publishers.

——, —— and —— (2003). Concurrent dynamic epistemic logic for MAS. *Proceedings of the Second International Joint Conference on Autonomous Agents and Multiagent Systems*, pp. 201–08. ACM.

——, —— and —— (2007). *Dynamic Epistemic Logic*, Synthese Library vol. 337. Dordrecht: Springer.

van Fraassen, B. (1966). Singular terms, truth-value gaps, and free logic. *Journal of Philosophy* 63(17): 481–95.

—— (1969). Facts and tautological entailments. *Journal of Philosophy* 66(15): 477–87.

van Inwagen, P. (2008). McGinn on existence. *Philosophical Quarterly* 58(230): 36–58.

Vardi, M. (1986). On epistemic logic and logical omniscience. In J. Halpern (ed.), *Proceedings of the 1986 Conference on Theoretical Aspects of Reasoning About Knowledge*, pp 293–305. San Francisco: Morgan Kaufmann.

Voltolini, A. (2006). *How Ficta Follow Fiction: a Syncretistic Account of Fictional Entities*. Dordrecht: Springer.

Wansing, H. (1990). A general possible worlds framework for reasoning about knowledge and belief. *Studia Logica* 49(4): 523–39.

Whitehead, A. and Russell, B. (1910). *Principia Mathematica*, vol. 1. Cambridge: Cambridge University Press.

—— and —— (1912). *Principia Mathematica*, vol. 2. Cambridge: Cambridge University Press.

—— and —— (1913). *Principia Mathematica*, vol. 3. Cambridge: Cambridge University Press.

Wiles, A. (2000). Interview with Andrew Wiles. Nova Magazine, www.pbs.org/wgbh/nova/physics/andrew-wiles-fermat.html.

Williams, D. (1953). On the elements of being. *The Review of Metaphysics* 7: 3–18 and 171–92.

Williamson, T. (1992). Inexact knowledge. *Mind* 101(402): 217–42.

—— (1994). *Vagueness*. London: Routledge.

—— (1996). Knowing and asserting. *Philosophical Review* 105: 489–523.

—— (1998). Bare possibilia. *Erkenntnis* 48(2–3): 257–73.

—— (2000a). *Knowledge and its Limits*. Oxford: Oxford University Press.

—— (2000b). The necessary framework of objects. *Topoi* 19(2): 201–08.

—— (2007). *The Philosophy of Philosophy*. Oxford: Wiley-Blackwell.

Wilson, G. (1991). Reference and pronominal descriptions. *Journal of Philosophy* 88(7): 359–87.

Wittgenstein, L. (1922). *Tractatus Logico-Philosophicus*. London: Routledge & Kegan Paul.

—— (1953). *Philosophical Investigations*. Oxford: Blackwell.

Yagisawa, T. (1988). Beyond possible worlds. *Philosophical Studies* 53(2): 175–204.

—— (2001). Against creationism in fiction. *Noûs* 35: 153–72.

—— (2010). *Worlds and Individuals, Possible and Otherwise*. New York: Oxford University Press.

Zalta, E. (1993). Twenty-five basic theorems in situation and world theory. *Journal of Philosophical Logic* 22(4): 385–428.

Index: Authors

Index: Terms